Advance Praise for *Undoctrinate*

"For too long, educators across America have relied on the ignorance of parents to indoctrinate students as young as five with one-sided and, now, divisive ideas. That is why Bonnie Snyder's *Undoctrinate: How Politicized Classrooms Harm Kids and Ruin Our Schools—and What We Can Do About It* could not be more timely. This fair and balanced book details what is truly happening and, in turn, this knowledge empowers us to pursue the right course of action to ensure that our kids receive the best and most comprehensive education possible."

—Eli Steele, Filmmaker, "Illiterate Revolutionaries"

"'Children are our future,' goes the politician's cliché, and we may be jeopardizing that future by allowing schools to bully students into ideological conformity, racial reductionism, and tendentious activism. *Undoctrinate* is a timely and disturbing call to action."

—Steven Pinker, Johnstone Professor of Psychology, Harvard University, and the author of *Enlightenment Now* and *Rationality*

"Indoctrination is not education. It is the antithesis of education. Far from liberating the intellect, indoctrination shackles it. Yet today in countless schools across the United States—public and private alike—indoctrination is masquerading as education. Parents of schoolchildren are rightly alarmed and appalled by it, but most have no idea what to do about it. What they need is a guidebook, and Bonnie Snyder has provided an excellent one. She has done the entire nation a service."

—Robert P. George, McCormick Professor of Jurisprudence and Director of the James Madison Program in American Ideals and Institutions, Princeton University

"In this remarkable book, Bonnie Snyder shows that in too many of the nation's primary and secondary schools, the marketplace of ideas has been overwhelmed by a monopoly of ideology. The same orthodoxy which has narrowed the minds of college students for years, is now working its way through the more vulnerable populations of children and adolescents. *Undoctrinate* shows how this is happening, why it's happening, and why it's wrong—pedagogically, ethically, psychologically, and legally. As the title suggests, *Undoctrinate* is not just a diagnosis but a prescription, and in the final chapters Snyder gives parents and their children reason for hope by giving them plans for action. In the fight to save our schools from partisan ideologues of any stripe, this is an indispensable armory of analysis and ideas."

—Lyell Asher, Associate Professor of English, Lewis & Clark College, "How Ed Schools Became a Menace"

"Bonnie Snyder's *Undoctrinate* is more than just a rallying cry against the epidemic of thought reform in K-12. This well-researched book traces the multiple vectors by which 'critical theory' replaced critical thinking in our education system, and why this 'learning without liberty' presents such a grave threat both to the well-being of students and the future of our country. Drawing on the experiences of dozens of families, and grounded in a deep understanding of censorship law and our nation's foundational principles, this book offers practical insights that will empower parents and teachers to defend our children's right to speak their conscience in the classroom."

—Paul Rossi, former math teacher, Grace Church School, and volunteer with the Foundation Against Intolerance & Racism

"The world is complex, and our challenges are changing. If we hand our children a set of answers, however well-intentioned, rather than the skills to find their own answers, then we really will not be preparing them for success. Bonnie Kerrigan Snyder's *Undoctrinate* is an important read for parents and educators who want their children and students to grow up able to think for themselves."

—Cynthia Meyersburg, Ph.D., Instructor, Harvard Summer School and Lecturer, Harvard Division of Continuing Education

"My daughter's middle school is teaching all sixth graders about the world's major religions. I think that's great. But what if the school chose one of the religions and pressured all the children to practice its rituals in every class, including math, gym, and health? In *Undoctrinate*, Bonnie Snyder shows us that this is exactly what is happening in many school districts across the country. She explains how this came to pass, what it does to our kids, and how you can organize with other parents to stop it. Every parent of children younger than eighteen should read this book, as should anyone who thinks education is important."

—Jonathan Haidt, Thomas Cooley Professor of Ethical Leadership, New York University— Stern School of Business, author of *The Righteous Mind*, co-author of *The Coddling of the American Mind*

UNDOCTRINATE

HOW POLITICIZED CLASSROOMS HARM KIDS AND RUIN OUR SCHOOLS— AND WHAT WE CAN DO ABOUT IT

Bonnie Kerrigan Snyder

BOMBARDIER
BOOKS

A BOMBARDIER BOOKS BOOK
An Imprint of Post Hill Press
ISBN: 978-1-64293-912-5
ISBN (eBook): 978-1-64293-913-2

Undoctrinate:
How Politicized Classrooms Harm Kids and Ruin Our
Schools—and What We Can Do About It
© 2021 by Bonnie Kerrigan Snyder
All Rights Reserved

Post Hill Press
New York • Nashville
posthillpress.com

Published in the United States of America
1 2 3 4 5 6 7 8 9 10

Dedicated to parents who stand up for their children
and students who think for themselves

"Education ought to foster the wish for truth, not
the conviction that some creed is the truth."
—Bertrand Russell, 1916

Contents

Foreword by John H. McWhorter

Something has been happening at the tony Dalton School in New York City since the fall of 2020. A letter circulated anonymously by parents paints the picture:

> Every class this year has had an obsessive focus on race and identity, 'racist cop' reenactments in science, 'de-centering whiteness' in art class, learning about white supremacy and sexuality in health class.

> In place of a joyful progressive education, students are exposed to an excessive focus on skin color and sexuality, before they even understand what sex is. Children are bewildered or bored after hours of discussing these topics in the new long-format classes.

> What Black parent wants the other children to feel sorry for their kid and look at them differently? We have spoken with dozens of families, of all colors and backgrounds, who are in shock and looking for an alternative school for their children.

More than a few enlightened folk may dismiss this as a mere anecdote, especially since Dalton caters to such an elite cohort who are assumed not to have many problems in the grand scheme of things. However, this transmogrification of education into obsessively "antiracist" cultural reprogramming has become nothing less than a norm nationwide.

It is by no means restricted to elite private institutions: schools public as well as private are being infected by a meme that goes under the name "social justice" but is actually a new, unintellectual, prosecutorial religion dedicated to "decentering whiteness." As I write this in the spring of 2021, I am receiving at least one missive every single day from a parent or teacher appalled at this virus infecting what they once knew as a school that is quickly becoming a struggle session academy.

This new movement is officially titled "antiracism," but this word is as euphemistic, foggy, and misleading as that of a department called "human resources" (human in what sense? What kinds of resources?). The "antiracist" approach to black kids, for example, is that it is racist to expect them to come up with real answers because precision is "white." One of the new movement's leading prelates Ibram X. Kendi, in his best-selling testament *How to Be an Antiracist*, openly derides standardized tests as racist and posits "What if we measured intelligence by how knowledgeable individuals are about their own environments? What if we measured intellect by an individual's desire to know?" Meanwhile, a document on math education teaches that it is racist to teach math in a linear fashion with skills taught in sequence, to require students to show their work, or to raise their hand before speaking.

In general, this "antiracist" approach to learning distrusts most of the Western academic heritage as "white supremacy." Then, an especially grievous aspect of this new wisdom is the idea that children must be separated by race and taught that whiteness is inherently oppressive while being non-white is definitionally to be oppressed by whiteness.

The people promulgating this ideology are closed to meaningful dialogue, as we see from how often teachers in dissent are simply fired for it. In this excerpt from an article by a top administrator at Riverdale Country School, we see an ideologue confidently asserting this new vision as truth incarnate:

Thus, private schools who find parents unwilling to accept moves toward culturally responsive schooling are free to draw a line in the sand, so to speak, and assert firmly and positively a philosophy of education that is explicitly anti-racist, decolonizing, and culturally affirming. In light of the problematic elements of neoliberal ideology evident in the structures of independent schools, it is not merely a freedom they have to construct their environment in this way, but in fact an obligation.

My two children are white-black biracials, and I shudder at the prospect of them exposed to this horror. At six and nine as I write, living an upper-middle-class existence in a very diverse neighborhood, they process race but dimly at this point. I will not tolerate that their understanding of it constitutes learning that the kind, enlightened whites around them are bad people, and that their essence as brown girls is as victims of white supremacy.

In his own "antiracism" testament, Ta-Nehisi Coates writes of seeing his child playing easily with white schoolmates and being worried that his child didn't know what white people are capable of. That would have made sense until roughly 1969, but for Coates to have felt this way in the twenty-first century on the Upper West Side of New York City was a feigned battle pose. Yet this new educational movement chimes in with people like Coates (and assigns his writings as text).

These are people under the naïve, unthinking misimpression that they are the first humans to have come upon unassailable truth, of a kind that justifies trampling opposition. They are the faceless menace familiar from 1984—except they are real. The "antiracist" commitment strangling America's educational system, which includes colleges and universities as well, is couched in elaborate verbiage. Too, in involving whites actually voluntarily giving up their power, it is an unprecedented development in human social history. This is part of why its participants are so narcotically devoted to the paradigm. They feel anointed, like people blazing a path towards, well, redemption. They are parishioners amidst a religion.

Unfortunately, it is a religion committed to illogic, dehumanization, and destruction, sacrificing all civic sense, as well as genuine concern with black and brown people's fate, to a focus on virtue signaling. Dedication to being non-racist leads them to construct a movement, *modus operandi* and policing system that thrives by leaving people cowering to be called racist, forced into accepting actions, opinions, and programs they never would under other circumstances, such as excusing brown students from having to do real work or behave themselves.

This is a collapse of post-Enlightenment thought, forced by people many of whom will quite openly condemn the Enlightenment as—what else?—too "white." We are witnessing a reversal of intellectual, moral, and artistic culture most familiar until now from the Dark Ages. It forces upon us a challenge.

The white professional "antiracists" have challenged themselves to give up their power as whites. The rest of us—who at this point are a cowering majority—must stand up and challenge ourselves.

The modern "antiracists" hold us in their grip solely via their ever-looming threat to call us racists in the public square. Our challenge is to get used to hearing that noise and walk on regardless. We must gather our resources, protest, refuse, walk away, decry, and utilize social media in the same way that they do until they realize that their scare tactics will no longer work.

It is us who are the vanguard to a better future, not them. And it's one thing to make a private pact with yourself as an adult to just lie low—confrontation is difficult and life is multifaceted. But remember—these people are coming after your kids.

John H. McWhorter, New York City, April 2021

Associate Professor of Linguistics, Columbia University; Contributing Editor of *The Atlantic Magazine*; and host of Slate's language podcast Lexicon Valley.

PART
ONE

The Problem in Our Schools

1

Thought Reform in Education

Gabrielle Clark was worried about her children.

Something was off, but she couldn't put her finger on the problem. Gabrielle was temporarily disabled and unemployed, so her son William worked as a fast food shift manager to help make ends meet while taking his high school senior classes remotely. As a single mom—William's father died before he was old enough to know him—she had to figure this out alone.

One day, she decided to sit down and watch her son's distance-learning classes from his magnet school. She tuned into a required course, "The Sociology of Change," and what she saw on screen shocked her. Her son, unbeknownst to her, had been taught lessons that were completely antithetical to her family's values…and common sense.

William's deceased father was white, which means William is biracial. However, his light skin, light hair, and green eyes mean that some people assume he is white. He's sometimes described as "the only apparent white boy in his class."

Being "apparently white" was enough for his teacher to target him.

For years, schools have had "anti-bullying campaigns" to stop kids from picking on each other. But what if the bullying is coming from the teacher and school administrators? According to the family's recently filed lawsuit, William was singled out and subjected to derogatory name-calling and hurtful labelling, based on his physical appearance.[1] His teacher delivered regular "privilege checks" for William, which his mother described as "deliberate and protracted harassment" and "emotional abuse." The classroom materials even implied that William's white father probably physically abused his black mother, because—according to his lessons—that's what white men do.

This is a far cry from Martin Luther King Jr.'s dream of a nation where people "will not be judged by the color of their skin, but by the content of their character." And what a way to sully the legacy of this young man's father!

Gabrielle claims her son, as well as the other students, were forced to profess their identities which were then subjected to open, official scrutiny that assigned negative character attributes and worldviews based on unchangeable personal characteristics, such as race and gender. Even students' religious upbringings were judged. The curriculum also explicitly instructed William to "unlearn" the "traditional Judeo-Christian principles" his mother taught him.

When students, including William, attempted to object, discussions were terminated and their speech effectively chilled. However, William refused to complete certain "identity confession" assignments, or to avow certain politicized statements he could not in good conscience affirm. That was enough to earn him threats of a failing grade.

As a senior, that was bad news. He had planned to spend the year applying to colleges and dreaming about his freshman year in which he'd study music.

But this bad grade would put all of that in jeopardy.

Gabrielle had her attorney write a letter to the school, which prompted a meeting. But Gabrielle didn't feel the school was taking her concerns seriously. "That's when I withdrew my daughter and got the lawyers for my

---

[1]   "Schoolhouse Rights," International Organization for the Family, December 22, 2020, https://www.schoolhouserights.org/the-lawsuit.html.

son," she wrote. "I'm not playing with these people."[2] She filed a lawsuit against the school, claiming they violated the mother's constitutional due process right to "family integrity and autonomy" by interfering with her "right and covenant to guide and direct the upbringing" of her children.

This case may have some of you scratching your heads. Others of you—having experienced similar interactions at school—might be nodding your head at the familiarity of the story.

How did America get to a place where a black mom has to sue her son's school for bullying him, simply because of the color of his (light?) skin?

Our nation has a problem. Recently, in both urban and rural communities, young children are being indoctrinated, bullied, and harassed by their fellow students and teachers for not falling into line on various topics.

In Arizona, Roberto Sandoval, the son of a Mexican immigrant who worked hard to achieve the American dream, was alarmed when his teen showed him her high school homework. "I have an assignment that's asking me how I am privileged," she told him.

The homework included statements such as *My skin color gives me privileges I didn't earn…Your skin color gives you struggles you didn't deserve.* And *For every $1 a White Man earns (with comparisons)…, [S]taying silent in times of injustice is privilege,* and *No one is asking you to apologize for being privileged; people want you to stop using your privilege in ways that require an apology.*

"I'm not white, and my daughter's not either," Sandoval said. "To me, this is teaching them that you're a victim. It's fine to have a conversation

---

2   Greg Piper, "Family Filed Civil Rights Lawsuit against Charter School for Mandating Anti-White 'Critical Race Theory' Class," *Tennessee Star*, December 29, 2020, https://tennesseestar.com/2020/12/29/family-files-civil-rights-lawsuit-against-charter-school-for-mandating-anti-white-critical-race-theory-class/.

about it, but…trying to create a divisive environment through race? It just doesn't belong."[3]

In Seattle, teachers explain that "Western" mathematics has been used "to disenfranchise people and communities of color." Then, they attempt to "rehumanize" math by incorporating curricular content such as explaining "how math dictates economic oppression" and "economic movements that have led to liberation," and asking, "How can we change mathematics from individualistic to collectivist thinking?"[4]

An exasperated eighth-grade student in that city recorded her art teacher's extended monologue about how peace was racist and that their art lessons came from a "European Eurocentric white supremacist point of view."[5]

Third-grade students in Cupertino, California (famous as the headquarters of Apple computer), were told to deconstruct their racial and sexual identities, ranking themselves on the intersectional hierarchy from "oppressor" to "oppressed." One scandalized parent objected, saying, "They were basically teaching racism to my eight-year-old."[6] When questioned, the principal acknowledged that the lesson was not part of the "formal curricula."

3   "Gilbert Parent Outraged by Child's Homework Assignment on Privilege," MSN News, September 24, 2020, https://www.msn.com/en-us/news/us/gilbert-parent-outraged-by-childs-homework-assignment-on-privilege/ar-BB19qzYN.

4   Jarrett Stepman, "Woke Math Aims to Teach Seattle Kids That 'Western' Math Is Racist," Daily Signal, October 24, 2019, https://www.dailysignal.com/2019/10/24/woke-math-aims-to-teach-seattle-kids-that-western-math-is-racist/ and George Leef, "A Racially 'Woke' Agenda Is Now Hardwired in Public Schools," Minding the Campus, November 4, 2019, https://www.mindingthecampus.org/2019/11/04/a-racially-woke-agenda-is-now-hardwired-in-public-schools/.

5   Jason Rantz, "Seattle Art Teacher Tells Kids 'Peace' Is 'Racist' and Trump Is Divisive," MyNorthwest, October 13, 2020, https://mynorthwest.com/2220892/rantz-seattle-teacher-peace-racist-and-trump-is-divisive/.

6   Christopher Rufo, "Woke Elementary," *City Journal*, January 13, 2021, https://christopherrufo.com/woke-elementary/.

Billionaire hedge funder John Paulson noticed an "alarming pattern" of "anti-white indoctrination" at his daughter's prestigious Spence School in Manhattan. A school play depicted two white girls pushing a black girl because she didn't summer in the Hamptons. Her required literature reading depicted a white father raping his daughter and another book included this observation: it's amazing that "rich people could be nice."[7]

Minnesota police complained to the governor about the lopsided nature of their public elementary school's curriculum. "Language in this book leaves the impression unchecked that police officers routinely pull over, arrest, and kill black people without consequence," their letter read. "It says cops are 'mean to black people' or 'shot them because they were black' or police officers 'stick up for each other' to help police officers get away with doing bad things. This book encourages children to fear police officers as unfair, violent, and racist."[8]

Students at Environmental Charter High School in Lawndale, California, had to write a "breakup letter with a form of oppression," such as toxic masculinity, heteronormativity, or the Eurocentric curriculum.[9]

The Chicago Public School District headlined its recently released "toolkit to help foster productive conversations about race and civil disobedience" with an epigraph by Angela Davis, the former Communist and criminal fugitive who supplied the guns used in the Marin County Courthouse massacre in 1970.[10] In a case of extreme irony, a teacher

---

7   Emily Smith, "Billionaire John Paulson Rips Elite Spence School for 'Anti-White Indoctrination," Page Six, July 7, 2020, https://pagesix.com/2020/07/07/billion-aire-john-paulson-rips-elite-spence-school-for-anti-white-indoctrination/.

8   "Minnesota Police Group Rips State for Using Anti-Cop Book, Materials in Elementary School," College Fix, November 2, 2020, https://www.thecollegefix.com/minnesota-police-group-rips-state-for-using-anti-cop-book-materials-in-elementary-school/.

9   "Notable & Quotable: California Teaches Kids to Be Woke," *Wall Street Journal*, September 17, 2019, https://www.wsj.com/articles/notable-quotable-california-teaches-kids-to-be-woke-11568759986.

10 Max Eden, "There Is No Apolitical Classroom: The Culture War Could Be Headed for Public Schools—Whether Parents Like It or Not," *City Journal*, June 19, 2020, https://www.city-journal.org/rise-of-woke-schools.

educator favorably quotes Bill Ayers, co-founder of the communist revolutionary Weather Underground, which conducted a campaign of bombing public buildings, including the U.S. Capitol and the Pentagon, in a prepared slideshow exhorting teachers to use their classrooms to interpret current events for students using an activist lens.[11] This same resource is then recommended as a helpful way to prepare teachers to inform students about dangerous riots at the U.S. Capitol.[12]

A student in an Illinois school reported that teachers called students in class "batsh*t crazy," "losers," and "pathetic" for supporting the losing candidate in a contentious election, causing several to leave required Zoom classrooms abruptly. The student sent a pleading message to the administration asking them to "[p]lease stop our teachers from making students feel isolated and uncomfortable when having these important discussions."

Students at a California private school were told to evaluate how "racism is the bedrock of the USA," while another student reports that her private school has formed "diversity pods" from which students of certain races are excluded. Meanwhile, teachers at the Dalton School in Manhattan issued a list of demands that caused parents to remove their kids from the school. Their expectations include sending half of all incoming donations to NYC public schools, eliminating AP courses if there are racial disparities in scores, requiring annual "anti-racism"

[11] Alyssa Hadley Dunn, "Teaching on Days after: Post-Election Pedagogy for Equity and Justice," Michigan State University, https://docs.google.com/presentation/d/1hQ_aBr95gU6xf0OAHPBTOaSkThvzZexf6-dBrROODb4/edit?fbclid=IwAR2j0jjhAT7v2P2KrLMFSh85ye5rrcg1T5BVFlnwzh-V86I9zYOZb2KDzXwM#slide=id.g35f391192_00.

[12] Jennifer Bradley, "Resources for Teachers on the Days after the Attack on the U.S. Capitol," Beyond the Stoplight, January 6, 2021, https://beyondthestoplight.com/2021/01/06/resources-for-teachers-on-the-days-after-the-attack-on-the-u-s-capitol/.

statements from employees, and enforcing mandatory diversity plot lines in school plays.[13]

The specific topics of the complaints in the examples above are not the point of this book. They change from year to year, or even from week to week. Over the past few years, the following issues have waxed and waned in intensity: global warming, Occupy Wall Street, weapons of mass destruction, voter suppression, immigration reform, the border wall, DACA, Black Lives Matter, gun control, same-sex marriage, reproductive rights, abortion, patriotism, election integrity, and the Me Too movement. In all of these examples, well-intentioned people of good faith can agree on underlying problems, while disagreeing on what to actually do about them.

Increasingly, however, children who are too young to have developed solid or informed opinions on these and other topics are being forced into premature ideological conformity with some teachers and administrators who seem intent on pushing their own particular worldviews in K–12 classrooms. This is my own book and it represents my own opinions. However, my opinions are informed from my vantage point as director of High School Outreach at the Foundation for Individual Rights in Education (FIRE). My job allows me to hear these kinds of transgressions regularly, often from people on the political Right. But it also happens from the Left.

A Minnesota public bus driver wanted to evangelize his Christianity, so he led prayers on the bus during his work hours.[14] A Georgia teacher was yanked from class after telling the students that President Barack

13 Keith Griffith, "Parents at Manhattan's $54K-a-Year Dalton School Pull Their Kids after It Imposes Anti-Racism Manifesto That Focuses on 'Challenges to White Supremacy,'" Daily Mail Online, December 22, 2020, https://www.dailymail.co.uk/news/article-9072155/Parents-Dalton-School-balk-staffs-eight-page-list-anti-racist-demands.html.

14 Janissa Delzo, "School Bus Driver Who Led Prayer with Students Removed from Job," Newsweek, April 21, 2018, https://www.newsweek.com/school-bus-driver-george-nathaniel-fired-prayer-students-896215.

Obama was a closeted Muslim.[15] In a widely shared TikTok video, a high school student angrily objected to the prominent display of politicized flags (Blue Lives Matter and "Don't Tread on Me") in their classroom, saying, "As a teacher, you're here to educate students, and putting up a f**king political flag that some people might be offended by that is not responsible of you as a teacher." The person who uploaded the video later said that the flag was subsequently taken down by the superintendent.[16] In Alabama, a geometry teacher actually taught a math lesson by asking students to evaluate the best angles to assassinate President Obama.[17] In Wisconsin, a high school social studies teacher was placed on leave after instructing students to watch a one-sided video questioning the integrity of election results.[18] In a shared screenshot of the assignment, he also apparently made sure to inform students that he would be protesting what he saw as unfair election results because it was "too important" not to do so, in a pretty clear attempt to influence them on this issue.[19] Teachers in Virginia, Florida, and Pennsylvania have also been subjected to disciplinary actions for classroom discussions related to attendance at

---

15   Doyle Murphy, "Georgia Teacher Pulled from Classroom for Anti-Obama Rant," *New York Daily News*, April 28, 2015, https://www.nydailynews.com/news/national/georgia-teacher-pulled-classroom-anti-obama-rant-article-1.2202604.

16   James Crowley, Student Confronts Teacher for Having Blue Lives Matter Flag in Classroom," Newsweek, January 12, 2021, https://www.newsweek.com/white-student-yells-teacher-blue-lives-matter-flag-classroom-1560865

17   Richard Adams, "Teacher Suspended for President Obama Assassination Lesson," *Guardian*, May 19, 2010, https://www.theguardian.com/world/richard-adams-blog/2010/may/19/teacher-alabama-assasination-obama.

18   Scott Williams, "Burlington High School Teacher Suspended; Allegedly Directed Students to Watch Video Questioning Election Results," *Journal Times*, January 7, 2021, https://journaltimes.com/news/local/burlington-high-school-teacher-suspended-allegedly-directed-students-to-watch-video-questioning-election-results/article_d193258b-806a-5a6b-a90c-12390d9e9530.html.

19   Sam Wunderle (@Sam_Wunderle), tweet, January 7, 2021, https://twitter.com/Sam_Wunderle/status/1347251433851203585/photo/1.

or personal views on the election-related demonstrations and subsequent riot at the Capitol.[20]

No matter the specifics of the heavy-handed "thought reform," we should all be against it. "Citizens of both parties should adopt a legal corollary to the Golden Rule—fight for the rights of others that you would like to exercise yourself," wrote former FIRE president and *Time* magazine contributor David French. "And one of the most important and vital of those rights is the right to speak and act in accordance with your deepest beliefs."[21]

In fact, I've noticed that liberal parents are—in some ways—even more alarmed over the rapid transformation of their children's schools and surprised to find themselves opposed to it. If it ever was once a partisan issue, the problem of school indoctrination has steadily worsened to the point that people across the political spectrum have found themselves allied against it.

FIRE defends free speech and other student (and faculty) rights at colleges throughout the country, and has recently become alarmed at the growing threats to these rights before students even arrive on campus. As a nonpartisan organization, we strive to stand on principle against unhealthy, dialogue-destroying censorship and for academic freedom and attempt to call balls and strikes fairly, as challenging as that can sometimes be. When I'm asked to explain what FIRE does, I often summarize it by saying that "we protect dissenters and defend your right to disagree." This is one of our most precious and basic freedoms in America.

For a number of principled reasons, FIRE has also long opposed what can be referred to as "thought reform" in academia. Our free speech rights derive from the same Enlightenment philosophy that brought us the American Revolution and our founding documents, so it's no surprise that FIRE was co-founded by an esteemed professor of seventeenth- and

---

[20] Sierra Fox, "Prince William teacher on leave after Capitol riot comments during class," Fox5, January 22, 2021, https://www.fox5dc.com/news/video-prince-william-teacher-on-leave-after-capitol-riot-comments-during-class.

[21] David French, "Religious Liberty: Not Just for Social Conservatives," *Dispatch*, February 5, 2020, https://thedispatch.com/p/religious-liberty-not-just-for-social.

eighteenth-century intellectual history, intent on defending the First Amendment freedoms of his students. Of the dangers of encroaching ideological enforcement on campus, Alan Charles Kors writes, "From the Inquisition to the political use of Soviet psychiatry, history has taught us to recoil morally from the violation of the ultimate refuges of self-consciousness, conscience, and private beliefs." More than twenty years ago, Kors observed the growing thought reform efforts on campuses throughout the country and wrote of them, concerningly, "Even traditionalist campuses now permit the ideologues in their offices of student life to pursue individuals into the last inner refuge of free men and women and to turn students over to trainers who want them to change 'within themselves.'"[22] Now, these same invasive efforts have filtered down to younger students not attending college by choice, but K–12 schools by legal compulsion.

Attorneys Harvey A. Silverglate and Jordan Lorence further describe this increasingly widespread phenomenon in FIRE's *Guide to First-Year Orientation and Thought Reform on Campus.* They distinguish between preventing and commanding speech, explaining that "[i]n our legal tradition, it is a worse violation of the First Amendment to force someone to say that which he does not believe (which we might describe as an affirmative form of censorship) than to prevent him from saying that which he does believe (which we might describe as a negative form of censorship)." They then explain:

> [T]he Affirmative form of censorship...goes beyond prohibiting "bad" speech and ideas. It instead seeks to impose on a student, and coerce the student to adopt, and to believe in, the "approved" point of view advanced by the authorities. Official acts that invade this private sphere of thought and conscience—what we call, in its starkest form, "thought reform"—are related to the more familiar concept of censorship of public speech,

---

[22] Alan Kors, "Thought Reform 101," *Reason*, March 2000, https://reason.com/2000/03/01/thought-reform-101-2/.

but reach far deeper. Instead of preventing students from expressing their views and beliefs, thought reform seeks to coerce students into contradicting those views and beliefs by saying things that they do not believe and that may, in fact, violate their most deeply held beliefs, with the ultimate goal of forcing change in those beliefs themselves. This act reaches deep into the mind and heart of a human being and seeks to force him not only to abandon his own beliefs, but also to mouth and indeed adopt the beliefs of those in positions of power and authority over him. Censoring speech is bad enough, but requiring people to adhere to, and even to believe (or at least to proclaim belief) in an official, orthodox ideology is completely incompatible with a free society and is the hallmark of totalitarian social control.[23]

Sound scary? It is. Sound un-American? Yep.

Many of you don't want to think about this, and I understand. You'd rather send your kids to school and trust implicitly in the system, as your own parents probably did. After all, it worked out okay for you. However, ignoring this problem won't make it go away. This fight will come to you, whether or not you want it. It doesn't matter if you live in a city or the rural South. A very specific ideology which developed in "elite" academia has jumped its boundaries and is seeping out into our culture…possibly into your home.

In this book, I'm going to explain how this "thought reform" is playing out at grade levels you probably assumed were protected and immune. And, more importantly, I'll explain what you can do as a parent or grandparent to help protect your family and community from these violations. It's a difficult subject, but one we must learn in order to combat the perilous "thought reform" happening across our nation.

---

[23] Harvey Silverglate and Jordan Lorence, *FIRE's Guide to First-Year Orientation and Thought Reform on Campus* (Philadelphia, PA: Foundation for Individual Rights in Education, 2005), 3–4.

2

The Way Schools Used to Be

We all have an idea of how school is "supposed" to be. This conception is based on personal experience, longstanding cultural traditions, and customary expectations for educator behavior. Undoubtedly, some of us have fonder memories of the "schools of yesteryear" than others. What evokes warm nostalgic reminiscences in one might stoke shudders of bad recollections for another.

Schools, as democratic institutions, represent their communities and generally uphold and model majoritarian community values. Those in the minority may have felt their perspective was less valued and pushed to the margins of classroom activity in traditional classroom arrangements. There are many types of minority positions: racial and ethnic backgrounds, religious beliefs, language challenges, gender, socioeconomic class, learning disabilities, and other differences—some of which are invisible. Some students have distinct advantages, such as educated parents who provide scholastic enrichment and homework support, that others lack.

It's unreasonable to expect every student will experience his or her ideal learning environment each day, no matter which school he attends. While we educators are likely always to fall short of perfection, and will surely disappoint some of our students (and parents) on some days, we can and should always strive to improve our professional practice. However, the current jettisoning of longstanding academic practices in order to correct perceived deficiencies in society is creating new problems greater than the ones educators purport to be solving.

For instance, American schools naturally have a great deal of student viewpoint diversity. On any given topic, students—and educators—may bring a range of conflicting perspectives based on their own individual backgrounds and unique experiences. But Americans have a right to hold divergent opinions, and this includes at school. As the Supreme Court ruled in 1969 in the landmark case of *Tinker v. Des Moines Independent Community School District*, students do not "shed their constitutional rights to freedom of speech or expression at the schoolhouse gate."[24] Diverging views must be respected and allowed.

Basic tolerance for student ideological diversity is a longstanding cultural expectation in American schools. Preserving this involves upholding normative social agreements and certain implicit assumptions that govern how we treat one another in civil society. Part of this mindset includes the presumption that we all have something worthwhile to learn from others who are different from us, which has long been a cherished, integral part of the K–12 experience, particularly for those of us who attended public schools.

These practices are based in common sense, wisdom, and mutual respect. Traditionally, educators are expected to function as impartial temporary guardians of others' children, acting *in loco parentis*, which means that they are to do what the parents would do if they were there. They never exceed their assigned occupational boundaries and defer to recognized parental authority regarding beliefs, which are in the "hands-off," "no-go" zone. Educators did not presume to dictate to students what values they should hold, beyond insisting upon adherence to established school rules. Responsible educators refrained from using their access to impressionable children in order to exert influence upon them, but

---

[24] 393 US 503, 506 (1969).

instead respected the sanctity of each child's individual free will and emerging understanding of the world.

School should be a place where every child is able to become the best possible version of themselves, with the opportunity to develop their own specific abilities and ideas. It should be a place to gain perspective of both the triumphs and errors of the past in order to properly and appropriately contextualize current events. It should be a laboratory for developing the critical thinking skills necessary to meet the challenges a person will confront in a lifetime. It's also a place to assimilate crucial cultural norms, such as respecting the right of other citizens to their own opinions, and the accompanying attitude of scholastic openness to competing ideas that has long been foundational for incoming college students. Teachers, in their proper roles, serve as guides, not interpreters, of information, and instruct students on how to think rather than telling them what to think. They are referees—not players on a favored team, trying to deflect the ball into their own goal. Students retain the crucial and necessary autonomy to reach their own independent conclusions as developing, self-directing citizens capable of living in a free society under self-government.

For so many decades, the trust between parents and teachers was unspoken and well deserved. Good faith and shared aims were presumed. Educators were revered as some of the most selfless, sacrificing, hard-working public servants in the community, upholding high standards and molding responsible, dutiful, informed citizens. Parents relied on them not to subvert their authority, undermine their values, or, worse, mislead them about their intentions under the guise that they somehow "know better."

Tragically, this trust has eroded. Whether it is retrievable remains to be seen. In the meantime, responsible parents absolutely must take off the misty, sentimental glasses of yesteryear and take a fresh, unfiltered look at what's actually going on in their children's classrooms today.

3

Things Have Changed

Educational fads come and go with predictable regularity. I've personally experienced (as a student, teacher, or parent) New Math, open classrooms, collaborative learning, whole language, outcome-based education, mastery learning, No Child Left Behind, and Common Core, to name but a few. However, some current enthusiasms are being pushed with greater fervency and insistence than previous iterations, to the exclusion of almost everything else. This is largely because current educational trends comprise not just teaching methods, but an entire political worldview. This is interfering with several important scholastic norms. Most concerningly, the new practices are silencing classroom discourse and chilling speech in ways that impoverish the educational experience for everyone. If there's one thing we're passionate about at FIRE, it's defending open discourse in academia and the essential right of individuals to speak up and to disagree, even (especially!) when their views are unpopular. Instead, what we're seeing are young students cowed into unnatural stony silence, in uncomfortably "chilly" classrooms, and conditioned to second-guess their own naturally erupting thoughts, lest they stumble upon an invisible tripwire that could blow up their futures.

"Critical theory" is having a cultural moment. It is certainly, arguably, worthy of academic coverage as an existing theory that seeks to explain certain aspects of the world. It's been ascendant in higher education for years, and its premises are now being carried to secondary, middle, and elementary schools by recent graduates. As a philosophy that interprets events, culture, politics, and art primarily through the lens of power relationships between participants, it tends to reach certain conclusions and seeks to redress perceived imbalances in society. One of the ways it does this is by silencing voices it associates with power and by "privileging" (giving more space to) those it considers to be or to have been disadvantaged. When this plays out in the classroom, we get the "chilling" effect on free speech that sometimes actively seeks to shut down unwelcome discussions and otherwise encourages some students to voluntarily self-censor. This, then, can run up against students' rights, as spelled out in school handbooks and as enshrined in established case law. Now we have a conflict.

Perhaps not surprisingly, critical theory has spawned passionate critics. According to Christopher Rufo, a journalist who has published numerous "whistleblower" documents exposing ideologically biased school programming and who has declared "a one-man war against 'critical race theory' [CRT] in the federal government:"[25]

> CRT is kind of an umbrella term for a lot of different approaches. Originally it was critical theory, then critical legal theory, then critical race theory, and then critical social justice pedagogies, but the kind of overall orientation of these programs is the same. In the American context, it's the idea that America is a fundamentally and irredeemably racist country and that all of America's social institutions provide this camouflage of ideals like freedom and equality but in practice uphold a system of white supremacy, capitalism, and patriarchal oppression.

---

[25] Victor Garcia. "Journalist declares 'one-man war against critical race theory' after nuke lab holds 'white privilege' training." *FoxNews*, August 13, 2020.

Rufo goes on to explain that critical theory is, "at heart, a Marxist theory, that abandons the old economic categories of bourgeoisie and proletariat and replaces them with the racial categories of white and black or white and people of color. But the basic theoretical foundation and the basic proposal of a solution are the same: it's that this oppressive society must be identified, must be subverted, and must be overthrown." The critical race theorists and their literature make their aims very clear, says Rufo.

They believe in a suspension of constitutional rights, they believe in a suspension of a right to property, mass wealth and land seizures and redistribution, based on group identity, and then they express deep pessimism and outright hostility to the American constitutional political regime. It's not anti-American in the sense of cheap partisan insults. It's actually in their own theoretical work, explicitly anti-American as an institution as a country as a nation state and for those reasons it's totally inappropriate to be teaching in American public schools. Aristotle knew, in antiquity that you have to educate children INTO the regime, into the society, into the constitutional republic, you have to inculcate them with the virtues that will lead not only to their happiness but also to the greatest expression of that society's structure, which in the united states is the constitutional republic. Critical race theory is opposed to it. And it violates this basic Aristotelian insight: that children should be educated into the regime. And in fact, CRT as it's translated into school curricula and school lessons in the classroom explicitly educates students *against* the regime, *against* the republic, *against* the constitution. It's a revolutionary ideology that only a foolish and corrupt educational class would voluntarily select as the official state dogma.[26]

---

[26] Personal interview, Feb. 23, 2021.

Essayist Wesley Yang has coined the term "successor ideology" to describe an emerging academic radicalism centered around concepts such as intersectionality, social justice, and identity politics that may be replacing traditional liberal values of pluralism, freedom of speech, color blindness, and free inquiry in schools. He describes it as "authoritarian Utopianism that masquerades as liberal humanism while usurping it from within."[27]

Another outspoken critic, Columbia professor of Linguistics and American Studies John McWhorter compares so-called "wokism" to actual religion and suggests that antiracism efforts have moved from Martin Luther King back to Martin Luther. McWhorter points out that one aspect of a religion is that "one is to accept certain suspensions of disbelief."[28] In other words, the ideology is so sacrosanct that you are not allowed to ask questions, and are expected to accept incoherent positions as articles of faith. To interrogate illogical premises is to be told you just don't "get it" and to be cast out as a "heretic."

Critical theory is a popular academic theory, and some K–12 teachers want to teach it, having studied it themselves in college. Here's the thing: while it is *a* theory, it is not *the* theory, and it is definitely not the *only* theory. Whether or not it is included in the existing curriculum is a reasonable discussion, but it is unreasonable to assert that it should replace and exclude all other theories. It mustn't consume all the oxygen in the classroom. It shouldn't preempt, conclude, or disallow all other discussions. It definitely shouldn't prevent and preclude the possibility of any disagreement. (Nor is it exempt from analysis, discussion, and criticism, like every other academic attempt at explaining the world.) When it attempts to do so, it interferes with the pedagogical function of a classroom, which includes allowing the exchange of ideas.

Though it may be taught informationally, so that students understand it, it can't be promoted as a system of belief in a public school, any

---

[27] Wesley Yang Twitter thread, May 24, 2019, https://twitter.com/wesyang/status/1132128661556142080?lang=en

[28] John McWhorter. "The Elect: The Threat to a Progressive America from Anti-Black Racists." *Substack*, February 23, 2021. https://johnmcwhorter.substack.com/p/the-elect-the-threat-to-a-progressive

more than religious precepts can. American students, like all citizens, have the right to reach their own conclusions and to decide for themselves what they believe. This is the essence of the First Amendment. To develop properly, students need to be exposed to multiple perspectives as their minds and opinions form and allowed to deliberate openly and honestly in an environment free of intimidation and fear.

Let me explain. By way of illustration, for a number of years, I taught developmental psychology courses, mainly to college sophomores, many of whom were education majors. One of the topics I was expected to cover according to the established syllabus was introductory genetics, which entailed some rudimentary knowledge on evolution—both Darwinian and Lamarckian. Back when I was in college, you were expected to believe Charles Darwin (most famous for his theory of natural selection) was 100 percent irrefutably correct and to laugh derisively at the mere mention of the name "Jean-Baptiste Lamarck" (who proposed a competing view of acquired adaptation) as an utterly misguided fool. How times have changed! Emerging research on epigenetics has revealed that Lamarck may have been more correct than previously believed. It was shortsighted to dismiss him so completely and so readily.

The point is not about evolution. It's that it can be foolish and unscholarly to shut down discussions or potential lines of inquiry. If you do, you risk losing out on crucial information that can lead to amazing discoveries down the line. My other point is this: most semesters, teaching where I did, I knew that I probably had a couple of fundamentalist students in the class whose families had taught them "creationism"—a Bible-based view of the world that rejects the theory of evolution.

I still taught it, of course, but I would generally preface my lectures by acknowledging this possibility and saying something like, "You don't have to believe in it, but you do have to know it. Not only will it be on the test, but you want to be sure to know what it is you don't believe!" Students would chuckle and then we'd get down to business, without any objections. (And, if they had objected, I would have covered it anyway, as part of the required curriculum for credit in the course.) In any case, they had the freedom to believe whatever they wanted in my classroom. Their business, not mine. My business was to teach them.

Multiple worldviews will always compete for precious curricular space, and teachers should strive to expose students to as many worthwhile ones as possible in the time allotted. As a matter of perspective, a case can be made that critical theory deserves to occupy some of it, but it certainly does not get to occupy all of it, crowding out the rest, in the zero-sum game of available class time.

If we accept its own premises, we must be cognizant not just of the presumed power disparities between men and women, different races, classes, orientations, and religions, but also of the tremendous amount of power that adults have over children and that teachers wield over students. *This* enormous power differential must never be misused, and it is precisely why the education profession operates according to long-established codes of ethics and norms of professional practice. As minors, children lack basic rights and some cognitive capacities. This is why they can't vote. In school, they comprise what's known as a "captive audience." They are compelled by law to attend and are, by virtue of their immature status, entitled to certain protections. Regardless of their temporarily diminished state, they are future citizens in the process of developing their own independent minds and self-directing aims. They are never to be used as mere means to another's end; they are autonomous ends in themselves whose boundaries are to be respected.

However, certain aspects of critical theory interfere with the crucial task of fostering open inquiry in school. One way in which this is revealing itself is over the seemingly ridiculous statement that sometimes $2 + 2 \neq 4$.

Some ardent critical theorists contend that even the simplest statement of reality is hopelessly tainted by our subjective perspectives, that one person's claim that "$2 + 2 = 4$" and another person's claim that "$2 + 2 =$ Blue" are both equally valid. What makes that math equation more significant than a person's feelings? Or someone's superstition? Critical theory suggests we elevate science over more experiential phenomenon, because we've been trained from birth to believe the West (and correlating advancements) is better than other cultures. In *Cynical Theories: How Universities Made Everything about Race, Gender, and Identity—And Why*

This Harms Everybody, Helen Pluckrose and James Lindsay explain how the origin of this thinking correlated with the rise of post-modernism during the 1960s and 1970s. According to critical theory, the very concept of knowledge is elitist non-sense. Instead, "lived experience" is just as valuable, if not more so.

According to Pluckrose and Lindsay, critical theorists aren't as concerned about *what is* as they are about *what ought to be.* "This leads to a belief that rigor and completeness come not from good methodology, skepticism, and evidence, but from identity-based 'standpoints' and multiple 'ways of knowing,'" they write.[29] This is all well and good, and can make for interesting cogitation, as do exercises in lifeboat and trolley dilemmas in an ethics or philosophy class, but it still doesn't get to paralyze or hijack the classroom or consume an entire curriculum.

When it comes to education and academic life, the process is as important as—or perhaps even more important than—the product. A functioning community of properly trained scholars knows you don't work backwards from desired conclusions, retrofitting evidence to conform to a preconceived narrative. That pathway can lead to serious error.

In the process of investigative inquiry, you never know where a good answer is going to come from; you must leave open the process of potential discovery. For instance, when a long-predicted pandemic strain of virus struck unexpectedly, the world faced a novel problem. Solving it involved reliance upon wide-ranging open-ended brainstorming, grounded in painstakingly acquired training in virology, coupled with the application of sound principles of rigorous scientific testing to produce an effective vaccine in record time. The SARS-CoV-2 virus couldn't care less about the lived experience, social class background, or ethnicity of the scientists fighting it; what mattered was the process by which unworkable solutions were rapidly disproven and discarded until the remaining viable possibilities, those able to withstand unyielding attempts at disconfirmation, emerged as the best existing solutions so far uncovered.

Perfect? No.

---

[29] Helen Pluckrose and James Lindsay, *Cynical Theories* (Durham, North Carolina: Pitchstone Publishing, 2020), 78–79.

But in an imperfect world, a solution that comes with a proven 94 to 95 percent effectiveness rate in record time is the best we've got, pending new information. Since so many of modern life's dramatic achievements and advancements rely upon academic principles of scientific neutrality and objectivity, we impugn them at our collective peril. If future generations are not given a thorough grounding in these essential scholarly practices, who will have the requisite training and mindset to develop the medical breakthroughs for the medical challenges in the year 2120?

This is serious. A matter of life and death.

I'm very concerned about our future when I read that in Rye, New York, Naomi Schaefer Riley said teachers at her kids' private school only assigned books to her biracial children about civil rights and immigrants (to prevent "research bias") and dedicated a portion of math class to meditation exercises (because the children's feelings are as important as learning the subject).[30]

Or how about when this theoretical ethos enters journalism? *New York Times* journalist Bari Weiss recently resigned from her job there, because "truth isn't a process of collective discovery, but an orthodoxy already known to an enlightened few whose job is to inform everyone else."[31] In a piece entitled "Stop Being Shocked," Weiss wrote that we used to believe that "everyone is equal because everyone is created in the image of God." She continues:

> The belief in the sacredness of the individual over the group or the tribe. The belief that the rule of law—and equality under that law—is the foundation of a free society. The belief that due process and the presumption of innocence are good and that mob violence is bad. The belief that pluralism is a source of our strength;

---

[30] Naomi Schaefer Riley, "My Kids and Their Elite Education in Racism," RealClearPolitics, September 16, 2020, https://www.realclearpolitics.com/ 2020/09/16/my_kids_and_their_elite_education_in_racism_523526.html.

[31] Bari Weiss, "Resignation Letter," accessed October 18, 2020, https://www. bariweiss.com/resignation-letter.

that tolerance is a reason for pride; and that liberty of thought, faith, and speech are the bedrocks of democracy.… Crucially, this liberalism relied on the view that the Enlightenment tools of reason and the scientific method might have been designed by dead white guys, but they belonged to everyone, and they were the best tools for human progress that have ever been devised.[32]

Weiss describes the problem as some mixture of "postmodernism, postcolonialism, identity politics, neo-Marxism, critical race theory, intersectionality, and the therapeutic mentality." Either way, it so dominated the *New York Times* that classical liberals are no longer welcomed, and Weiss resigned from her prestigious position there.

Meanwhile, blogger and former *New Republic* editor and *New York Magazine* columnist Andrew Sullivan wrote that "[c]ritical theory was once an esoteric academic pursuit. Now it has become the core, underlying philosophy of the majority of American cultural institutions.… [T]he CRT advocates have brilliantly managed to construct a crude moral binary to pressure liberals into submission. Where liberalism allows neutrality or doubt or indifference, CRT demands an absolute and immediate choice between racism and anti-racism (defined by CRT)—and no one wants to be a racist, do they? Legitimate anguish about racial inequality and the sheer terror of being publicly labeled a bigot have led liberals to surrender their core values to the [F]ar [L]eft.[33]

This problem is not unique to America, but is becoming a worldwide pandemic, at least certainly a huge Western one. Recently, in London, Kemi Badenoch, the women and equalities minister for the United Kingdom, warned members of Parliament of the dangers of such curricular encroachments in their schools.

---

32 Bari Weiss, "Stop Being Shocked: American Liberalism Is in Danger from a New Ideology—One with Dangerous Implications for Jews," *Tablet*, October 14, 2020, https://www.tabletmag.com/sections/news/articles/stop-being-shocked.

33 Andrew Sullivan, "Why Is Wokeness Winning? The Astonishing and Continuing Success of Left Illiberalism," *Weekly Dish*, October 16, 2020, https://andrewsullivan.substack.com/p/why-is-wokeness-winning.

"This government stands unequivocally against critical race theory. [But schools] have a statutory duty to be politically impartial.... It is a political movement.... [T]here is a lot of pernicious stuff that is being pushed and we stand against that. We do not want to see teachers teaching their white pupils about white privilege and inherited racial guilt," she said. "Let me be clear, any school which teaches these elements of critical race theory as fact or which promotes partisan political views, such as defunding the police, without offering a balanced treatment of opposing views is breaking the law."[34]

This same problem in American K–12 education seems to have started and appears to be most advanced in selective private schools that feed elite colleges and universities (and thereby emulate the schools their students aspire to attend, which are also sometimes the schools from which their teachers graduated). From there, it spread to public schools in affluent areas, and on to school districts nationwide.

It's pretty well accepted that political correctness dominates the scene in American higher education, but when this same problem appears at the K–12 level, it is potentially far more damaging because it targets children. This infiltration is hardly surprising since K–12 educators must go to college to earn their teaching credentials. Under the social sciences umbrella, schools of education have a well-documented, steep, politically leftward tilt.

It's already taken hold and it will increase more rapidly as aging teachers with more "traditional" views retire. Baby boomer educators, taught by the more ideologically balanced professoriate of the World War II generation, are reaching the ends of their careers and ceding their classrooms to younger millennials and Gen Z, who experienced less academic rigor, less balance, and more applied activism in their schooling.

Previous generations have to stand up now for the youngest among us, so that Generation Z (and whoever will come afterwards) can learn how to think for themselves, rather than being told what to think by others.

---

[34] Fraser Nelson, "Kemi Badenoch: The Problem with Critical Race Theory," *Spectator*, October 24, 2020, https://www.spectator.co.uk/article/kemi-badenoch-the-problem-with-critical-race-theory.

4

The Way Schools Are Now

Today's K–12 students are attending schools that are fundamentally different from the ones their parents and grandparents attended.

Students are increasingly expected to adapt their value system to what could be called an "orthodoxy"—an established set of opinions or beliefs that few dare to question for fear of negative repercussions. As more students inevitably yield, the pressure for the remaining students to conform intensifies and the range of acceptable opinions narrows. This constriction of thought and withholding of opinion is inconsistent with and unacceptable for the education of free people in a democratic republic.

Accompanying this growing ideological conformity is a troubling lack of transparency between the schools and the community, with new philosophical commitments being undertaken without full disclosure, open discussion, or buy-in from the people with final responsibility and ultimate authority over the education of children: the parents. In some cases, this lack of transparency is deliberate, with the intent to conceal motivations, when an activism-oriented teacher senses that not everyone in the community shares the educator's allegiances. This can be undertaken paternalistically, with the assumption that those who are "better educated" are justified to withhold contentious information in the service of a righteous cause and for the improvement of those less ennobled or less aware (less *woke*, in the current parlance).

One North Carolina teacher decided language arts was less interesting than dividing students by ideology. In Spanish class, the teacher held a "silent session," where students were not permitted to talk; instead, she asked the class questions about religion, politics, mental health, and abortion, and had students stand at different sides of the room according to their responses.[35] Early reports claimed students were told not to discuss the activity; the district's subsequent investigation found the teacher had not made that instruction, and a news report attributed mistaken claims to a misunderstanding by parents of participating students. "It is not appropriate for a teacher to even ask a student what their beliefs are," the superintendent stated. "Our school system takes very seriously the rights of students in these areas and students should never be instructed to not share classroom activities with their parents."[36] The teacher apologized and was returned to the classroom after a brief suspension.[37]

However, not all situations are exposed and not all school districts are as clear. In these situations, the teacher-parent relationships have undergone a very unfortunate shift from the traditionally assumed collaborative relationship to an adversarial one. A Philadelphia high school teacher was apparently so concerned about the potential for parents "overhearing the discourse" when engaged in what he characterized as "equity/inclusion

35 "Punishment Increased for Johnston County Teacher Who Segregated Students Based on Beliefs," ABC11, November 21, 2019, https://abc11.com/education/johnston-co-teacher-suspended-for-segregating-students-based-on-beliefs/5660625/; see also "Teacher under Investigation for Segregating Students Based on Religious, Personal Beliefs," Johnson County Report, October 30, 2019, https://jocoreport.com/teacher-under-investigation-for-segregating-students-based-on-religious-personal-beliefs/.

36 Matthew Wright, "Teacher Is Suspended after 'Segregating Her Students Based on Religious Beliefs and Whether They Supported Abortion," Daily Mail Online, November 4, 2019, https://www.dailymail.co.uk/news/article-7646177/A-North-Carolina-teacher-suspended-allegedly-segregated-students.html.

37 "Punishment Increased for Johnston County Teacher."

work" during virtual lessons that he asked other teachers online, "How many of us have installed some version of 'what happens here stays here' to help this?"[38] Should classrooms have the same slogan as Las Vegas? What exactly was he trying to hide?

A slideshow for educators about "Pedagogy for Equity and Justice" included the following thoughts from a Michigan middle school teacher: "I wanted to do something about Kavanaugh and the hearings. God, I wanted to soooo bad. But I was just afraid of what parents would say if they found out, let alone if my principal did. I know you taught us about creative insubordination and all that, but I just didn't know if THIS was the time to be creatively insubordinate. I really… [whispering] [H]old on, I think they might be outside my door… [long pause] Okay, okay, it's fine. [sighs loudly] It's not them."[39] "Creative insubordination"? School administrators, are you paying attention?

Another teaching resource guide refers to other teachers as "co-conspirators," an apt phrase, especially since the same guide said, "I don't actually think the classroom SHOULD be safe for all viewpoints."[40] Teacher training at one North Carolina district indicated that parents should be considered an impediment to social justice and suggested that the way to deal with parental pushback is to "ignore parental concerns and push the ideology of antiracism directly to students. 'You can't let

[38] Hank Berrien, "Philly Teacher: Parents with Access to Virtual Classrooms Would Do Damage to 'Honest Conversations about Gender/Sexuality,'" Daily Wire, August 10, 2020, https://www.dailywire.com/news/philly-teacher-parents-with-access-to-virtual-classrooms-would-do-damage-to-honest-conversations-about-gender-sexuality.

[39] Dunn, "Teaching on Days After."

[40] Bradley, "Resources for Teachers on the Days after the Attack on the U.S. Capitol."

parents deter you from the work,'" implying that "teachers have an obligation to subvert parental wishes and beliefs."[41]

Good faith relationships can only exist when both parties respect each other as autonomous actors with good and true intentions, backed up with honest representations and no intent to mislead, undermine, or cause harm. Regrettably, the teacher/parent relationship has shifted into "bad faith" territory, where some teachers have a fundamental disrespect for the rights, dignity, and/or autonomy of the parents, and a hidden, unrevealed agenda.

At some schools, the institutional ideological buy-in is so complete that educators and administrators are sincerely unaware that other positions on social issues even exist, and hence they see no need to disclose, discuss, or justify their actions, since there is no alternative reasonable position to hold, in their limited view.

I call this book *Undoctrinate* to refer to the opposite of *indoctrination*, which is imparting a "body of principles presented for acceptance or belief, as by a religious, political, scientific, or philosophic group." While there may be various ways of defining school indoctrination, I'm referring here to heavily one-sided curricular content that does not include or allow balanced presentation of competing views, or that seeks to alter students' values and attitudes without allowing them the freedom of conscience and thought to reach their own voluntary conclusions, without coercion from those in authority over them. Professor of educational psychology David Moshman puts it more concisely: "Learning without liberty is indoctrination, not education."[42] People typically associate the root word "doctrine" with church, which isn't far from the truth of the matter, as the

---

[41] Christopher Rufo, "Subversive Education: North Carolina's Largest School District Launches a Campaign Against 'Whiteness in Educational Spaces." *City Journal*, March 17, 2021 and A.P. Dillon, "Records Request Reveals 'Whiteness in Ed Spaces,' 'Affinity groups' at WCPSS EdCamp Equity," *Lady Liberty1885*, September 5, 2020.

[42] David Moshman, *Liberty and Learning: Academic Freedom for Teachers and Students* (Portsmouth, New Hampshire: Heinemann, 2009), ix.

worst offenders do promote systems of expected belief in the classroom. But secular schools are not meant to be Sunday schools.

Tendentious, agenda-driven, biased teaching yields compliancy, complacency, obedience, and listlessness. It weakens mental capacity, and its one-sidedness renders it incomplete and insufficient. The importation of critical theory aims and methods into the classroom (the most common form of school indoctrination now being confronted) seeks to enact desired political and societal ends regardless of the means required to achieve them, which is typical of Marxist actors, and it relies inordinately upon power in enacting its aims. (As such, it may conversely breed resentment, distrust, and outright rebellion against its premises, among those who perceive their educational rights as being violated, which would be another way it falls short.) Either way, such imposition is unwise, ill-considered, and damaging, particularly when implemented without proper notification, full disclosure, and buy-in from the community.

Sometimes, these teachers are fired up with missionary zeal as they deliver their sermons on ambiguously defined conceptions of "social justice" or "equity." Sometimes, they are unwittingly using outside curricular materials that seem innocuous, but have been prepared by partisan groups and do not align with established, democratically adopted curricular standards or practices.

Whether deliberate or accidental, these teachers do their young, impressionable charges a great disservice by treating them as mere means to be exploited in furtherance of a cause. Their unique access to minor children places them in a position to potentially harm them. It is precisely for this reason that public school teachers are *licensed* by their respective states.

Though many teachers remain fair and unbiased, thankfully, others forget that they themselves were (presumably) once given the chance to reach their own independent conclusions and to form their own personal opinions. It is foolhardy and immature for a teacher to abandon the long-term standard of neutral classroom management in pursuit of some short-term partisan aim. For whatever perceived "gains" are made, much more of greater value is lost.

At best, such efforts are misguided and self-centered; at worst, they represent educational malpractice and malfeasance. They chip away at the core of the student-teacher relationship while undermining and eroding community faith in the local school system, upon whose support it relies. That's not the job at all.

Imbalance in the Teaching Ranks

Another development which has created a lopsided environment is that academia decisively tilts to the Left. According to Federal Election Commission data, there are 79 Democrats in the teaching profession for every 21 Republicans. At the high school level there are 87 Democrats for every 13 Republicans. And in elementary schools there are 85 Democrats for every 15 Republicans.[43]

The teachers' unions, to which most public school teachers belong, give overwhelmingly to Democrats. Since 1990, the K–12 teachers' unions gave close to 80 million dollars to Democrats (95 percent); they gave only 3.4 million of those dollars to Republicans.[44] A 2016 study published in *Econ Journal Watch* that examined faculty voter registration showed an imbalance of 11.5 to 1 in social science fields overall (education, of course, is a social science field), but the disparity is much greater in certain fields. In psychology, for instance, the imbalance is 17.5 on the Left to 1 on the Right and in history, the ratio is a staggering 33.5:1 (and the one faculty member on the Right is likely to be older.)[45] A 2017 study shows that over

---

[43] "Democratic vs. Republican Occupations: The Best American Infographics 2016," Verdant Labs, accessed November 15, 2020, http://verdantlabs.com/politics_of_professions/index.html.

[44] "Teachers Unions," OpenSecrets.org, accessed November 22, 2020, https://www.opensecrets.org/industries/indus.php?ind=l1300.

[45] Mitchell Langbert, Anthony Quain, and Daniel Klein, "Faculty Voter Registration in Economics, History, Journalism, Law, and Psychology," *Econ Journal Watch*, September 2016, https://econjwatch.org/articles/faculty-voter-registration-in-economics-history-journalism-communications-law-and-psychology.

60 percent of education faculty describe themselves as "liberal" and the more liberal the respondent, the greater the willingness to discriminate against a conservative whether they are applying for a job, submitting a research paper, or seeking a grant. Not surprisingly, conservatives in the same study reported experiencing a "hostile climate" in the academy more than those of other political affiliations.[46]

Demographic trends indicate that this disparity will tilt much more heavily to the Left in coming years since the faculty on the Right tend to be nearing retirement. This process of accelerating tilt has already begun, as baby boomers age. According to University of California Professor Emeritus John Ellis, author of the upcoming book *The Breakdown of Higher Education: How It Happened, the Damage It Does, and What Can Be Done*, the steep leftward tilt among newly hired junior faculty reaches an astonishing 50:1.[47]

According to an American Institute for Economic Research study, as recently as twenty years ago the academy exhibited a relatively stable diversity of political perspectives. Now it is skewed heavily toward a single "consensus" ideology that constitutes a clear majority of the professoriate. At the same time, non-leftist voices have been squeezed out of the academy due to a combination of retirements and an emerging bias in faculty hiring that appears to privilege progressive political beliefs.

The political skews have also played out unevenly across academic disciplines, concentrating heavily in subjects that lend themselves to political content. Professors in the humanities and social sciences skew much further to the Left than the physical sciences. Over 80 percent of English professors, for example, identify on the political Left. Subjects such as history, political science, sociology, and fine arts typically approach or

---

[46] Nathan Honeycutt and Laura Freberg, "The Liberal and Conservative Experience across Academic Disciplines: An Extension of Inbar and Lammers," *Social Psychological and Personality Science*, March 2017.

[47] "Professor John Ellis Discusses How American Universities Became 'One-Party Campuses," Life, Liberty, and Levin interview, June 22, 2020, https://video. foxnews.com/v/6166221789001#sp=show-clips.

exceed 70 percent. In short, the humanities and social sciences have become ideological monoliths.[48]

Heterodox Academy, an organization recognizing that diverse viewpoints and open inquiry are critical to research and learning, has described the imbalance problem. "American universities have leaned left for a long time. That is not a serious problem; as long as there are some people with a different political perspective in every field and every department, we can assume that eventually, someone will challenge claims that reflect ideology more than evidence. But things began changing in the 1990s as the Greatest Generation (which had a fair number of Republicans) retired and were replaced by the Baby Boom generation (which did not).... In the 15 years between 1995 and 2010 the academy went from leaning left to being almost entirely on the left."[49]

Faculty political affiliations at 39 percent of the colleges sampled in a recent survey showed zero Republicans. Nearly four of five academic departments across the board (78.2 percent) did not employ a single Republican. The remaining 61 percent had political affiliations that were "absurdly skewed in favor of Democratic affiliation." The tilt is pronounced in certain key disciplines, including environmental studies (25 to 1), humanities (32 to 1), and sociology (44 to 1).[50]

As the Iron Curtain crumbled, people often joked, "Marxism is dead everywhere—except American universities." Academics Neil Gross and Solon Simmons provide some notable evidence of this aphorism. In their surveyed

---

48 Phillip W. Magness, "Here Is Proof That the Leftist Tilt on Campus Has Gotten Dramatically Worse," American Institute for Economic Research, May 1, 2019, https://www.aier.org/article/here-is-proof-that-the-leftist-tilt-on-campus-has-gotten-dramatically-worse/.

49 Heterodox Academy, accessed July 21, 2016, https://heterodoxacademy.org/the-problem/.

50 Mitchell Langbert, "Homogeneous: The Political Affiliations of Elite Liberal Arts College Faculty," April 19, 2018, https://link.springer.com/epdf/10.1007/s12129-018-9700-x?shared_access_token=gp2rvi_iDtlQtFfwLwOT9fe4RwlQNchN-Byi7wbcMAY6VS-9n0WALCjqT8pEbO7-xadb0R244aaF16x6E-Ch-26FU5Z9ZKqKu88HBAJCKZSTb4_cMutGPHtjmD0_OnmTYdgYS5-VdrB0XC1ka4Sl19hVSvhDopTS6__WZeCjiR0Sk%3D.

sample, they found that nearly one out of five professors in the social sciences self-identifies as "Marxist," and as many as 25 percent in sociology. These numbers are shocking but probably on the low side. Even the most strident Marxists don't like the descriptor, since the word Marxism is immediately off-putting to so many Americans and political self-identification is so unreliable. Many Marxists in academia might call themselves "radical," "activist," "socialist," or even the innocuous term "progressive."[51]

Lance Izumi of the Pacific Research Institute points out that the teaching profession is more liberal than the acting profession. "Among English teachers, there are 97 Democrats for every three Republicans, with the proportion being even more one-sided among health teachers, with 99 Democrats for every one Republican. While there are slightly more Republicans among math and science teachers, among high school teachers overall, there are 87 Democrats for every 13 Republicans."[52] It's important to understand the influence of schools of education, which train prospective teachers, on the political and ideological leanings of teachers.

Imagine you want to become a teacher, but you're a conservative or a libertarian. You will have to sit through hours of Far Left indoctrination that most Democrats would shun, and do it in a classroom of people hostile to your beliefs. In a review of hundreds of syllabi from three top education schools, one researcher found them dominated by figures who embrace extreme ideologies such as communism and critical race theory.[53]

---

51 Neil Gross and Solon Simmons, "The Social and Political Views of American College and University Professors," in N. Gross and S. Simmons, eds., *Professors and Their Politics*, (Baltimore, Maryland: Johns Hopkins University Press, May 29, 2014), and Ellis, John, "A Crisis of Competence: The Corrupting Effect of Political Activism in the University of California," National Association of Scholars, March 30, 2012.

52 Lance Izumi, "Why Are Teachers Mostly Liberal?" Pacific Research Institute, April 3, 2019, https://www.pacificresearch.org/why-are-teachers-mostly-liberal/.

53 Jay Schalin, "The Politicization of University Schools of Education: The Long March through the Education Schools," James G. Martin Center for Academic Renewal, February 19, 2019, https://www.jamesgmartin.center/2019/02/schools-of-education/.

Lamenting the profession's inability to attract and train more capable prospects, Dr. Greg Forster wrote, "[T]he whole [educational] experience will be of little value to you as a teacher. I would be tempted to say the apparent bankruptcy of teacher education has been a major scandal in the field for decades."[54]

What would the training of a typical middle-aged teacher in, say, California have been like? Lance Izumi says the philosophy of the state university education school would've been "influenced by Brazilian leftist education philosopher Paulo Freire, who *The New York Times* termed the foremost 'radical educator in the world.' Freire famously wrote *The Pedagogy of the Oppressed*, which [has been] described as 'a utopian political tract calling for the overthrow of capitalist hegemony and the creation of classless societies.'"[55]

A 2009 study by the executive director of the Johns Hopkins Institute for Education Policy found that *The Pedagogy of the Oppressed* was one of the most frequently assigned books in philosophy of education courses.[56] (I can attest to that: it was assigned to me in graduate school in an ed program at a state university.)

"The central concept in the ideology that rules education schools, with an iron fist, is that real pedagogy means the liberation of the oppressed," writes Greg Forster. "The idea is that good education is primarily a tool of political liberation. Therefore, if you want to teach people how to educate, teach them how to liberate. With that as a starting point, the actual teaching part goes out the window, and it's off to the races with every nutty political fad that comes along." In other words, indoctrination is simply a new form of oppression.[57]

---

[54] Greg Forster, "Forming Teachers: The Education School Challenge," Oklahoma Council of Public Affairs Perspective, August 2019, https://www.ocpathink.org/uploads/assets/img/Forming-teachers-the-education-school-challenge.pdf.

[55] Izumi, "Why Are Teachers Mostly Liberal?"

[56] David Steiner, "Skewed Perspective," *Teachers and Teaching* 5, no. 1 (2009).

[57] Greg Forster, "Who Teaches the Teachers?" Oklahoma Council of Public Affairs Perspective, April 20, 2018, https://www.ocpathink.org/post/who-teaches-the-teachers.

Consequently, the classroom is now a crockpot of advocacy. What kind of advocacy? The only kind they are being taught.

I saw this with my own eyes.

Academic Pressure

In ninth grade, my daughter's teacher assigned *The Communist Manifesto*, written by Karl Marx with Friedrich Engels. I didn't mind it. The pamphlet is arguably the most influential one in history, and understanding communism is vital to understanding global history. At Harvard, six separate professors assigned *The Communist Manifesto* (the only book I was assigned more than once as an undergraduate), and, consequently, I was familiar with its claim that "the history of all hitherto existing society is the history of class struggles" and that the victory of the working class would end class society forever.

I didn't buy that, but I understood it.

In my daughter's roundtable discussion, students were asked to debate the relative merits of capitalism versus communism. All of these American students swiftly and defensively sided with communism… correctly intuiting that this was the apparent point of the exercise.

Well, almost all of them.

My daughter argued for capitalism. But before she'd made an effective argument, she was cut off and informed by a classmate she was "wrong" because "capitalism is *evil*." Heads nodded all around.

This would've been a great teaching moment. An unbiased teacher might have required several of the "pro-communist" students to change sides to even out the odds and asked them to examine the issue from another position, deepening their understanding. Or, she could've stepped in to bolster the argument of a lone, dissenting student, in order to challenge the others to refine and enrich their thinking.

As John Stuart Mill wrote in *On Liberty*, it's important for people not to silence others' unpopular opinions. "If the opinion is right, they are deprived of the opportunity of exchanging error for truth: if wrong, they lose, what is almost as great a benefit, the clearer perception and livelier impression of truth, produced by its collision with error."

A fair teacher certainly shouldn't have allowed the lazy ad hominem descriptor "evil" to be assigned to a student without scrutiny. Political science Professor Joshua Dunn explains the power teachers have over students: "Teachers are in a position of authority and can dramatically affect the life prospects of students [who] understandably will self-censor to avoid offending the person who controls their grade."[58] A school (with the possible exception of a private religious school) has no business operating like this, yet increasingly they do.

"I tried to take the side of capitalism," my daughter told me after school. Her voice began to break. "But I didn't have the tools to do it."

I didn't understand. Don't Americans learn about capitalism not only by living in this country, experiencing the benefits of capitalism, but by going through the school system?

"No, they never *taught* me anything about capitalism," she explained. "The only book we read on the subject was *The Communist Manifesto*."

Like many of you, I felt a gnawing apprehension and disquieting suspicion growing within me. What was happening?

Social Pressure

The next year at my daughter's school, things got worse. The school's diversity club led weekly school-wide assemblies during which students formed a circle and were asked to stand publicly to signal their support for various, shifting causes. Students who did not stand at the appropriate, indicated times were targeted by upperclassmen for corrective action in the hallways, afterwards, while teachers turned blind eyes. Students had to support all of the causes or risk social ostracism…a nightmare for high

---

[58] Joshua Dunn. "Free Speech Accountability and Public Trust: The Necessity of Neutrality," in Meira Levinson and Jacob Fay, *Democratic Discord in Schools: Cases and Commentaries in Educational Ethics* (Cambridge, MA: Harvard University Press, 2019), 254.

school students already living through the indignities of adolescence. On the mornings of these assemblies, my daughter inevitably had stomach-aches and tears, as she prepared to face the miserable Hobson's choice of either being internally dishonest or risking public judgment and scorn resulting from these public litmus tests.

Just as some religious ideologies require complete adherence, these academic ideologies demand public professions and seek to expose "heretics," and punish disbelievers. This process of "outing" and prosecuting/persecuting dissenters—those who refuse to publicly profess assent—can sometimes resemble an inquisition. Those who dissent or depart from the narrow opinion corridor are often punished with social disapproval, rejection, and ridicule. Young people quickly discern which views are allowed and which will earn them approval or social harm, and they (seeking to fit in and earn teacher approval) conform.

If you don't conform, your social life (and perhaps your academic future) is at stake.

How I Entered This Battle

I didn't want to write a book about K–12 school indoctrination. I used to dream of being a professor of literature, someone who could teach the beautiful words of Shakespeare to curious minds.

I was on my way.

After attending a public school in New Jersey, I attended Harvard in the 1980s, where reason predominated, students backed up assertions with evidence, and intellectual disputes rarely resulted in mean-spirited name-calling. After college, I earned my first teaching certification in secondary English and taught public school in New Jersey. Ultimately, I earned three teacher certifications (including Elementary Education and Secondary Guidance) in four different states.

Soon, I'd be enlightening a new generation about *Macbeth*.

But when I returned to academia a few years later, the tone had noticeably shifted. So-called literary theory, which had made only minor appearances during my undergraduate education, was now enjoying a heyday, and sapping the joy and color from what should have been, and once was, one of the most congenial of the humanities. "Criticism" ruled, and literary "appreciation" was out the window. Rich texts that could have been fruitfully explored from multiple deep, creative angles were reduced to repetitive, superficial, and easily predictable exercises in rote drudgery.

In one literature class, a persistent student invariably described every writer we studied as "sexist" with nary a peep from each easily intimidated instructor. "What if the Wife of Bath didn't want to be a wife?" she asked. "What if she wanted to be a lawyer, instead?"

As I listened to her complain day after day, I decided to put Shakespeare on the shelf and become an education reformer, someone who could cut through all of this classroom morass so that truth and knowledge could prevail. (Incidentally, I was far from alone in abandoning the increasingly dreary and inhospitable humanities. According to the *Chronicle of Higher Education*, at many institutions, the decline in humanities majors since 2010 is over 50 percent.[59]) To accomplish this, I earned a doctorate in higher education administration—a frightful experience in itself—ready to plunge myself into the murky waters of "thought reform" and save us from drowning in it. But higher education didn't want to be saved. After spending a number of years as a freelance writer and adjunct professor of education, I realized I was an "ideological mismatch" for the now staunchly orthodox academy. I wouldn't fit in.

Fine. Apparently, I wasn't destined to wade into those waters after all.

However, after seeing my daughter's classroom communism indoctrination and morning shaming rituals, the same feelings rose in my chest. Education should be uplifting, ennobling, eye-opening, and horizon-expanding. It shouldn't fill our children with canned ideas and daily dread. I regularly approached the administration during my daughter's years there, but they weren't persuaded by my view of education. Eventually, we removed our child from this school, transferring to a

---

[59] Eric Hayot, "The Humanities as We Know Them Are Doomed. Now What?" *Chronicle of Higher Education*, July 1, 2018, https://www.chronicle.com/article/the-humanities-as-we-know-them-are-doomed-now-what/.

reputable cyberschool, supplemented with homeschooling. This experience was incredibly disruptive, disappointing, and dispiriting, but at the time, I thought it was an unusual outlier.

As I now listen to so many similar stories from frustrated, stunned, disillusioned, and occasionally distraught parents across the country facing thought reform efforts in their own children's schools, I empathize, because I've been there as a parent, but also because I recognize that the same strain of ideological orthodoxy that drove me out of the humanities decades ago has swelled to an enormous wave that is engulfing us all, threatening to wipe away many significant standing structures with it.

5

Shrouded in Silence

This might feel like drinking from a firehose, especially if you hadn't heard about these types of incidents before this book. It might even seem like these anecdotes can't possibly be real. If this was happening all across America, parents would certainly rise up. Wouldn't they?

There are at least a couple of reasons why parents are reluctant to talk about these incidents. First, the bias problem is no longer an individual teacher here or there, but rather an institution-wide phenomenon, often publicly stated. School districts advertise their district-wide commitments, and proclaim their "diversity" efforts. School districts hire expensive "diversity consultants" who often lack teacher training and licensure credentials, but who nonetheless are empowered to recommend and impose dubious and insufficiently vetted materials designed to alter students' personal views, values, and thoughts.

It takes courage to stand up to an organized, determined phalanx of educators. After all, who wants to oppose "diversity" and other anodyne-sounding pleasantries? However, it is perfectly reasonable and responsible to take a close look and, when necessary, a principled stand against some of these efforts, especially when they are not as advertised.

Young people have an intuitive sense of right and wrong and keenly perceive when their rights are being violated, when teachers are pushing an agenda, and when they're being silenced. Yet it takes incredible bravery and considerable provocation for young students to oppose their adult teachers. One group of frustrated, fed-up upper school students at a private school on the West Coast banded together to produce a largely anonymous publication in order to protest the uniform squelching of non-approved views at their school. They wrote of a "deepening intellectual totalitarianism of the PC thought police that is metastasizing throughout the country and at this very school."

In a "Declaration of Intellectual Independence," the students recounted school events in which they were silenced or intimidated for sharing their views. For example, several students discussed a discouraging town hall debate held at the school, on the topic of affirmative action. One student came armed with statistics and facts to support the "con" side. But he wasn't really able to properly convey his thoughts as order was disrupted.

"People began raising their hands as if it was treasonous to not do so in opposition to what this student had said. People snickered, laughed, and gasped at what this student had said while he was still speaking. One teacher constantly added his own opinion into the mix. It reached the point where this teacher, along with many other teachers, no longer felt the need to raise their hand and be called on to speak but to begin speaking and cut off students who were speaking at the same time," wrote the student.

He said the pressure from the teachers was untenable. "As a Christian since birth, I have felt that some teachers at [this school] have harassed my religious views. As a conservative, I feel that some teachers at [this school] have shunned my views. Whether it is a teacher telling me why Christianity and the existence of higher deity is impossible or a teacher explaining why Bernie Sanders is unarguably the best candidate and that there are no Republican candidates worth talking about...[i]t is impossible for a student to voice opposition without ruining their relationship with the teacher."

A student's relationship with his teacher is important, because teachers hold inordinate power over the student's future. Anonymous or not, these young people rightly fear the consequences of their unwillingness to fall in line.

"I am no longer comfortable being open about my political opinions after seeing what transpired at the town hall. While I completely stand behind my beliefs, no amount of 'safe space stickers' will compel me to be open with my peers and make me believe that this is truly a safe space. People should be debating political preferences and are allowed to disagree. This is the key of a healthy democracy," wrote another student. "We pride ourselves on our advancements in stopping bullying in areas such as race or sexual orientation. Yet we pay no attention to how students are shunned and suppressed because of their political views."

One parent group at another private school invited members of the community to submit their anonymous experiences about the intimidation they'd received. The responses were eye-opening.

"During my senior year, the administration had a poet speak to the entire upper school campus. This speaker openly praised Marxist ideals and called for the destruction of the 'capitalist system.' While this was the most radical speaker I witnessed, [the school] would routinely invite leftist speakers on campus to indoctrinate students. Not once did I witness a conservative speaker come to campus," wrote one student.

"My French teacher would consistently give the right-leaning kids lower grades on essays in which they argued a side she disagreed with. The class was able to identify this phenomenon and joked about it light-heartedly. From then on, I'd always argue the liberal perspective instead of what I thought," another admitted.

One student summed up the problem in one sentence: "During multiple classes they make me feel guilty about being white."

Another one said his French teacher made every lesson political. Though the Supreme Court has nothing to do with speaking French, that's what one lesson was focused on. "One day, we were analyzing the poetry of Jean de la Fontaine and she turned the whole day into a vitriolic tirade about [Justice] Kavanaugh."

They had to fall into line on sexual issues as well, according to this student: "During the all-school assembly in which transgender speakers came to 'dismantle gender construct' I wanted to ask a question. I held back, and a like-minded student asked it instead. He was shunned by most of the school and teachers decried him in private club meetings according to kids who attended them."

One student's English teacher mocked the president at the time and said she "hated him," and thought he was the "worst president she has seen in her lifetime." Students received an email from another teacher saying, "Let's start a revolution together." Another letter from a teacher to freshman students explained that "I'm committed to justice across intersections of gender, race, class, sexuality, religion, etc. with our planetary ecosystem in mind." Ironically and inappropriately, it was signed "with love."[60]

A public high school student on the East Coast was pressured to walk out of school in support of a cause he didn't support. This was a nationwide "walkout event" (there have been two large ones, recently, both for left-wing causes) in which students were supposed to express their strong feelings about certain current events by walking out of the school building, being marked absent, and presumably taking the consequences, as a form of protest. In this particular case, the school administrators were so excited about the particular cause, that they decided that the entire school including the teachers and staff would walk out in solidarity, as well.

Technically, this is dereliction of duty, but let's leave that for the moment. The student reached out to FIRE because he didn't support this particular cause (gun control), which violated his beliefs, and he didn't want to be forced to support it, against his will. He asked if he could please just go to school that day like normal. The school administrators told him that that would not be possible because there would be no one in school to supervise him, but they suggested an alternative. Since they had decided that the students were all going to march in a circle around the school track for this cause, they suggested the dissenting student

60   Woke at Harvard-Westlake (@wokeathw), Instagram, 2020, https://www.instagram.com/wokeathw/?hl=en.

stand alone in the middle of the track while the entire school marched around him.

I suggested to this student that he inform his school counselor that in no way did he feel comfortable standing in the center of the school track while the entire student body, teachers, and administrators marched around him in a circle. She, wisely, saw to it that the whole idea was called off.

Tragically, in too many of our schools today, students do not feel they have the right to disagree or to state their opinions or beliefs anymore. They recognize a reigning orthodoxy of beliefs and opinions that will gain them approval, and they understand that deviation from that well-worn path of accepted thought will gain them negative consequences and social disapproval—sometimes of the most extreme variety. Many feel they have no choice but to self-censor in order to avoid repercussions ranging from subtle but pernicious to the most drastic and intimidating kind, including lowered grades, public ridicule, smear campaigns, diminished college and career prospects, ostracism, and social rejection.

Secondly, parents don't want to expose their children to retaliation. When even adults fear the possibility of being smeared, mischaracterized, targeted, "cancelled," or ostracized, imagine how children feel about it! This *is* happening to children, often at the hands of those charged with their care.

Children are effectively hostages of the school until they graduate, and so many fall uncomfortably silent in what winds up amounting effectively to emotional blackmail.

6

Reading, 'Riting, 'Rithmetic No More

It's baffling that teachers are spending so much time on social engineering. It's not as if they're exactly knocking it out of the park when it comes to their basic job responsibilities and looking for ways to occupy the remainder of the school day. After all, according to the Nation's Report Card, by fourth grade fewer than half of America's students achieve reading or math proficiency (35 percent and 41 percent, respectively) and those numbers fall further by eighth grade (34 percent for both subjects).[4] That's pretty humbling, as is the fact that only 15 percent of eighth graders achieve proficiency in U.S. history.[61] *Yikes.* Students struggle with basics such as identifying where Los Angeles, Tokyo, London, or Mumbai are on a world map while a majority cannot accurately identify times in different time zones.[62]

By their senior year, a majority are below reading proficiency and a small minority are proficient in U.S. history, geography, civics, math, and

---

[61] "National Achievement-Level Results," Nation's Report Card, accessed November 24, 2020, https://www.nationsreportcard.gov/reading/nation/achievement/?grade=8.

[62] Ibid.

writing.[63] A national survey reveals that most Americans cannot pass a basic citizenship test, with a majority believing that the Constitution was ratified in 1776. (Astonishingly, 12 percent think that Eisenhower led troops in the Civil War and 37 percent believe that Benjamin Franklin invented the light bulb!) Most older adults passed, but a whopping 81 percent of those under age forty-five failed.[64] Meanwhile, civic knowledge remains abysmal. A recent survey found that only two in five Americans can name all three branches of government and one in five can't name any.[65]

According to the National Literacy Directory, one out of every six adults lacks basic reading skills—that means thirty-six million Americans can't read a job application or understand basic written instructions.[66] A reading efficiency study found that today's students read considerably slower than their counterparts of fifty years ago and many of today's high schoolers are still spending a lot of time simply decoding words—a strategy typically used by people just learning to read that interferes with basic comprehension.[67]

From my perspective, having worked with thousands of freshmen and sophomores in introductory college courses at a regional state university over a number of years (both in writing and in educational/developmental psychology), many of these students struggle to memorize vocabulary words, comprehend textbook paragraphs, and write reliably in complete

---

[63] Ibid.

[64] Woodrow Wilson National Fellowship Foundation, "National Survey Finds Just 1 in 3 Americans Would Pass Citizenship Test," October 3, 2018, https://woodrow.org/news/national-survey-finds-just-1-in-3-americans-would-pass-citizenship-test/.

[65] *Annenberg Civics Survey 2019*, Annenberg Public Policy Center, September 12, 2019, https://cdn.annenbergpublicpolicycenter.org/wp-content/uploads/2019/09/Annenberg_civics_survey_2019.pdf.

[66] "Facts," National Literacy Directory, accessed November 24, 2020, https://www.nld.org/page/facts.

[67] Alexandra Spichtig, et al., "The Decline of Comprehension-Based Silent Reading Efficiency in the United States: A Comparison of Current Data with Performance in 1960," *International Literacy Association Reading Research Quarterly*, April 2016.

sentences. Most would be hard-pressed to say for certain whether World War I preceded or followed the American Civil War. Nearly all would be challenged to interpret a few lines of Shakespearean iambic pentameter with any degree of accuracy.

Despite these basic challenges, their even younger K–12 counterparts are effectively being asked to apply a Marxist-feminist or equivalent critical theory lens to already-challenging content, which is by no means an introductory level of analysis. This entails advancing directly to the predictable, expected, pre-foregone conclusion of assessing and denouncing most topics (Hemingway, physics, the Constitution, Lincoln, or [fill-in-the-blank]) as some version of an unenlightened oppressor and dismissing the topic as therefore unworthy of serious, effortful examination.

As for actually exploring the philosophical, universal, transcending meaning of, say, Shakespearean passages themselves, to quote *Macbeth*: "That is a step on which I must fall down, or else o'erleap." How convenient to be able to skip over this hard part and to have one useful, ready, easily memorizable, dismissive, critical standby with which to sidestep all such scholastic difficulties!

The problem, however, is that the o'erleaping comes at the expense of the hard-won development of deep engagement and acquired understanding. Critical theory might be appropriate, fruitful fodder for a late-night, graduate-level seminar analysis by adult students well versed in depth and breadth of background content knowledge, but it is being superimposed on secondary students who possess only the most shallow and rudimentary grasp of the basics. The phrase for this is: developmentally inappropriate. Theory may also be an interesting angle for an adult teacher to apply to familiar material, but it's frustrating for K-12 students and does not serve their academic needs appropriately.

The statistics cited above are national, but to highlight a more illustrative, isolated example, let's look at one school in Milwaukee. According to the MacIver Institute: "Out of the 350 students at Marshall High School in Milwaukee, only one—one student—is proficient in math. None are proficient in English.... Despite its zero percent proficiency rate, Marshall spent the entire first week in February getting students on board with the

Black Lives Matter agenda." Meanwhile, over at James Madison High School, "student achievement is just as dismal. It also only has one student who is proficient in math and none in English."[68]

This poorly performing district pursued thematic emphases on topics such as restorative justice, globalism, collectivism, queerness, and transgenderism, rather than algebra, grammar, and American history. They also organized coordinated, time-consuming school walkouts for approved causes ranging from bullying and climate activism to defending DACA and gun control. They took photos of protests, which were traced, transferred, and transformed into celebratory illustrations.[69] Even elementary school students were included in the out-of-class activism; at one staged event protesting Wells Fargo and Chase Bank, students as young as age six met up with local activist organizations and were treated to the spectacle of their smiling teacher being arrested. Meanwhile, the high school marching band played loudly to disrupt business while students chanted and blocked the sidewalk for customers.[70]

This, instead of attending class.

With so little seat time devoted to academics, you might rightfully wonder how these students are ever going to master the fundamentals. Charles Love, the assistant executive director of Seeking Educational Excellence, is also concerned.

---

68 "Black Lives Matters in Milwaukee Classrooms," MacIver Institute, October 22, 2020, https://www.maciverinstitute.com/2020/10/questionable-curriculum-black-lives-matters-in-milwaukee-classrooms/.

69 "Questionable Curriculum: Schools Walk Out on Education," MacIver Institute, July 2, 2020, https://www.maciverinstitute.com/2020/07/questionable-curriculum-schools-walk-out-on-education/ and "Milwaukee Students Risk Arrest during Climate Protest against Banks Funding Fossil Fuel Industry," *Milwaukee Independent*, December 10, 2019, http://www.milwaukeeindependent.com/articles/milwaukee-students-risk-arrest-climate-protest-banks-funding-fossil-fuel-industry/.

70 Mrinal Gokhale, "Hundreds Protest against Wells Fargo and Chase Bank Fossil Fuel Investment," *Milwaukee Courier*, December 14, 2019, https://milwaukeecourieronline.com/index.php/2019/12/14/hundreds-protest-against-wells-fargo-and-chase-bank-fossil-fuel-investment/.

"Today, in too many predominantly minority areas, the schools are failing," he says. "Instead of improving these schools academically, the leaders of these race-focused movements want to teach the 1619 Project and BLM theories of white guilt. Not only will this create a generation of depressed whites and angry blacks, but it will do nothing to address the achievement gap. While white students are learning code and calculus, our kids will be given an excuse to fail. If they want equality, they should be demanding a focus on STEM and personal responsibility."[71] Perhaps a good place to start would be differentiating what teachers want to cover from what students need to learn, and by rightly prioritizing students' needs over teachers' ambitions and inclinations.

It's happening across the country. While students are obediently taking to the street to protest for teacher-sanctioned causes, and are so quick to parrot approved solutions to societal ills, more than a quarter of last year's college graduates could not name a single freedom guaranteed by the First Amendment,[72] a third failed to identify the Bill of Rights as "a group of Constitutional amendments," and 15 percent were unable to identify First Amendment freedoms such as freedom of speech, freedom of assembly, or the right to petition the government as being protected by the First Amendment.[73] According to *The People vs. Democracy: Why Our Freedom Is in Danger and How to Save It*, fewer than a third of U.S. millennials "consider it essential to live in a democracy,"[74] while nearly one out of four believes that democracy is a bad form of government. More than one-third of Americans aged eighteen to twenty-four now favor some sort of strongman rule, unchecked by Congress or elections.[75]

---

[71] Email to author, November 10, 2020.

[72] *2018 State of the First Amendment Report*, Freedom Forum Institute, accessed November 26, 2020, https://www.freedomforuminstitute.org/first-amendment-center/state-of-the-first-amendment/2018-report/.

[73] "Deficient High School Civic Education Contributing to Issues on Campus," FIRE Newsdesk, July 26, 2017, https://www.thefire.org/deficient-high-school-civic-education-contributing-to-issues-on-campus/.

[74] Yascha Mounk, *The People vs. Democracy: Why Our Freedom Is in Danger and How to Save It* (Cambridge, MA: Harvard University Press, 2018), 106.

[75] Ibid.

How could American youth understand and appreciate so little of the value of the culture they are inheriting? Perhaps because they have been fed a steady diet of nothing but one-sided criticism.

The American Council of Trustees and Alumni, in a report titled "A Crisis in Civic Education," wrote: "What knowledge students do receive of their history is often one-sided and tendentious. Lately, student protesters have sought to expunge historic figures like Thomas Jefferson or Woodrow Wilson from campus, deeming these men too flawed to deserve monuments or buildings that bear their names. These protesters properly remind us of the cancer of racism that has infected our nation, but their demands are made on campuses where there is little reason to believe that students are sufficiently grounded in knowledge and understanding of the history of America and its civic institutions to make sound judgments."[76] The reason for these huge gaps in knowledge, it concludes, is the "proliferation of programs that do not address the problem" and a persistent tendency to deliberately "confuse community service and student activism with civic education."[77]

It's also much harder to hit a moving target or to hold teachers accountable for deficits when these same educators make no claims to be instilling measurable rudimentary knowledge but are instead focused on far loftier but ultimately unquantifiable aims.

No-Test, Anti-meritocracy Efforts

Given the de-emphasis of measurable book knowledge and its replacement with approved opinion-holding and expected activism, it's hardly surprising that we're simultaneously seeing the rise of a coordinated anti-test, anti-meritocracy agenda unfolding at some of the most selective, prestigious magnet schools in the country. So-called "exam

---

[76]   *A Crisis in Civic Education*, American Council of Trustees and Alumni, January 2016, 1–2, https://www.goacta.org/wp-content/uploads/ee/download/A_Crisis_in_Civic_Education.pdf.

[77]   Ibid, 6.

schools," which limit entry to top-scoring students, include Stuyvesant and Bronx Science in New York, Central High School in Philadelphia, the Thomas Jefferson High School for Science and Technology in northern Virginia, and Lowell High School in California. Ongoing efforts seek to replace rigorous high-stakes testing with a lottery system to determine who gains entrance.[78]

In an article titled "Everyone Has a Right to Be Here," one parent wrote, "Most of our families…are Asian families and immigrant families who came to this country because we believe in the American dream of hard work and meritocracy.… What a lottery does is take admission to our high school and put it in the bucket for random chance. It ultimately will not increase diversity, it will increase the number of white students at the school, and ultimately the phenomena that we have today of the American dream will be decimated."[79]

---

[78] Eliza Shapiro and Vivian Wang, "Amid Racial Divisions, Mayor's Plan to Scrap Elite School Exam Fails," *New York Times*, June 24, 2019, https://www.nytimes.com/2019/06/24/nyregion/specialized-schools-nyc-deblasio.html; Christina Samuels, "Selective Virginia Public High School to Drop Standardized Admissions Test," *Education Week*, October 12, 2020, https://www.edweek.org/leadership/selective-virginia-public-high-school-to-drop-standardized-admissions-test/2020/10#:~:text=Thomas%20Jefferson%20High%20School%20for,the%20school's%20enrollment%20more%20diverse; John McWhorter, "Don't Scrap the Test, Help Black Kids Ace It," *Atlantic*, May 9, 2019, https://www.theatlantic.com/ideas/archive/2019/05/dont-abolish-nyc-high-school-admission-test/589045/; Jeanine Martin. "Admission Test for TJHSST Eliminated," Bull Elephant, October 9, 2020, http://thebullelephant.com/admission-test-for-tjhsst-eliminated/; and Jay Barmann, "SF School Board Members Suggest Racism Is at Play in Blowup over Lottery Admissions for Lowell High," SFist, October 14, 2020, https://sfist.com/2020/10/14/meeting-discussing-lottery-lowell-high-school-gets-chaotic/.

[79] Kolbie Satterfield, "Everyone Has a Right to Be Here: Protests Continue over Proposed Admission Changes to Prestigious FCPS High School," WUSA9, October 5, 2020, https://www.wusa9.com/article/news/education/protests-over-proposed-admission-changes-to-thomas-jefferson-high-school-for-science-and-technology/65-a656b423-ef6d-4769-b3ff-d341b36d1564.

The "anti-test" movement is expanding to include more general standardized testing practices, which conveniently spare educators from being held accountable for students who don't measure up. Here's how another New York City parent described the pressure he and his family experienced confronting emerging orthodoxies regarding testing in his child's school:

> Every spring, starting in third grade, public-school students in New York State take two standardized tests geared to the national Common Core curriculum—one in math, one in English.... Opting out became a form of civil disobedience against a prime tool of meritocracy. It started as a spontaneous, grassroots protest against a wrongheaded state of affairs. Then, with breathtaking speed, it transcended the realm of politics and became a form of moral absolutism, with little tolerance for dissent.
>
> We took the school at face value when it said that this decision was ours to make. My wife attended a meeting for parents, billed as an "education session." But when she asked a question that showed we hadn't made up our minds about the tests, another parent quickly tried to set her straight. The question was out of place—no one should want her child to take the tests. The purpose of the meeting wasn't to provide neutral information. Opting out required an action—parents had to sign and return a letter—and the administration needed to educate new parents about the party line using other parents who had already accepted it, because school employees were forbidden to propagandize.... I took a sounding of parents at our bus stop. Only a few were open to the tests, and they didn't say this loudly. One parent was trying to find a way to have her daughter take the tests off school grounds. Everyone sensed that failing to opt

out would be unpopular with the principal, the staff, and the parent leaders—the school's power structure.

A careful silence fell over the whole subject. One day, while volunteering in our son's classroom, I asked another parent whether her son would take the tests. She flashed a nervous smile and hushed me—it wasn't something to discuss at school.... The week of the tests, one of the administrators approached me in the school hallway. "Have you decided?" I told her that our son would take the tests.... Later that afternoon we spent an hour on the phone. She described all the harm that could come to our son if he took the tests—the immense stress, the potential for demoralization. I replied with our reason for going ahead—we wanted him to learn this necessary skill. The conversation didn't feel completely honest on either side: She also wanted to confirm the school's position in the vanguard of the opt-out movement by reaching 100 percent compliance, and I wanted to refuse to go along. The tests had become secondary. This was a political argument.

Our son was among the 15 or so students who took the tests. A 95 percent opt-out rate was a resounding success. It rivaled election results in Turkmenistan.[80]

The pressure to conform to reigning orthodoxies is immense, and even the adults are feeling it.

---

[80] George Packer, "When the Culture War Comes for the Kids: Caught between a Brutal Meritocracy and a Radical New Progressivism, a Parent Tries to Do Right by His Children While Navigating New York City's Schools," *Atlantic*, October 2019, https://www.theatlantic.com/magazine/archive/2019/10/when-the-culture-war-comes-for-the-kids/596668/.

7

Collective Belief

During Brett Kavanaugh's confirmation hearings for the Supreme Court of the United States, the nation watched as Dr. Christine Margaret Blasey Ford testified about uncorroborated allegations of sexual abuse. No matter how one felt about Kavanaugh's guilt, the hearings were emotionally arduous and difficult to watch.

During the hearings, a California math teacher expressed his frustration and confusion over the process. "I'm a teacher, and I don't know what I'm going to say to my students if Kavanaugh gets confirmed," he tweeted. "Do I tell them that this country doesn't take sexual assault seriously? Do I tell them that truth and integrity don't matter? What do I say?"

The tweet was "liked" twenty-four thousand times and retweeted seven thousand more.

Thomas Fordham Institute Senior Fellow Robert Pondiscio suggested he tell his students that "his views carry no more or less weight than theirs, their parents, or any other citizens. And that the Republic will endure only as long as we accept the rule of law and agree to abide by lawful outcomes—even those we don't agree with."[81]

Though I agree with Pondiscio's sentiments, the whole idea that a math teacher would need to instruct his students at all about a Supreme Court appointment is misplaced. Politics should not eke its way into every single aspect of American life, and it certainly shouldn't creep into every subject taught in K–12 classes. What does the chemistry teacher have to teach the students on the national debt? What does the gym teacher have to say about immigration reform?

These teachers are hired to teach their area of expertise within the confines of their licensure and certification, not to express their political opinions on every issue that arises in freewheeling fashion. However, teachers increasingly believe that "all people should agree on this matter," even if the subject is complicated and difficult.

These thorny topics include, but are not limited to, how to welcome immigrants in a legal and socially beneficial way, how to ensure the rights of protestors and property owners, how to stop tragic police shootings, how to support police during racially charged times, how to cast one's vote in hotly contested elections, and how to deal with climate issues on an individual and national level. Though these issues are presented in "black and white," they are actually quite nuanced and require serious investigation in order to come up with an educated, thoughtful response.

But intellectual curiosity on these matters is not encouraged. Remember, schools are no longer teaching how to think, but what to think—even if the school's positions go against the students' values, their parents' religious beliefs, or the dominant view of the school's community.

School districts now assume everyone should think in exactly the same way politically. Instead of educators acting *in loco parentis*, they are acting *in loco punditis*, offering themselves as the main interpreters and deliverers of "how we should think about this difficult topic"…even if they were hired to teach, in this example, math.

---

[81] Robert Pondiscio, "Teachers, Curb Your Activism," Thomas B. Fordham Institute, October 24, 2018, https://fordhaminstitute.org/national/commentary/teachers-curb-your-activism.

This new embrace of "collective belief" is happening everywhere. For example, public school districts in Oregon published a letter encouraging people to vote for Democrats, donate to campaigns of progressive politicians who are trying to unseat incumbent Republicans/conservatives, and to "actively fundraise for and campaign on behalf of progressive/radical politicians (especially non-white people)."[82]

The vice president of the National Education Association offers multiple resources for educators, including Black Lives Matter lesson plans, ideas for passing community resolutions, and tips on school board activism.[83] Meanwhile, the New York public school system adopted an entire BLM curriculum, whose second objective was stated as "We are committed to disrupting the Western-prescribed nuclear family structure." This seems a far cry from the literal interpretation of the appealing statement that "black lives matter." (In fact, many are recognizing a need to distinguish between the lower-case assertion that "black lives matter," for which there is near-unanimous support, versus the upper-case organization "Black Lives Matter," which incorporates many political positions and conclusions with which reasonable people might disagree.) Room must remain in the curriculum and among educator prerogatives to parse fine points like these; a key part of being a well-educated individual is resisting the impulse to paint complicated topics with a broad brush and instead grasping and enunciating important distinctions.

News personality Megyn Kelly was alarmed when her children's New York City private school sent out a letter asserting white children are inherently racist and that "white school districts across the country [are] full of future killer cops." "Which boy in my kid's school is the future killer

---

[82] Jeff Reynolds, "Oregon School Districts Say White People Should Vote Democrat to Be Less Racist, May Have Broken the Law," PJ Media, July 7, 2020, https://pjmedia.com/election/jeff-reynolds/2020/07/07/oregon-school-districts-say-white-people-should-vote-democrat-to-be-less-racist-may-have-broken-the-law-n612452.

[83] "Black Lives Matter at School – Resources," National Education Association EdJustice, accessed November 24, 2020, https://neaedjustice.org/black-lives-matter-school-resources/.

cop? Is it my boy? Which boy is it?" she asked. This caused her to pull her children from this school. "They have gone off the deep end," she said.[84]

But it's more than the fact that the school is pushing such an extreme agenda. They shouldn't be pushing an agenda at all. A Northern California school sent out an email which instructed community members to dismantle institutional racism, to "Take the Equity Pledge of Support," give money to specific organizations, and read polemical books like *White Fragility* by Robin DiAngelo, which claims all whites have "a deeply internalized sense of superiority and entitlement," are racist, and are complicit in society's racism. Are you white and suddenly feeling defensive about this accusation? Well, your "fragility" is showing. (As I recall from my counseling training, this kind of *damned-if-you-do-an d-damned-if-you-don't*, lose-lose situation is known as a "double-bind" dilemma, and is often found in unhealthy or abusive relationships, but should never be found in school.) Also, they suggested members be trained in avoiding microaggressions and implicit bias.[85]

Fifth- and sixth-grade students are receiving instruction on novel, apparently values-laden concepts such as "collective value" and "restorative justice." Seventh- and eighth-grade students receive a lesson titled "Think about It George Washington: The Beginnings of 273 Years of Hypocrisy in America." In high school, students learn about "Confronting Whiteness in Our Classrooms," with corresponding lessons on the concept of "white privilege." The high school curriculum includes a unit that expresses "moral approbation" regarding riots—not just peaceful protests, but

---

[84] Frances Mulraney, "Megyn Kelly Says She's Leaving New York and Taking Her Kids out of Their 'Woke' $56K-a-Year School after Letter Circulated Saying 'White Kids Are Being Indoctrinated in Black Death' and Will Grow Up to Be 'Killer Cops,'" Daily Mail Online, November 18, 2020, https://www.dailymail.co.uk/news/article-8963261/Megyn-Kelly-says-shes-leaving-New-York-far-left-schools-gone-deep-end.html.

[85] "IN SOLIDARITY," San Juan Unified School District Fall Stakeholder Forum October 29, 2020, accessed November 21, 2020, https://www.sanjuan.edu/standtogether.

deliberate property destruction and the setting of fires.[86] Moral approbation? Is this church or school?

One of the problems is that administrators have forgotten why they go to work. This was made very clear in Omaha when several school districts had students walk out of school to protest gun violence. At Papillion-La Vista High School, 250 students left.

When I was a kid, they called this "skipping school," and we'd get punished for doing it. But Principal Jerry Kalina had a different approach: he actually protested with the students. "Kids don't need to hear me being upset and mad at them, and throwing discipline at them," he said. "Kids needed to hear someone who was going to be comforting, caring, loving and hey, we'll get through this, let's go together."[87]

Did you get that? He viewed his job as primarily being "comforting, caring, [and] loving" to the student, though these historically have been the realm of the family unit. Perhaps the kids' parents need to learn biology so they can take care of that over dinner? Or maybe they can teach calculus on Saturday mornings since they're missing out on school time because of protesting?

New York City allowed 1.1 million students to skip school without penalty for climate change "strikes."[88] Here's a thought experiment. Would they make the same sweeping exception for a pro-life march? Unlikely. It also puts the students who do not take advantage of this day out of school in a peculiarly exposed position, as they have now

---

[86] Max Eden, "Critical Race Theory in American Classrooms: The Radical Curriculum May Already Be at a Public School Near You," *City Journal*, September 18, 2020, https://www.city-journal.org/critical-race-theory-in-american-classrooms.

[87] Erin Duffy, "Area Students Stage Walkouts in Reaction to Florida Shooting; Papillion Principal's Approach: 'Let's Go Together,'" *Omaha World-Herald*, February 22, 2018, https://omaha.com/news/education/area-students-stage-walkouts-in-reaction-to-florida-shooting-papillion-principals-approach-lets-go-together/article_5f78274e-7b6c-5d9d-83b9-19015ec2bc1e.html.

[88] Anne Barnard, "1.1 Million Can Skip School for Climate Protest," *New York Times*, September 20, 2019, https://www.nytimes.com/2019/09/16/nyregion/youth-climate-strike-nyc.html.

been involuntarily "outed" as likely being opposed to whatever cause is being promoted, regardless of whether or not they want to take a public stand on the issue. Does this not make them targets and expose them to potential repercussions, for their failure to display the right sensibilities at the right moments? Probably.

My point is not to argue the topics of climate change, racial discrimination, the Second Amendment, or abortion. Rather, I am stressing that public schools (which are actors of the government) should not be directing our children on these political issues at all. They are supposed to practice viewpoint neutrality, so that young people, eager to fit in and please those who formally evaluate them, won't feel the need to conform and yield to the clear dictates of this messaging.

Yet, it happens again and again.

A private school in the Northeast issued a unity statement by members of their student diversity club explaining how to be anti-racist and even supplied a pre-written email template for complaining to police departments.[89] One district in Texas outlined a plan to create a process for campus administrators to "document microaggressions and discriminatory behaviors in the discipline offense history for students…for tracking purposes." This includes anonymous reporting by other students of "everyday verbal or nonverbal, snubs or insults, whether intentional or unintentional." Subjective interpretations and anonymous reporting of peers by adolescents…what could go wrong?

All of these programs cost a great deal of money, which is interesting considering the constant assumption that schools never have enough funding. It reminds me of the old bumper sticker that reads, "It will be a great day when our schools get all the money they need and the Air Force has to hold a bake sale to buy a bomber." Well, this Texas district must've had some amazingly good cookies to sell, because they are planning to spend $425,000 the first year and then $250,000 the next four years for

---

[89] "A Guide to Being an Ally in 2020," Rivers School BRIDGE, accessed November 24, 2020, https://bbk12e1-cdn.myschoolcdn.com/ftpimages/54/misc/misc_187692.pdf.

a total of $1.4 million to pay for their program to fight "discrimination" and "microaggressions."

Sometimes the political message is broadcast to students in signs and symbols. In North Chicago, a student snapped photos of a teacher's laptop with stickers on it, aimed at students when it's open, one of which says: "I'M VOTING FOR DEMOCRATS!" Written on the blackboard in a high school classroom in Oregon was an admonition against the then-president: "He is a threat to everything we stand for as a democracy. Please, young people, fight back!"[90]

Young, impressionable students might get the impression that they should adopt these positions, or suffer the consequences...with good reason. In Seattle, a public school teacher asked his middle school class to "tell who your hero is and provide multiple sources to explain your reasoning." When one thirteen-year-old's was the president of the United States, he was held after class alone as the teacher then worked one-on-one to change the student's view. The student filmed the encounter which recorded his obvious discomfort at his teacher's obvious attempt to get him to adjust his opinion.[91]

Seattle Public Schools, as revealed in a "document dump," tells teachers that the education system is guilty of "spirit murder" against black children and that white teachers must "bankrupt their privilege in acknowledgement of their thieved inheritance." They also learn that they "must commit to the journey of anti-whiteness," even if their "lizard-brain" objects, and that "American schools murder the souls of

---

[90] Jamie Wilson, "Portland Teacher Forced to Remove Anti-Trump Message in Classroom," Fox 12 Oregon, May 16, 2017, https://www.kptv.com/news/portland-teacher-forced-to-remove-anti-trump-message-in-classroom/article_79f841d8-8b2b-5c97-b0d7-c5eeeec456be.html.

[91] Jason Rantz, "Video Shows Teacher Telling 13 Year Old That Trump's Comments 'Racist,' Immigration Policy Wrong," MyNorthwest, October 27, 2020, https://mynorthwest.com/2258047/rantz-video-teacher-trump-racist-immigration/?.

Black children every day through systemic, institutionalized, anti-Black, state-sanctioned violence."[92]

As Helen Pluckrose and James Lindsay point out in *Cynical Theories*, these new ideologies finding their way into K–12 classrooms have religious elements in the way in which they attempt to compel allegiance and command obedience, and in the way in which they demonize and shun perceived "heretics" or disbelievers. As such, they contend that they have moved out of the realm of academic inquiry and into the realm of proselytizing.

"An academic theory that prioritizes what it believes *ought* to be true over the aim of describing what *is*—that is, one that sees personal belief as a political obligation—has ceased to search for knowledge because it believes it has The Truth," Pluckrose and Lindsay write. "That is, it has become a system of faith, and its scholarship has become a sort of theology. This is what we see in Social Justice scholarship. Declarations of *ought* have replaced the search for what *is*."[93]

However, promoting belief or faith systems in secular schools violates the legal principle of the "separation of church and state." You are entitled to your own belief system, and to behave according to the dictates of your own conscience, but not to impose it on others. This is foundational to the social compact we pledge to one another in our pluralistic society. As stated in the lawsuit involving William at the opening of this book, the alleged actions of the school "deliberately invade the sphere of intellect and spirit which it is the purpose of the First Amendment to our Constitution to reserve from all official control."[94]

Another way of describing this split, in academia, is the divide between the traditional, objective inquiry-based academic disciplines, such as physics and chemistry, and the newer, subjective advocacy-based disciplines (which are often politically and identity-based), such as

---

[92] Christopher Rufo (@realchrisrufo), tweet, December 18, 2020, https://twitter.com/realchrisrufo/status/1339937490954686465.

[93] Pluckrose and Lindsay, *Cynical Theories*, 263.

[94] Clark v. State Pub. Charter Sch. Auth., No. 20-CV-02324-RFB-VCF (D. Nev. filed December 22, 2020).

women's or gender studies programs. Whereas inquiry-based disciplines are open-ended, faithfully following evidence wherever it might lead, advocacy-based programs begin with a conclusion and expect students and practitioners to promote it, to enact it, and not to question it. (The furor with which they attack those who do is reminiscent of the enforcement of a taboo.)

8

Partisan Outside Curricula

Sometimes teachers, in an effort to supplement their approved curricula, will understandably use outside sources to drive home their lessons. Though it is reasonable for educators to access supplemental materials to boost their curricular content ideas, sometimes they select sources that have one-sided, political, or partisan aims that might conflict with a student's family's values. Concerned parents will want to be alert for this, and ready to investigate the origins of biased materials that find their way into their children's classrooms.

I've received complaints about certain outside curricula from parents and educators, for years. One such example that's received a lot of attention is the 1619 Project, which sounds pretty educational. "The 1619 Project is an ongoing initiative from *The New York Times Magazine* that began in August 2019, the 400th anniversary of the beginning of American slavery," the *New York Times* reported.[95] "It aims to reframe the country's history by placing the consequences of slavery and the

---

[95] Nikole Hannah-Jones, et al., "The 1619 Project," *New York Times Magazine*, August 18, 2019, https://www.nytimes.com/interactive/2019/08/14/magazine/1619-america-slavery.html.

contributions of black Americans at the very center of our national narrative."

Turns out, putting slavery at the very center of our American story wasn't historically accurate. Princeton Professor Allen Guelzo, an acclaimed scholar of American history, pointed out that the 1619 Project is "riddled with mistakes and exaggerations." Following historical fact-checking and pushback from skeptical individuals and organizations, the Pulitzer Prize-winning 1619 Project was quietly edited to remedy some misleading or flat-out wrong statements. For example, the organization claimed the American Revolution was designed to protect slavery, even though evidence for this assertion is lacking.[96] The original iteration also claimed that plantation slavery was the model for capitalism, that Lincoln was a racist, and that the nation's "true founding" occurred with the arrival of African slaves.[97]

In spite of the controversy surrounding this project, it became very popular, very fast. More than 3,500 classrooms in all fifty states have adopted this mostly as supplemental curriculum, according to the annual report of the Pulitzer Center, which partnered with the *New York Times* on the project. Five school systems, including Chicago and Washington, DC, have adopted it district-wide. Because this is supplemental, optional classroom teaching material, the "school systems are adopting the project by administrative fiat, not through a public textbook review process."[98]

"Some of the poorest school districts in the country, with the lowest performance levels in reading and math, have adopted the 1619 Project as

[96] Allen Guelzo, "Pulitzer Overlooks Egregious Errors to Award Prize to *New York Times*' Fatally Flawed '1619 Project,'" Heritage Foundation, May 6, 2020, https://www.heritage.org/american-founders/commentary/pulitzer-overlooks-egregious-errors-award-prize-new-york-times-fatally.

[97] Ibid.

[98] John Murawski, "Disputed *NY Times* '1619 Project' Already Shaping Schoolkids' Minds on Race," RealClearInvestigations, January 31, 2020, https://www.realclearinvestigations.com/articles/2020/01/31/disputed_ny_times_1619_project_is_already_shaping_kids_minds_on_race_bias_122192.html.

a mandatory curriculum for their high school students," said Ian Rowe, resident fellow at the American Enterprise Institute. "In cities such as Chicago, Newark, and Buffalo, with high concentrations of minority students, what will these young minds now be learning?... Black students growing up in low-income communities are inundated with messages from many adults in their lives that they will be preyed upon because of their race. Rather than reinforce this false idea of powerlessness in the face of a system rigged against them, why not educate young people of color about the forces within their control that are most likely to put them on a path to power and economic success?"[99]

The largest teachers' union, the National Education Association, suggests resource recommendations for teachers to use on DACA, police violence, restorative justice, racial justice, and social justice, and invites them to "join the EdJustice League" and "sign the pledge" to "take actions...by highlighting inequities and increasing awareness, organizing for change, and growing the movement." They also offer a rapid response text program where they "organize to win on the issues we care about" and the opportunity to "learn from our activists."[100]

There really is no shortage of freely available, prepared curricular material promoting progressive ideas for educators to choose from, but are any of them balancing it with comparable opposing ideas from competing perspectives? Are they teaching students to "consider the source" and to apply a skeptical, critical lens to these materials?

Unlikely.

The antidote to all of these attempts at curricular insertions is transparency. Parents deserve to know exactly what their children are going to be taught, where the lessons fit into their statewide learning standards, and what sources teachers are accessing in preparing lesson plans. To help

---

[99] Ian Rowe, "The 1619 Project Perpetuates the Soft Bigotry of Low Expectations," 1776 Unites, February 10, 2020, https://1776unites.com/essays/the-1619-project-perpetuates-the-soft-bigotry-of-low-expectations-by-ian-v-rowe/.

[100] "Growing the Movement to Win Education Justice for Our Students, Schools and Communities." National Education Association EdJustice, accessed November 24, 2020, neaedjustice.org.

you pinpoint this information, we've prepared a Parental Transparency Protocol, which is available in the appendix of this book. Parents have every right to pre-notification of lessons that enter the realm of family values and the prerogative to object and to opt their children out of such lessons.

9

Diversity Consultants in Schools

You know those random days during which your kids are out of school for apparently no reason? Those teacher in-service days sometimes put a kink in your schedule, but they also might be filled with a toxic training that could ultimately be detrimental for your children.

The diversity consultant industry, which exploded throughout corporate America, is now carving deep inroads into K–12 education. One of the main problems with this new surge in popularity is that this industry is unregulated, with no licensure or certifications, as other school personnel who work around children are required to have. Alan Kors, in an article titled "Thought Reform 101" described the field thusly: "The desire to 'train' individuals on issues of race and diversity has spawned a new industry of moral re-education.... This growing industry has its mountebanks, its careerists, its well-meaning zealots, and its sadists. The categories often blur."[101] Meanwhile, parents of public school students are required by law to send their children to schools where outside actors may be imparting unproven ideas and contestable notions without passing through the democratic curriculum adoption process.

---

[101] Alan Kors, "Thought Reform 101."

The lucrative training—formerly a "Diversity, Equity, and Inclusion" (DEI) model before it was expanded to IDEA, adding an *A* for "Accountability"—is often delivered during "professional development" days for teachers. For students, it tends to take place outside of the classroom, assembly-style, removing kids from their Carnegie-unit seat time (progress towards their diploma) for the duration.

A great deal of information exists on these consultants' stated aims and high ideals, but not much on their effectiveness in achieving them or how participants (voluntary or involuntary) feel about their participation afterwards. Much of this programming appears hastily assembled and half-baked, as the rush is on to cash in. You can guarantee it's full-priced, diverting precious district dollars from other purposes such as textbooks, school supplies, and building maintenance. One northern Virginia district spent $422,500 in taxpayer funds for critical race theory training for staff and $314,000 for social justice "coaching,"[102] while a California district has paid more than $1 million since 2013 to provide a variety of services "centered on implicit bias and cultural proficiency."[103]

When I was in elementary school, I was subjected to "Up with People"—a funky experience for children of the seventies that was parodied expertly as "Hooray for Everything" on *The Simpsons*. Though a pretty innocuous program (aside from the quasi-religious, compulsory-attendance, encounter, "rap"-session nature of it all), students collectively groaned whenever "Up with People" came to town.

How do today's students feel about their experiences with this sort of training? I checked in with students I know, and here's how one characterized his experiences with such training. "Although I appreciate

---

[102] "Loudoun County Public Schools Spent $422K on Controversial Critical Race Theory Curriculum in Past Two Years." West Nova News, September 22, 2020, https://westnovanews.com/stories/555367615-loudoun-county-public-schools-spent-422k-on-controversial-critical-race-theory-curriculum-in-past-two-years.

[103] Joshua Molina, "Judge Strikes Down Portion of Fair Education Santa Barbara's Lawsuit over Implicit Bias Training," *Noozhawk*, July 15, 2020, https://www.noozhawk.com/article/judge_anderle_strikes_down_portion_of_fair_education_implicit_bias_training.

diversity, my school's program focused more on dividing the student body as opposed to celebrating our differences. Also, viewpoint diversity was scarcely mentioned and not a priority to the program," he said. "Many students simply tuned out because they were tired of being lectured."

Students are lectured, because much of today's DEI programming works backwards from the presumption of guilt. They also may veer into circular reasoning where some attendees are presumed guilty of certain transgressions and questioning this starting assumption is considered proof of the accusation, leaving targeted individuals understandably feeling vulnerable and scapegoated, with no apparent escape. (This is known as a "Kafka trap," in which denial of an accusation is considered evidence of guilt, in a staged show trial.) This creates an emotionally threatening environment, to say the least. Where are the school employees expressing concern for the welfare of the students?

DEI firms across the country have strikingly similar mission statements.

A firm in North Carolina claims it "brings not only a structural/systems lens but also an integrated analysis that connects racism to other power systems such as classism and sexism and to a larger movement for social change." It also exposes and dismantles unjust systems. A Boston firm wants to "build capacity among white people of diverse backgrounds to discuss, understand, identify, and tackle racism." Another Boston firm, which has branches in Minnesota and New Jersey, wants to create societal change toward social justice. They also want to create "conversational communities that drive change."[61] Yet another Boston firm trains boards, search committees, and admission committees about implicit bias and educates on issues of equity, inclusion, and justice. A California firm beats on the same drum. It "collaborates and compassionately rethinks diversity, equity and inclusion, [and] implements 'proactive intentionality,' social justice advocacy, and grassroots community and coalition building."

Even though these organizations span the country, you'd think they share the same central office. Note the repetitive use of similar copycat buzzwords, the instantly recognizable embedded mindset, and, ultimately, the vague meaninglessness of it all. One agency's mission includes specialization in "heart work" and "stretching hearts and minds." What does that even mean? What if I don't want my heart "stretched?" (This sounds, after all, extremely painful, if not medically ill-advised.) This sounds ominous, indeed.

After reviewing several of these mission statements, I quickly internalized the most common buzzwords and was able to mindlessly manufacture my own: *Through courageous conversations, we unpack biases and confront privilege to create inclusive spaces in which to push past resistance and center the marginalized to foster intentional change, drive institutional equity, and engage in social justice advocacy and activism.* But what did I just say? And how many kids are learning the same exact strategy of mental regurgitation to get through this sort of "programming?" My cynical mind says nearly all of them, and this lack of authenticity is its own huge problem.

Make no mistake: no matter where the materials are originating, or what language they use, they will reach your child eventually.

How Effective Is This Training?

The above organizations tout unbalanced assertions and opinions, most of which are presented as unquestionable articles of faith. But let's ignore that very troubling aspect of these programs for one second to consider a very salient question: Do these organizations actually solve the problems they seek to solve?

Some testimonials sound more reminiscent of EST training or seventies-style "encounter" sessions than scholastic content.

"[This is] a life-changing program. It is something that simply can't be taught. You have to experience it and live it. It was much more than diversity work. It was life work, hard work, heart work," said an unnamed high school teacher. "[This] is impactful in ways you could never imagine. Sometimes the greatest impact is within you. I can assure that you will never view the world in the same way," said a "trustee of a K-12 school in Illinois."

Um…what? Once again, I'm grasping for something solid but left clutching vapor. How would you measure anything as indistinct as that? When researchers tried, it indicated that these kinds of programs not only fail to live up to their vague promises, but can actually intensify the problem they're brought in to solve.

According to *Harvard Business Review*'s "Why Diversity Programs Fail," such corporate training is frequently ineffectual and actually breeds resentment. "It shouldn't be surprising that most diversity programs aren't increasing diversity and often make things worse, not better," wrote the authors. This kind of "force-feeding can activate bias rather than stamp it out."

A number of studies indicate any positive results are a mirage. People, you won't be surprised to realize, are good at gaming the system. They quickly learn how to correctly respond to a questionnaire about their biases but the effects "rarely last beyond a day or two."

According to professors Frank Dobbin and Alexandra Kalev, this approach also "flies in the face of nearly everything we know about how to motivate people to make changes. Decades of social science research point to a simple truth: You won't get managers on board by blaming and shaming them with rules and reeducation." Doesn't it make sense that this would apply to educators and students too?[104]

Plus, there's no end or finished product. Journalist Nora Zelevansky writes, "[O]ne-off training doesn't shift culture in the direction we want to see it go: building empathy. Inclusion is an ongoing process." In other words, it sounds like it will never be done.[105] This is good for diversity consultants, whose very lessons create the need for more training. However, it's bad for our students and bad for society.

---

[104] Frank Dobbin and Alexandra Kalev, "Why Diversity Programs Fail," *Harvard Business Review*, July–August, 2016, https://hbr.org/2016/07/why-diversity-programs-fail.

[105] Nora Zelevansky, "The Big Business of Unconscious Bias," *New York Times*, November 20, 2019, https://www.nytimes.com/2019/11/20/style/diversity-consultants.html.

Let's be real. Anything that attempts to reform and realign a person's settled ways of thinking is going to provoke internal resistance and create discomfort. That's the nature of cognitive dissonance, which is never enjoyable, regardless of who encounters it or when. But these thought reform attempts transcend normal school boundaries and educator competence. Certainly, educators need to be mindful of the limits of their own professional training and avoid anything that smacks of conducting "unlicensed therapy." Delving into private beliefs can easily unearth unexpected emotional responses K–12 school personnel are underequipped to handle. For that reason, such programming is extremely problematic in a school setting, but even more so when dealing with others' minor children and without parental pre-notification and consent to "treatment."

Remember the self-help book from the sixties *I'm OK—You're OK*? The new programs transmit an alarming, contrary message: *I'm OK, but There's Something Seriously Wrong with YOU*. A dystopian, discouraging, fault-finding, resentment-breeding, and hopeless worldview is embedded in this programming. How much criticism can a person take? What about a young person, with a very fragile and still-developing ego? How about a hypersensitive teen, already riddled with crippling self-doubt? Programming that begins with the presumption that the attendees are irredeemably broken precludes positive behavior modification.

Educator David Ferrero described the destructive problems he observed with DEI programming in a private school where he worked. He said the students were "stressed" and the programming was "fatalistic," "demonizing," and fueled "feelings of helplessness." Ferrero decried the programs' "pessimism" and recommended replacing the "trauma-based condemnatory approach" with "affirmative" alternatives to these "shaming tactics."[106]

---

[106] David J. Ferrero, "How Private Prep Schools Get Diversity, Inclusion and Social Justice Wrong," *Areo Magazine*, August 24, 2020, https://areomagazine.com/2020/08/24/how-private-prep-schools-get-diversity-inclusion-and-social-justice-wrong/.

Schools spend millions of dollars for programs that make children anxious, ashamed, and bitter toward their fellow classmates...at the expense of math, science, and the arts.

Does that sound right to you?

Me either.

10

The Injustice of "Social Justice" in Class

Your conception of what is "just" depends on your values, which likely derive from your faith tradition, or at least your developed understanding of right and wrong. Our society's understanding of "justice" is enshrined in our laws and legal system. But the version of "social justice" now blithely being "embedded" across K–12 school curricula is quite different. It is more aligned with particular partisan aims and ends that may profoundly violate the personal, individual ethics and private values of many members of the student body and their parents, who are acknowledged, legally, to have the primary responsibility for their education and upbringing.

There is an implicit attempt to gloss over a deep, meaningful discussion of how we reach our conceptions of what is right and wrong and to impose a particular set of conclusions on impressionable school children without examining or even acknowledging the disputable assumptions behind them.

For one thing, in the United States we already have a system of justice. Students need to learn about the origins of this system, the philosophy that undergirds it, and the legal protections it affords them. One of these, of course, is the concept that an accused person is "innocent until proven guilty." Another is the expectation that an accused person will enjoy the benefits of "due process" and fair procedures in determining his/her guilt or innocence. Obviously not everyone understands or believes fully in this central tenet of our existing legal/justice system, or we would not be seeing accusations being treated as akin to convictions, as is now sometimes happening in the "court of public opinion." Justice in our cultural system means following established procedures, gathering credible evidence, weighing it impartially, and treating people equally, among other things. "Social justice" appears to be a second conception of justice at odds with the first. The evolution of American jurisprudence is certainly a large, academically demanding body of material to consume and master in itself, with a long history undergirding its development. It cannot be skipped or bypassed in order to reach some predetermined political conclusion.

"Social justice," as the vague and elastic term now bandied about in education, seems to be focused on attaining a certain desired social "end" whereas ordinary justice is centered on finding the truth. The term "social justice" is benign-sounding, and certainly appeals to those wishing to be perceived as "good people," but it carries a host of unacknowledged baggage that seems deliberately obfuscated in an attempt to place clearly contestable issues beyond dispute in an attempt at invalidating, disqualifying, and dominating all competing views. The implication of those pursuing "social justice," of course, is that any others are "unjust."

Everyone desires "social justice," but many policies are sometimes under this term's umbrella that actually go against simple "justice." Enlightenment scholar Alan Charles Kors, for example, claims "*social justice*" means "*not individual* justice."[102] In other words, group or collective justice.

In the United States, however, we deliberately practice a system of individual justice, and teaching children otherwise is misleading and seriously misinforms them. This is an extremely important foundational principle. We already have a justice system and a system of established laws, with sound historical antecedents, worthy of deep academic examination. Calling for justice used to mean appealing to the legal system, but "social justice" appears to be calling for something extra-legal. Does it mean working to change the laws? What do high school kids know about our existing laws and their origins, before asserting which of them, if any, need changing? Shouldn't kids learn first what our laws are and why they were set that way in the first place before trying to upend them? Wouldn't that be the work of legal scholars and people with years of legal training? People with law degrees, at the very least? Without such grounding, agitators attempting to impose wholesale change are more likely to represent what education reformer Nathan Hoffman refers to as "illiterate revolutionaries."[107]

The term "social justice" is far too vague and abstract to be very meaningful, but it appears to be sufficiently mutable to suit many capricious ends. It simultaneously means everything and nothing, according to expedience. It means whatever its purveyors want it to mean, but whatever it means, it is clear that a "social justice orientation" (as it's sometimes called) is not values-neutral; it is values-laden.

Feel free to go ahead and look up some definitions and see if you can get a coherent, consistent grasp of the slippery contours of this malleably useful concept; meanwhile, I'll share a few I've found (while pointing out that insisting on precise definitions on all obscure, potentially loaded terminology is one of the better tactics for slowing their spread). Educators frequently promote "social justice," but fail to define what they mean by "social justice." It's almost as if they don't want you to know.

Some are more precise in explaining what they mean by the term. Here's a more direct definition from a "leading scholar in education":

> Social justice-oriented approaches in education refer to standpoints and scholarly traditions that actively address the dynamics of oppression, privilege, and isms, recognizing that society is the product of historically rooted, institutionally sanctioned stratification along socially constructed group lines that include race, class,

---

[107] "Illiterate Revolutionaries," February 21, 2021, Man of Steele Productions: https://www.youtube.com/watch?v=vECN2oJ2gMU

gender, sexual orientation, and ability. Working for social justice in education means guiding students in critical self-reflection of their socialization into this matrix of
unequal relationships and its implications, analysis of the
mechanisms of oppression, and the ability to challenge
these hierarchies.[108]

My favorite source for wrapping my head around cryptic terminology
is NewDiscourses.com, which not only defines heavily loaded language,
but offers analysis and commentary. Of "social justice," they write that it
is "the ultimate 'Trojan Horse' term, where it seems to mean one (good)
thing as most people understand it—social justice, a more fair and equal
society—but actually means something else. That something else is very
specific, and most people, if they knew what they were encountering,
would be unlikely to accept it. The idea advertised by the phrase 'social
justice' doesn't match the ideology and worldview bearing the seemingly
identical name."

Social justice seems to borrow from Paulo Freire's concept of "consci-
entizacao," or consciousness-raising, a central tenet of critical pedagogy,
which, according to Wikiversity, is "a teaching approach inspired by
critical theory and other radical philosophies, which attempts to help
students question and challenge posited 'domination,' and to undermine
the beliefs and practices that are alleged to dominate."

What certification or licensure can teachers receive in "social justice,"
"dynamics of oppression, privilege, and isms," or "historically rooted,
institutionally sanctioned stratification"? None. This is the language
of someone who should be running for political office, not signing up
to be paid by the public to instruct other people's children. The closest
approximation to a "justice" certification would be held by a lawyer or a
judge, while issues such as "fairness" are more in the realm of a religious
leader, such as a rabbi or priest. Teachers are no better qualified to instruct
on value matters than students, when we get right down to it. They are

---

[108] Marilyn Cochran-Smith, *Walking the Road: Race, Diversity, and Social Justice
in Teacher Education* (New York, NY: Teachers College Press, 2004).

empowered to enforce school rules, but are not all-purpose, omnipotent authorities in judging or ruling on existential matters of "right" or "wrong." And, even more to the point, what recognized learning standards are being addressed by "social justice" instruction? It's more likely that such instruction reflects the private interests and concerns of the teacher, who is misusing the classroom to pursue some personal crusade.

Ominously, many schools are adopting "social justice commitments" and "embedding" social justice "throughout" the curriculum, as administrators proclaim their allegiance to the concept—despite the fact that this content likely meets no existing or recognized statewide learning standards or teaching objectives.

One concerned parent described how this trend played out in her family's life. "My child's school recently sent out a notice that they will be implementing a new plan for responding to incidents of bias and intolerance. I am in favor of addressing these issues, as I think we need to find ways to treat each other with mutual respect and dignity. However, I became concerned when I saw that the school will achieve this goal by integrating the work of a partisan group which has a blatant political agenda organized around "Social Justice" principles—not recognizing that people might have different conceptions of justice and fairness (I say this as a political moderate)," the parent explained. "The centerpiece is identity politics, which in my view does not promote honest dialogue nor social cohesion."

Social justice now occupies curricular space in physics, calculus (see radicalmath.org), physical education, and so on. Some schools administer pre- and post-intervention surveys to collect personal information from minors and track the adjustment of their "attitudes" and "beliefs" of perceived biases, power dynamics, privilege, and systemic racism in response to targeted instruction aimed at fostering preferred opinions. Are you allowed to collect psychological data from minors without parental permission? What does experimental research ethical protocol say? (Answer: no, you may not.)

Students at a California Bay Area high school even have a "Social Justice and Reform" career pathway to follow through school. This track is recommended for students interested in "careers in education, law, social work, and community organizations with a focus on social justice." They're not merely preparing kids academically to pursue these careers; they're telling them what ends these careers must be used for! The goal is that students will "become active participants in advocating change for their community." What kind of change? What kind of reform? This is unstated but implied by the name. Plus, students are being told they are to reform a society before they even have taken an adult place within it. This is placing the cart before the proverbial horse.

Two educators have published an entire anthology dedicated to teaching educators how to "infuse their curriculum" with "social justice concerns." The authors of *Promoting Social Justice through the Scholarship of Teaching and Learning* argue that teachers should use both "critical pedagogy" and "transformative practice" in their classes to promote social justice. But what if parents don't want their children "transformed"?[109]

In the book *Planning to Change the World: A Plan Book for Social Justice Educators*, the authors explain it is intended for educators who believe their students "can, will, and already do change the world." Change it how? Pictures on the cover depict raised power fists and activists marching with signs saying "Climate Justice," "Defund the Police," "Gun Reform," and "Abolish I.C.E." It is designed to help teachers "translate their vision of a just education into concrete activities."[110] Notice whose vision of "just" it is: the teacher's. Anyone attempting to coopt others' children in a captive classroom environment into their personal crusade for world transformation has transgressed their professional bounds.

"Changing the world" is not one of the recognized learning standards for public school education in any of the fifty states. Just to be clear, public school educators, who are paid with public funds, are expected

---

[109] Delores Liston and Regina Rahimi, *Promoting Social Justice through the Scholarship of Teaching and Learning* (Bloomington, Indiana: Indiana University Press, 2017).

[110] Gretchen Brion-Meisels, et al., *Planning to Change the World: A Plan Book for Social Justice Educators*, Rethinking Schools, 2020, https://rethinkingschools.org/books/planning-to-change-the-world-2020-2021/.

to adhere to established curricular guidelines as adopted democratically through state boards of education and administered by local school boards. This is their contractual obligation.

New Jersey, to take just one example, describes the process like this:

> In 1996, the New Jersey State Board of Education adopted the state's first set of academic standards called the Core Curriculum Content Standards. The standards described what students should know and be able to do upon completion of a thirteen-year public school education. Over the last twenty years, New Jersey's academic standards have laid the foundation for local district curricula that are used by teachers in their daily lesson plans. Revised every five years, the standards provide local school districts with clear and specific benchmarks for student achievement in nine content areas.... Developed and reviewed by panels of teachers, administrators, parents, students, and representatives from higher education, business, and the community, the standards are influenced by national standards, research-based practice, and student needs.[111]

The nine content areas in New Jersey are world languages, visual and performing arts, technology, social studies, science, mathematics, English language arts, health and physical education, and twenty-first century life and careers. The last area is the most vague, but under this area, we find value-neutral standards in categories such as "Career Ready Practices," "Personal Financial Literacy," and "Career Awareness, Exploration, and Preparation." Nowhere does it say that students are to be instructed in or to emerge from school with certain opinions, judgments, or belief systems. Such content is irrelevant to the established curriculum, which is, essentially, a misuse of public funds. Teachers have no business wasting

---

[111] New Jersey Student Learning Standards, State of New Jersey Department of Education, accessed November 23, 2020, https://www.nj.gov/education/cccs/.

state resources pursuing ends that are not geared toward achieving established curricular aims.

Whereas previous generations of teachers prized their scholarly neutrality and lived by the maxim that "politics stops at the classroom door," we are currently seeing open, proud abandonment of neutrality accompanied by self-righteous bragging among a small but vocal subset of activist educators. This tends to accelerate after unpreferred election results.

Activism at the college level has been going on a long time, and today's K–12 classroom teachers were yesterday's college students. There, some adopted the misguided view that the classroom, filled with a captive audience, is a setting to be used for personal political goals and activism. For instance, a study by UCLA's prestigious Higher Education Research Institute found that more faculty believe that they should teach their students to be agents of social change than believe that it is important to teach them the classics of Western civilization.[112]

Likewise, *Inside Higher Ed* shared a call to action from the senior director of the Office of Academic Diversity and Inclusiveness, who stated:

> Many people call for an end to politics in the classroom, as this is seen as the source of the problem. Rather than address systemic and structural oppression and discrimination, faculty are being asked to take "neutral" stances and just teach our disciplines, leaving politics to social media and in-person conversation. Yet for many scholars, this is our work. Many of us are trained to see and then speak on institutional and structural systems of oppression. I have been trained specifically to see and call

---

[112] Jennifer Lindholm, et al., *The American College Teacher: National Norms for the 2004–2005 HERI Faculty Survey*, Higher Education Research Institute (HERI), September 2005, https://www.heri.ucla.edu/PDFs/pubs/FAC/Norms/Monographs/TheAmericanCollegeTeacher2004To2005.pdf and Robin Wilson, "Social Change Tops Classic Books in Professors' Teaching Priorities," *Chronicle of Higher Education*, March 5, 2009, https://www.chronicle.com/article/social-change-tops-classic-books-in-professors-teaching-priorities-1564/.

out institutional racism through an intersectional lens. If we are being told to just do our job, then we are. So the real question becomes, is society ready to accept the true point of an education, which is to develop a group of critically thinking, conscious citizens?

She lists her general interests as "radical pedagogy, academic hustling and social justice."[113]

As popular as the term "social justice" currently is in K–12 education, it is currently in the process of being supplanted by the equally vague neologism "anti-racist" or "antiracist." This will surely be replaced and transcended quickly with a newer term, as the half-life of verbal enthusiasms in the educational community is roughly eighteen months.

Parents—not teachers—are the ones in charge of their children's educations, as we'll see when we review the law. While we're here, however, a word about teaching standards: these are found at state departments of education, clearly marked by grade level and subject. Do not confuse these with facsimiles masquerading as official standards which have in fact been created by partisan actors to resemble them. Go to the correct source for the right information: your statewide Department of Education.

Rejecting Overreach and the Proper Role of the Teacher in the Classroom

A good teacher is a guide, not an interpreter. Their assigned role is to faithfully instruct students in the curriculum as established by the school, which is overseen by a school board, and state boards of education in a

---

[113] Nicole Truesdell, "Front Line in the Fight against White Supremacy: People Today Often Call for an End to Politics in the Classroom, Yet for Many Scholars, This *Is* Our Work, Argues Nicole Truesdell," *Inside Higher Ed*, December 22, 2017, https://www.insidehighered.com/advice/2017/12/22/faculty-trained-speak-about-systems-oppression-should-not-be-required-be-neutral.

public school. Private schools have more flexibility in how they operate, but they still have a clear responsibility to communicate ethically and honestly with their customers (parents and students) in describing the mission, methods, and modes of instruction to be undertaken in the school, along with the curricular aims to be pursued. This is a simple matter of truth in advertising.

Some may dispute this. Some may argue that teachers have a duty to transform society according to some preferred vision that the educator holds dear. Teachers (and/or entire schools) who do, and who intend to act as interpreters in the classroom, or to push an ideological agenda, certainly have an ethical obligation to be up front and honest about their intentions, so that everyone can respond accordingly. Anything else is duplicitous, deceptive, and out of alignment with the ethical and professional norms that govern proper educational practice.

Hidden agendas and deceptive practices have absolutely no place in an educational institution, and concealed motives, once exposed, inevitably erode trust. Parents have a right to be properly and fully informed, so that they can make responsible decisions about what, if any, actions to take, and must be allowed to transfer children out of lessons or classrooms where a teacher has renounced non-partisanship and undertaken openly activist aims in opposition to their family's values and educational aims.

PART
TWO

How We Got Here

11

Downward Drift from the Academy

You may wonder how our public schools became apparent propaganda mills. Allow me to answer by paraphrasing a Hemingway character explaining how he went bankrupt: gradually, then suddenly.[114] Several cultural trends coalesced to bring us to this current tipping point. First, let's look at what's been happening to the curriculum in American colleges and universities, where the current crop of incoming teachers is prepared.

Does anyone else remember the "Hey, hey, ho, ho, Western Civ has got to go" protests at Stanford, back in the 1980s? In response, Stanford raced to replace its Western Culture requirement with a multicultural alternative called "Cultures, Ideas, and Values." Broadly speaking, this led to teachers abandoning our accumulated, inherited cultural wisdom and shared enlightenment values and replacing them with activism and newer identity-based departments. (I hesitate to call them disciplines, since their methodology tends to rely on circular reasoning, meaning that whatever a person occupying a particular identity-based position says it is, it is.)

The result has been a concomitant decline in civic understanding, appreciation for founding American principles, and respect for basic civic norms,

---

[114] Eden, "Critical Race Theory in American Classrooms."

such as respecting the rights of others to free speech and their own opinions. Some departments within modern universities reject traditional academic neutrality, replacing disinterested inquiry with partisan advocacy. They even frequently teach the "myth" of objective reality. Instead, they posit inarguable and irrefutable "standpoints." For the uninitiated, standpoint theory denies science and reason are the same for all humans, but posits they depend on your group. Also, it claims disagreement is not an option.[115] It is irrefutable.

Departments from the humanities to the social sciences (including ed schools) embraced relativism, which splintered disciplines by the people studying rather than the content being studied. Whereas traditional academic inquiry and science require withstanding attempts at disconfirmation (according to Karl Popper, the Falsification Principle is what demarcates science from non-science), advocacy/activism merely requires, nay, *demands*, genuflection and obedience.

Have you ever heard the tale of "The Blind Men and the Elephant"?

It's an Indian story about a group of blind men who've never encountered an elephant. Each one is allowed to touch a part of the animal, but only a part—for example, one might touch its ear while another feels its tusk. When they each describe what an elephant is, their descriptions vary wildly. They even begin to doubt the truthfulness of their friends, believing them to be lying about what they felt. The moral of the story is that we each perceive only a limited part of the entirety from our narrow, limited position. Each of us misses the whole, yet we claim absolute truth based on our limited, subjective experience.

This is happening over and over and over in academia.

Undergraduates used to learn formal logic, a requirement that was gradually removed from the liberal arts core, much to the decline of American discourse and reasoning skill. We now see easily disputable logical fallacies being promoted as "arguments" throughout academia and in the general culture. Casuistry and speciousness, unsound reasoning, and impenetrable, cloudy jargon, masquerading as "evidence," now substitute

---

[115] Samuel Hoadley-Brill, "The Cynical Theorists behind *Cynical Theories*," LiberalCurrents, August 19, 2020, https://www.liberalcurrents.com/the-cynical-theorists-behind-cynical-theories/

for the tedious hard work of collecting and verifying proof and applying disciplinary rigor to the analysis of perennial questions.

We have some people (who've felt a tusk) screaming, "An elephant is hard and made of ivory," while others (who've encountered only an ear) say, "No, an elephant is fleshy and very thin." We've lost the ability to take a step back and see the whole picture, and we're beginning to look at our fellow Americans with great suspicion and doubt.

Ed Schools and Enveloping "Theory"

The Marxian theories that underlie most of today's most troubling K–12 curricular incursions fall under critical theory, although they're so omnipresent and polynymous they're often simply referred to now as "theory." Critical race theory was largely pioneered in U.S. schools of education where a generation of teachers was trained in its toxic assumptions. According to the Manhattan Institute's Max Eden, racial unrest catalyzed a host of major education trade associations to publicly vow to "imprint this ideology onto the next generation."[116] These associations include the National Council of Teachers of English (NCTE), the National Association of Secondary School Principals, and the National Council for the Social Studies' Committee on Social Studies' Early Childhood/ Elementary Community. The last has promised to overhaul educational content: "We need to start early. WE, as educators, and family members, need to flood our children with counter messages."[117]

The Frankfurt School of thought gained "cultural hegemony" at Columbia University during the early twentieth century and heavily impacted the highly influential Teachers College there. Founded to advance Marxist studies, it was forced out of Germany in the 1920s and relocated to the United States, where it advanced relentless criticism of capitalist society and advocated a "long march through the institutions" to upend

---

[116] Eden, "Critical Race Theory in American Classrooms."

[117] Max Eden, "Public Education Has Gone 'Woke,'" Manhattan Institute, June 24, 2020, https://www.manhattan-institute.org/public-education-has-gone-woke.

it.[118] Even today, it leaves an indelible imprint on American educational practice. Consider the following current course offerings at Columbia Teachers College, taken from their 2020 website:[119]

C&T 6517 Contemporary Curriculum Studies

This course examines contemporary ideas on curriculum and forms of curricular inquiry drawn from a range of theoretical stances, including neo-Marxist, feminist, post-structuralist, postfoundational, critical race theory, and queer scholarship. In discussing particular approaches and studies, we will consider the contexts in which alternative theories of curriculum have arisen, what problems or critiques they respond to, and their usefulness in understanding concrete schooling practices and dilemmas. One topic that will be pursued in depth is the relationship between curricular knowledges (formal and informal) and student subjectivities/identities.

C&T 6010 Poststructuralist Theories and Education

The course is an introduction to some poststructuralist and feminist poststructuralist theories and their possible uses in educational research and practice. These theoretical orientations are widely used in education, in the humanities and social sciences, and in cross-disciplinary

---

[118] "The Marxist 'Long March' into the Age of Identity Politics," *Parrhesia Diaries* (blog), February 1, 2020, theparrhesiadiaries.medium.com/the-marxist-long-march-through-the-institutions-and-into-the-age-of-identity-politics-6a7042b-235dc.

[119] "Academic Catalog 2022-2021," Department of Curriculum and Teaching, Teachers College, Columbia University, accessed November 25, 2020, https://www.tc.columbia.edu/catalog/academics/departments/curriculum-and-teaching/.

fields such as cultural studies, gender and sexuality studies, postcolonial and transnational studies, etc.

C&T 6535 Freire Culture Circles: Critical Pedagogy in Action

This seminar is designed for doctoral students in education who are interested in critical pedagogy. In addition to engaging with the work of Paulo Freire, students will have the opportunity to critically problematize education inequities from a Freirean perspective, through culture circles. Students and instructor will work dialogically as a community to name, unpack, deconstruct, and reconceptualize historical and contemporary issues in education. This will entail reading the world and engaging in critical problem posing collectively.

C&T 6560 Critical Race Theory in Education

This course aims to help students explore and understand Critical Race Theory (CRT) as an analytical framework for studying inequities in education broadly defined--in pre/schools, community settings, etc. It provides a platform for investigating race-based epistemologies, methodologies, and pedagogies.

C&T 6025 Teacher Educator as Transformative Activist Researcher: Inquiry in Teacher Learning

This doctoral research course is designed to prepare future teacher educators to be researchers of teacher education. We focus on research on teacher education primarily in the U.S. contexts and examine what questions are absent in the published studies. Taking up a transformative, activist stance, we study various research methods and a wide variety of possible methodological tools. We use these to then design two research studies: one small-scale study examining a local pedagogical enactment; and one larger, mixed methods or longitudinal study designed to be conducted by a group.

C&T 6521 Mapping Literacy Research for Equity and Justice

Examines research on the inequities and exclusions produced by school literacy for children and youth from minoritized communities, and explores theories and methodologies that offer new imaginaries for literacy education for equity and justice.

Notice that repetitive sameness?

Just as the "consultant class" uses the same language, catchphrases, and tone, university classes use the same loaded, cryptic terminology advancing the same predictable ideology, over and over again, under different names. Lather, rinse, and repeat. These are not neutral explorations; there's an embedded ideology which lacks contextualization and counterbalancing opposition.

Do these sound like courses that will equip classroom teachers to raise the dismal mathematics and reading scores of their student charges—or to be prepared to accomplish something else, entirely?

The ed school's current tagline is: Prepare to transform. Transform what, into what? Shouldn't the education school's tagline have *something* to do with educating?

One recent graduate, a self-described progressive, confessed to me he was "traumatized" by the teacher training he endured there, citing "policing of speech," "cultish" behavior, "science denialism," "eradication of dissenting views," "anti-Western everything," "repackaged anti-Semitism," and "insane regurgitation."

George Leef, in an article from *Minding the Campus* titled "A Racially 'Woke' Agenda Is Now Hardwired in Public Schools," wrote, "Many college professors and administrators are eager to turn their students into ideological clones of themselves in hopes of ensuring that the U.S. will have the kind of governmentally controlled, collectivistic society they desire."

Leef explains that "the alliance between the public education establishment and the march of 'progressivism' is as natural as anything could be. Public education depends on the power of government: to tax, to build schools and hire teachers and administrators, to compel student attendance, to minimize or even prohibit competition.... Therefore, it's no surprise that public schools are ratcheting up their efforts at turning students into adults who will automatically vote to keep their political allies in power. And that calls for constant adjustments to the curriculum."[120]

In the past, classrooms were apolitical. However, national and statewide educator organizations are telling teachers there is no such thing. A group called Education Deans for Justice and Equity describe themselves as a "nationwide alliance of current and recent education deans, and directors/chairs of education…that aims to speak and act collectively regarding current policies, reforms, and public debates in order to advance equity and justice in education." Notice that they are not deans for high quality education; they are for something *else*.

They claim "that educational institutions, including colleges of education, have never been—and cannot ever be—neutral politically or ideologically." Now, remember that these deans oversee professors delivering the training that future high school educators must complete in order to earn their state licensing certifications.[121]

The messaging learned in the ed schools is often reinforced at ongoing professional conferences, designed to update skills and remain "current" in the field. To get a flavor for these, read this summary of the published "call for presenters" for the National Convention for Teachers of English (bolding is mine):

---

[120] Leef, "A Racially 'Woke' Agenda Is Now Hardwired in Public Schools."

[121] "Education Colleges for Justice & Equity: A Framework for Assessment and Transformation," version June 20, 2019, Education Deans for Justice and Equity, accessed November 25, 2020, https://educationdeans.org/edje-framework/.

Our students' voices matter. Their voices matter in our schools, our communities, and beyond. As teachers, we want our students to discover their own voices. We want them to know the power of their voices. We want them to know the power of others' voices, and we want them to know the power of their **collective voices**. Most important, we want to help them discover how their voices might **impact our world** and to be empowered to **use their voices to speak out for equity and justice**.... Connecting with others often builds understanding and **helps harness the power of a collective voice**.... Our classrooms can be places **where our students discover who they are, who they might become, and the issues that they care about**.... Teachers, and teachers of teachers, have both the opportunity and responsibility to create environments in which students can use their voices in powerful ways. **Doing so can be a gateway to equity and justice.** In thinking about this year's theme, begin with these questions:

- How can our students **use their voices to create change** in their communities?
- How can our students use writing **to speak out for equity and justice?**
- What is our role in **supporting our students in creating change?**
- How do we, as **educators, raise our voices against injustices, acting as models for our students to raise their voices?**[122]

---

[122] "2018 NCTE Annual Convention – National Council of Teachers of English," California Community Colleges, accessed November 24, 2020, http://plnlegacy.foundationccc.org/event/2018-ncte-annual-convention-%E2%80%94-national-council-of-teachers-of-english.

How can students discover their *own* voices while using their "collective voice"?

Teachers should not be telling students what the purpose of their voices is—in this case, they are to be used to "speak out for equity and justice," which sounds to me like their voices are to be used to amplify someone else's political message (who will "harness the power") that is being superimposed or grafted onto them…or maybe I should say extracted from them. (Now I have a mental image of the sea witch removing Ariel's voice and trapping it in a shell she wears around her neck, rendering the little mermaid mute.)

Harnessing others' voices for your purposes is usurpation, a completely unethical use of the classroom and a teacher's access to young people. Why shouldn't students decide for themselves what they'd like to use their voices for? Some students might prefer to use their voices to express gratitude and appreciation for many positive things that enrich their lives, right? But this possibility isn't considered.

For one statewide English teacher convention, the call for presenters was titled "Heroic Reading" and the Planned Workshops on Literacy & Learning focused on four key elements: Writing, Technology, Social Justice, and Classroom Strategies. (If it were my conference, I probably would have focused on Vocabulary, Reading, Writing, and Comprehension, referring back to the NAEP deficiencies, but no one asked me.) This is an odd assortment, but can you identify the one topic that really sticks out as anomalous?

Social justice appears to be some sort of hard-to-find itch that teachers in all fields can't resist scratching. Why does the word "justice" require a qualifier, at all? Both "social" and "restorative" justice imply the substitution of a new, apparently arbitrary, system for our existing justice system, which requires extensive examination for such a drastic action to be considered.

A recent theme for a regional social studies educator conference was "Social Studies: A Road Map for Social Justice." At this conference, a public school teacher taught a session called "Why Socialism? Transition in the United States" and the keynote address was called "Now More Than Ever: Youth Organizing and Why It Belongs in Schools."

This is what educators (and future educators) are up against. If they want to succeed, they have to get with the program.

12

Missing Voices in the Classroom

Many of the educational problems detailed in this book stem from a lack of balance, and steeply tilted one-sidedness. We're seeing this with the hyper-domination of one similar strain of thought in the education schools and with the supermajoritarian agreement found in teachers' unions. Without balance, without hearing from or representation from the other side, something essential is missing, the conversation becomes a monologue, potentially dissenting voices are chilled into stony silence, and distortion grows.

Our classrooms are occupied by roughly equal numbers of male and female students, but what is the gender representation like among the faculty? Teaching and nursing have long been conceived of as "female" professions—the only acceptable ones beyond homemaking. At least, they were before so-called "women's liberation," which presumably freed women from the restrictive limitations of traditional roles and empowered them to pursue careers in any field of their choosing.

How has this panned out? Despite lowered barriers and expanding opportunities elsewhere, the teaching ranks have grown even *more* female in recent years. While the number of male nurses has tripled since the

1970s,[123] the number of male teachers has not shown similar increases. According to a study led by University of Pennsylvania Professor Richard Ingersoll, the gender imbalance in education has increased from 67 percent female in 1980–1981 to 76 percent female by 2016—more than three out of four.[124] This means that male teachers are now underrepresented by a whopping 50 plus percent, relative to their proportion of the overall population.

We know that women are more likely to vote Democratic than men, but students in most classrooms are about as likely to come from Republican homes as Democratic ones, and regardless of their backgrounds, they all deserve to fully understand the reasoning behind the main political worldviews operating in the country they inhabit. Will they receive this information with accuracy and without partiality given such disparity in the teachers assigned to instruct them? If we presume that disproportionate representation of varying identity traits indicates systemic biases and discrimination, as proponents of critical theories do, what do these statistics tell us about the forces at play in K–12 education, which has so much to say about the faults in our larger society? Can this critical lens not be turned on itself, to its own chagrin? Or is critical theory somehow exempt from its own criticism?

Harvard Education Professor Carol Gilligan, in her landmark work *In a Different Voice*, argues that women "speak" differently than men. They develop differently, reason differently, and are likely to reach different conclusions than men will. She asserts that they are more influenced by their relationships with others, and hence it is unfair to judge them as

---

[123] "Male Nurses Becoming More Commonplace, Census Bureau Reports," United States Census Bureau, February 25, 2013, https://www.census.gov/newsroom/press-releases/2013/cb13-32.html.

[124] Alia Wong, "The U.S. Teaching Population Is Getting Bigger, and More Female, *Atlantic*, February 20, 2019, https://www.theatlantic.com/education/archive/2019/02/the-explosion-of-women-teachers/582622/ and Richard Ingersoll, et al., "Seven Trends: The Transformation of the Teaching Force—Updated October 2018," Consortium for Policy Research in Education, November 13, 2018, https://repository.upenn.edu/cgi/viewcontent.cgi?article=1109&context=cpre_researchreports.

deficient according to criteria developed for evaluating male development. This is why it is so important to include and respect their unique voices.

If this is so, then the same would also be true for men, whose distinct voices must also be included, but who are decreasingly represented in American schools. Where is the "equity" in this? Don't young boys deserve to have role models in the classroom from whom to draw inspiration? Would not males bring their own enriching and unique perspectives to academia and help teachers to recognize blind spots and to avoid dangerous groupthink and confirmation biases? We presume that the racial and ethnic backgrounds of teachers matter: Why not gender?

We possess brains with two hemispheres—each has its area of specialization. One side is more logical-mathematical and sees details while the other is more visual-spatial and better at grasping the big picture. Neither is more important; they work together and both are equally necessary. When we're young, in a process known as lateralization, we tend to lean towards our favored side. With age and ongoing development, most of us improve in our weaker side, becoming more "even" and coming to appreciate and benefit from the increased cognitive balance. From studies of people with hemispheric brain damage (to one side), we know that these deficits can cause enormous deficits in perception and will impair the ability to perceive accurately. Extrapolating from this, gender parity is yet another way in which our K–12 classrooms need to rectify the dramatically disproportionate overrepresentation and overinclusion of certain voices, lenses, and viewpoints, in order to draw closer to appropriate and educationally sound levels of egalitarianism. When both sides are present and functioning, we see and understand everything more clearly and completely.

13

Role Inflation

You've probably heard of grade inflation. This is the tendency, over time, for teachers and schools to start awarding higher grades for the same quality of work, mainly because it's hard to "hold the line" and often easier to give in to student whining and parental complaints. Soon enough, people relying on the integrity of the institution learn that an A no longer means what it once did.

Well, meet "role inflation," when people elevate their assigned roles in inappropriately expanding directions, leaving behind mundane, core tasks in favor of more appealing ones. No wonder our kids are struggling to keep up with the basics! Such foundation work is apparently too pedestrian or distracting for high-minded idealists whose agendas are fixed on far nobler aims than ordinary algebra, grammar, or civics. It's almost as if some teachers are looking through and beyond their students, towards more interesting goals than what their hired responsibilities are. Accordingly, there seems to be a growing misunderstanding of the clear and significant differences between college level and K–12 teaching and a concomitant blurring of the important boundaries between the two.

Colleges and universities are charged with conducting rigorous research and pushing outwards the boundaries of knowledge through the production and analysis of primary academic sources. In accordance with their higher levels of academic training and presumed expertise in narrow, respective fields, and taking into account the adult status of college students, professors are afforded greater latitude in classroom conjecture and the proffering of singular opinions.

This is not at all what happens in K–12. Secondary education teachers are concerned with passing along accumulated, established knowledge, mainly through the use of anthologized secondary sources. As such, they are expected to remain within the boundaries of their training and certification, conscious of their responsibilities to parents and the community, and cognizant of the enormous power disparity between them and their young charges. They are expected to faithfully act *in loco parentis*, not seeking to undermine parents or to subvert their authority. (Staff in colleges were once expected to act *in loco parentis* as well, which is why we used to see quaint-seeming customs like "parietal rules" governing dorm visits by members of the opposite sex. During the sixties, with the draft, the Vietnam War, and ensuing protests, this expectation was abandoned for those who've reached the age of majority.) The legal concept of *in loco parentis* remains in force for the protection and supervision of minors entrusted to educators for much of the day.

"Simply put, K-12 teachers do not have the broad academic freedom that is usually afforded to their counterparts in higher education," said Professor of education law, policy, and practice at University of Wisconsin-Madison Julie Underwood. "Courts have made a distinction between university faculty and K-12 teachers in the area of free speech, noting 'a special concern of the First Amendment' in higher education because of the university's unique role in participating in and fostering a marketplace of ideas."[125]

While some want to pretend they are college professors, others just want to "make friends" with their students. These are the so-called "cool" teachers who operate like youth group leaders, without realizing they

---

[125] Julie Underwood, "School Districts Control Teachers' Classroom Speech," *Phi Delta Kappan*, December 4, 2017, https://kappanonline.org/underwood-school-districts-control-teachers-classroom-speech/.

are misusing their authority over impressionable minors. (Think of Jack Black's character Dewey Finn who completely gives up the standard music curriculum and teaches his students to "rock." Fun for a ridiculous movie; simply annoying in real life.) These types of teachers have no awareness of the irony of the power disparity they exploit to teach ostensibly about the dangers of so-called systemic power-and-oppression dynamics. One can only hope that the irony isn't lost on the students.

Without having a very firm understanding of their functioning boundaries, teachers drift away from their cultural roles into something very different. K–12 schools are the perfect demonstration of the truth of O'Sullivan's law, which effectively states that any organization that is not expressly and deliberately right-wing will become left-wing over time.

Entropy might be another way of describing this depressing phenomenon, which must be resisted and counteracted through the application of matching levels of targeted and equally determined, opposing energy to restore equilibrium.

Sometimes teachers will say they just must speak out now. "Recent events," amplified by the news media, are used to justify the jettisoning of long-established "hands-off" treatment of politics in the classroom, and to embolden those inclined to use their classrooms for partisan goals. This is merely a convenient excuse, however, since these ratcheting efforts have been ongoing since at least the early twentieth century and have only accelerated recently. Anyone who lived through the 1960s knows that there is no reason to accept the argument that "this time it's different" or "we *have* to do this, because *now* it's an emergency!"

The reason we have established codes of ethics and professional practice, which instruct teachers to remain impartial and to adhere to principled neutrality in the conduct of their employment duties, is precisely to guide us when our passionate emotions threaten to override our better judgment. It doesn't matter how strongly a teacher feels or what compels him or her to depart from upholding professional standards in carrying out their classroom duties: it's still wrong and not why you're collecting a paycheck.

Like every other complex occupation requiring the constant exercise of professional judgment, K–12 educators require a period of extended, supervised training along with the enforcement of appropriate guardrails to ensure they remain quality practitioners and achieve high standards. Increasingly, both the training and the practice are becoming suspect by growing numbers of observers and constituents, which presents a dire situation for these institutions that must always rely on public support.

Being a K–12 educator is a noble, necessary endeavor in its own right, without needing to be elevated or inflated into something different, apologized for, or expanded beyond recognition. Done right, the proper cultivation of young minds remains one of the most rewarding jobs there is; done wrong, the potential damage to individuals and to society is incalculable.

14

Trojan Horses and "Creative Insubordination"

"The difference between the almost right word and the right word is really a large matter," wrote Mark Twain. "'Tis the difference between the lightning bug and the lightning."

Be extremely skeptical of novel terms introduced by your school. Words you thought you understood do *not* mean the same thing in social justice and critical pedagogy terms; these usages are very specific and loaded with implications. If you require teachers and administrators to fully define vague and ambiguous language, you are likely to discover that much of it directly opposes the values you hold dear.

Activists use the word "diversity" to mean something other than what most parents or students would mean if they used the word. Most consider "diversity" as simply welcoming people of all ethnic backgrounds to the table. But "diversity" on the lips of a critical social justice activist means something else. While an activist might occasionally claim to be tolerant of different ideas and political viewpoints and nod towards philosophical differences, he focuses almost entirely on physical and cultural differences, which he evaluates according to the critical social justice conceptions of privilege and marginalization. He therefore aims to privilege the marginalized and marginalize the privileged in order to redress the imbalances it sees in society.

Most people assume the word "inclusion" means to welcome everyone…not to exclude anybody. Inclusion, in a critical justice sense, refers to something subtly different. It means to create a welcoming environment specifically for groups considered marginalized, and the exclusion of anything that could feel unwelcoming to any identity groups (see also: safe space). This is because everything in critical social justice must be understood in terms of systemic power dynamics that it theorizes characterize all of social, if not material, reality.

Most people believe the word "equity" is the notion of being fair and impartial. In critical social justice, equity is different than equality. Equality means that citizen A and citizen B are treated equally, while equity means we must adjust shares in order to make citizens equal. Activists believe invisible systems of power and privilege hold some people back in invisible ways because of their race, gender, sexuality, or other marginalized identity factors. Therefore, equity requires giving some identity groups privileges in order to redress the perceived imbalance.

However, these are two totally different—even opposite—notions. Being equal is quite different than attempting to force equality of outcome by enforcing some resource allocation system. And if a parent has the audacity to say they believe in "equality of opportunity," a critical social justice activist might say this statement is as harmful as white supremacy.

Many embedded assumptions lurk below the surface of innocuous-sounding terminology. Stealthy deception is one of the main methods by which unpopular ideas are being smuggled into our children's classrooms. Using heavily loaded, cloaked, ill-defined, and ever-shifting impenetrable terminology is the hallmark of bad faith operators. (And, as we've already seen, teachers are being encouraged to use duplicitous means such as "creative insubordination" to sneak their activist aims past their own trusting, unwitting supervisors!) Innocent-sounding but loaded with suppositions, these Trojan horses look superficially nice and you might think you'd like to have one. So you wheel it inside, but then when you open it up, all sorts of problems come spilling out. Regrets!

French moralist Joseph Joubert said, "Words, like eyeglasses, blur everything that they do not make more clear." That's why words in America's classrooms should be clear. Without starting with precise definitions, parents cannot discern whether or not the programming will violate their family's belief system.

And that, my friends, is by design.

PART
THREE

Why It's Bad

15

(Why It's Bad) Philosophically

School indoctrination restricts access to competing ideas and censors unapproved thoughts and questions. It restricts the marketplace of ideas, thereby removing dialectical challenge from the classroom and undermining the rigorous application of liberal science to the exploration of topics. When you indoctrinate elementary-aged students and fill them with high levels of ideological certainty, they don't develop an appreciation for freedom of inquiry; instead, they arrive at college closed-minded, regurgitating reflexive ideological answers to every question. At that level of certainty there's kind of no need for free speech or free inquiry because you've got it all figured out. These college students enter society lacking familiarity with basic American principles.

The Enlightenment values of free thought and expression, which undergird our constitutional rights, derive from millennia of history during which "might equaled right"—whether that came in the form of religious or political persecution exercised by either unquestionable church authorities or the divine right of kings. The story of Galileo is perhaps the most famous example of authority asserting domination over plain scientific evidence. Fortunately, a revolution in 1776 freed us from paying obeisance to conclusions by fiat and allowed our culture to unleash a wave of creative and scientific advancement the likes of which the world had not yet seen.

Basic unifying principles of evidentiary rules and the presumption of innocence undergird our systems of knowledge-seeking, truth verification, governmental checks and balances, law enforcement, and justice. (In science, the concept of presumed innocence takes the form of the "null hypothesis.") This is no small matter, yet the incursion of imposed classroom orthodoxies in our schools, under many varied guises, threatens all of these.

The encroachment also directly undermines the "marketplace of ideas," an American ideal which teaches us that hypotheses are to be tested against competing thoughts and are expected to withstand rigorous criticism. As Oliver Wendell Holmes Jr. wrote, "[T]he ultimate good desired is better reached by free trade in ideas -- that the best test of truth is the power of the thought to get itself accepted in the competition of the market." Many of these indoctrinating ideas, which brook no dissent, are (as I've repeatedly reminded you) rooted in Marxism which does not believe in competitive markets—of ideas or anything else. By walling off criticism, these theories are doing a disservice to knowledge and the pursuit of truth itself.

As English philosopher John Stuart Mill wrote, "The peculiar evil of silencing the expression of an opinion is, that it is robbing the human race; posterity as well as the existing generation; those who dissent from the opinion, still more than those who hold it. If the opinion is right, they are deprived of the opportunity of exchanging error for truth: if wrong, they lose, what is almost as great a benefit, the clearer perception and livelier impression of truth, produced by its collision with error."[126]

Mill further asserts:

> He who knows only his own side of the case knows little of that. His reasons may be good, and no one may have been able to refute them. But if he is equally unable to

---

[126] John Stuart Mill, *On Liberty* (London: John W. Parker and Son, West Strand, 1859).

refute the reasons on the opposite side, if he does not so much as know what they are, he has no ground for preferring either opinion.... Nor is it enough that he should hear the opinions of adversaries from his own teachers, presented as they state them, and accompanied by what they offer as refutations. He must be able to hear them from persons who actually believe them...[and] he must know them in their most plausible and persuasive form.

Mill also famously defended dissenters and praised eccentricity, nonconformity, and individuality as key elements of well-being and societal flourishing. "If all mankind minus one, were of one opinion, and only one person were of the contrary opinion, mankind would be no more justified in silencing that one person, than he, if he had the power, would be justified in silencing mankind.... In this age, the mere example of non-conformity, the mere refusal to bend the knee to custom, is itself a service."

Are America's schoolchildren (or teachers in training) being taught about Oliver Wendell Holmes Jr. and John Stuart Mill anymore? If not, why not? When did they fall out of favor and what has replaced them? At what cost?

Dialectical reasoning is the process of arriving at truth by comparing and contrasting opposing positions. Dialectical tension is the back-and-forth pull between two competing propositions that can never truly be separated, typically expressed in dialogue or debate. For instance, in American politics, there exists a push-pull tension regarding the proper size of government. When it is too small, certain societal problems arise, but when it grows too large, different problems emerge. What is the right balance? The argument between these opposing forces is ongoing and intertwined.

Most students are surprised by the complexity of issues that superficially appear simplistic, when they face appropriate dialectical challenges from skilled teachers or capable fellow students in an open and free discussion. Few can pinpoint their own biases and omissions as accurately as a faithful opponent can. Thesis–antithesis–synthesis is the natural progression of thought leading to refined understanding. But indoctrination is thesis–thesis–thesis with an implied command to come swiftly to heel and to curtail mental exploration—a false imitation of actual knowledge building. It's also operating at the lowest level of Bloom's taxonomy, mere memorization, and requires nothing meaningful of students.

The new pedagogy eschews the chewing over of the finer points and complications of deep thorny issues in favor of pat responses, repeated but never fully debated. Strong students sharpen each other, by finding and pointing out the flaws in each other's reasoning; the new commitments in education demand the pulling of all mental punches and unquestioning affirmation. Consequently, mental muscles atrophy through disuse.

Balance is the antidote to competing biases. They cancel each other out, the same way that random selection works in compensating for sampling biases in experimentation. Opposing views function as checks and balances to keep one another honest and weed out erroneous conclusions. But today, students are presented with the sound of one hand clapping. This is a hollow appearance of an education without the true substance.

Liberal Science

We have a reliable method of sorting out what is true and false, which has evolved throughout the centuries, and part of it can be traced to the ancient philosophers of Greece. In fact, the Greek systems of logic used to be taught as a central part of a well-rounded liberal arts education. During the Enlightenment, it moved to preeminence. Using it has yielded numerous wonderful advances.

This process is so central and implicit to our way of life that we don't really have a name for it. It's simply the water in which we swim; at least, up until now. But since it is currently under direct challenge in academia, it merits discussion. Jonathan Rauch, in *Kindly Inquisitors*, suggests calling this process "Liberal Science." (Rauch calls his book *Kindly Inquisitors* because an "inquisition" is what happens to people who defy dogma. He argues that we have moved beyond dogma and developed a better system, but some still want to impose orthodoxy by authoritarian means.) The liberal science process is not intuitive; it must be taught. As adherence to it declines, inductive reasoning and dogmatic instruction has skyrocketed, with predictably poor results.

According to Rauch, the two rules of liberal science are:

1. No one is completely immune from error.
2. Any belief may be wrong; hence, no one can legitimately claim to have ended any discussion—ever.

This could be called the "principle of falsifiability." Essentially, if you do not try to check ideas by trying to debunk them, then you are not practicing science. Decisions about what is and is not true are always provisional, standing only until refuted by better arguments or more information.

In liberal science, no one gets special say simply on the basis of who he happens to be. "No one has personal authority," according to Rauch. Every assertion must be subjected to the same method of checking and double-checking—subjected to doubt—regardless of the identity of the checker and the source of the assertion. (Notice how this stands diametrically opposed to standpoint epistemology, which insists that certain people cannot possibly be wrong by virtue of who they happen to be.)

According to Rauch, identity does not make any difference regarding the veracity of results: whatever one person does to check a proposition must be something that anyone can do, at least in principle, and get the same result. *Who* you are doesn't count; the same rules apply to everyone, across the board. A test is valid only insofar as it works for anyone who tries it. Where different checkers (debunkers) get different results, no one's result overrides anyone else's, and no definitive result can be declared. The results are inconclusive. Truth is what survives persistent attempts at disconfirmation.

An essential aspect of this process is that no one, expert or amateur, gets to claim special authority simply because of who he happens to be. (Those familiar with logical fallacies will recognize this error as the "argument from authority or "appeal to authority." In Latin, this would be *argumentum ad verecundiam*, meaning "appeal to reverence"—the essence of dogmatism. Presuming that the source of an argument proves its veracity would be falling for a logical error known as the "genetic fallacy." (Subtly different, this fallacy would be assuming that everything printed in the *New York Times* is absolutely true while everything in the *National Enquirer* is automatically false.) Truth can come from any quarter, but all claims to truth must undergo equivalent, thorough testing before being accepted.

Furthermore, whatever one person does to become an expert in studying the problem must be something that others could, theoretically, do as well. One person might have a PhD in a subject, but you could also get one. (Another way of saying the same thing is that it's not a matter of birth, but a matter of effort—achievable merit; you can see how these multiple aspects of our culture are interwoven. Authority based on bloodline would cause us to revert to aristocracy/monarchy, which we rejected as an inadequate, flawed system long ago.) The views of experts, no less than those of laymen, are expected to withstand vigorous checking.

Unscholarly Certainty and Epistemic Humility

"Having pure intentions, steadfast goals, and an unwillingness to consider that you might be wrong is the formula for some of the worst evils mankind has ever wrought upon one another, from inquisitions to the twentieth century's disastrous experiments with totalitarian utopias," writes Greg Lukianoff, president and CEO of FIRE in his book *Unlearning Liberty*. "As pushy as those of us who defend civil liberties may seem, the right to freedom of speech and freedom of conscience rests on a deep-seated humility: I know I am not omniscient, and I suspect you aren't either. Therefore, I have no right to tell you what you can't say, certainly no right to tell you what you *must* say, and I wouldn't even imagine telling you what you must think, believe, or hold in your heart."[127]

The temptation to coopt classroom space to advance personal aims is nothing new. In the seventies, for instance, the justifying cause was a proposed nuclear arms freeze and teachers in thirty-four states admitted adopting a one-sided curriculum that recommended highly controversial solutions. When confronted, teachers were unapologetic and pretended that the material was not controversial, implying that they somehow possessed "an inside track on Truth." At least one activist, who, while sympathetic to the cause, nevertheless objected to the methods, properly admonished them, saying, "Some of the most destructive people in history have been certain of their righteousness."[128]

In academia, questions remain open to investigation in a spirit of free inquiry, not settled advocacy. The continual practice of cross-checking and collegial challenge is what keeps a discipline honest, vibrant, and productive. Likewise, feeling strongly that one is absolutely right is absolutely no guarantee that one is actually correct. Trained scholars with academic temperaments should not indulge this temptation.

The pursuit of pure science requires skepticism, curiosity, and humility—but today's educators too often exhibit certainty, incuriosity, and are anything but humble. To the contrary, they are supremely confident in their settled conclusions and rebuff all questions. Their unscholarly certainty justifies their open abandonment of attempts at neutrality (some even go so far as to claim that neutrality is "impossible" or representative of "white supremacy" or other forms of "oppression"). But when objectivity is abandoned in academia, any conclusions drawn automatically become suspect.

I'm reminded now of the popular signs currently popping up in yards and even in schools that inform us that "Science is real" (among other

---

[127] Greg Lukianoff, *Unlearning Liberty: Campus Censorship and the End of American Debate* (New York, NY: Encounter Books, 2014) 29.

[128] Jonathan Zimmerman and Emily Robertson, *The Case for Contention: Teaching Controversial Issues in American Schools* (Chicago: University of Chicago Press, 2017) 40–41.

unnecessary pronouncements, including "Water is life"). However, not if the practice of science has been degraded or corrupted. A quick review of Soviet Lysenkoism or Nazism's Welteislehre/Glazial-Kosmogonie plainly reveals the damage that results when pure science becomes infected and contorted to conform to political or cultural pressure.

"The worst characteristic of scholars is…the selective use, and avoidance, of evidence, in order to support what they already believe," according to enlightenment scholar Alan Charles Kors. "Ignoring what is inconvenient to that end and effecting a methodological complexity part of which is that no one outside of their own theoretical perspective is in a position to criticize, let alone judge, it. *THAT* is the end of serious intellectual life."[129]

Social psychologist Jonathan Haidt addressed these conflicting cross-purposes in "Why Universities Must Choose One Telos: Truth or Social Justice." A "telos" refers to an "end" or "goal." It could be equated to the school's "mission." "What is the telos of university? The most obvious answer and ubiquitous answer is 'truth' –- the word appears on so many university crests. But increasingly, many of America's top universities are embracing social justice as their telos, or as a second and equal [but contradictory] telos," calling to mind the adage that you "cannot serve two masters."[130]

After observing troubling signs in the academy, Haidt, a self-identified liberal, created Heterodox Academy to increase open inquiry, viewpoint diversity, and constructive disagreement. Detecting liberal bias and "a statistically impossible lack of diversity" in his field, Haidt fears that this overwhelming imbalance will "hinder research and damage their credibility—and blind them to the hostile climate they've created for

---

[129] Alan Charles Kors, "The Enlightenment and Academic Freedom," speech at Grand Valley State University, March 22, 2016, https://www.youtube.com/watch?v=fP1n5hElmSA&t=3708s.

[130] Jonathan Haidt, "Why Universities Must Choose One Telos: Truth or Social Justice," Heterodox Academy, October 21, 2016, https://heterodoxacademy.org/blog/one-telos-truth-or-social-justice-2/.

non-liberals."[131] Discussing the problem of "motivated reasoning," he points out that scholarship undertaken to support a political agenda almost always succeeds, and that the only way to maintain the integrity of such an enterprise is to rely on "institutionalized disconfirmation," in which competing scholars who do not share the same motives actively seek to disprove shaky claims.[132] When taking into consideration the growing ideological imbalance in education that is now filtering down to K–12, however, we can't count on competing academics to keep the scholarship honest anymore because there are hardly any more conservatives in the humanities and social sciences.

This troubling new dichotomy can be seen as a battle between "activism" versus "academics." You could also view it as a battle between neutrality versus partiality, objectivism versus subjectivism, or deductive versus inductive thought. Another helpful way of understanding this split is to conceive of it as a battle between inquiry versus advocacy.

Inquiry is open-ended. It means asking questions and then following certain protocol for collecting evidence impartially, in an attempt to find answers, with no preconceived expectations of what the "right" answer will be. The evidence will unfold and reveal the answers, if you follow the procedures faithfully. The scientific method is an example of the process by which a scholar would engage in inquiry, but in other fields, such as history or literature, you would have to use other reputable methods of analysis.

Blatant advocacy was not traditionally a stance associated with academia, but with the inclusion of identity studies departments (women's studies, gender studies, ethnic studies—which have been jokingly, collectively, called "studies studies"), activism is now widely practiced within certain segments of the academy. This means students and professors in these fields typically seek to advance a set ideology and policy positions, and political uniformity in those fields is nearly total. Agreement with often unstated aims is assumed at the outset.

---

[131] John Tierney, "Social Scientist Sees Bias Within," *New York Times*, February 7, 2011, https://www.nytimes.com/2011/02/08/science/08tier.html.
[132] Haidt, "Why Universities Must Choose One Telos."

These fields tend to be inductive, and the disciplines do not subscribe to the traditional methods of evidence-seeking—even rejecting them as forms of "structural oppression." Certain people, by virtue of their "identities," have "epistemic privilege" which means they are uniquely suited to interpret the world and are above question by others not sharing that identity (this could be considered to be the genetic fallacy or the fallacy of origin, by those bound to more traditional epistemologies like "logic" and "rhetoric.")

Let's look at this same problem from the neutrality/objectivity perspective. In 2017, a graduate teaching assistant presented a short clip of a controversial discussion about the use of new gender pronouns to describe people who do not want to identify as "he" or "she." She wasn't taking a stance on the topic: she was proposing it for discussion. When called in for questioning by her department (which she recorded), she attempted to defend her methods by citing neutrality, and was informed that her objective stance was the problem. She was supposed to be *critical* of certain positions.[133]

Another way of looking at the contrast between inquiry and advocacy is comparing open versus closed inquiry. A free and open inquiry would allow for the evidence to lead the conclusions wherever they may logically go, whereas closed inquiry begins with a preferred conclusion in mind, to which all arguments must then be retrofitted. This restrains the thought process unnaturally, forcing students into logical errors and bad mental habits. It is probably not even correct to refer to such a thing as closed inquiry, since it lacks questioning at all. It might be more accurate to refer to such "reasoning" as rationalization.

But perhaps the most apt way of looking at the new attempts to impose classroom conformity is as a system of beliefs, which seeks to impose itself on others. As Helen Pluckrose and James Lindsay put it in *Cynical Theories*, "you can hold whatever moral beliefs you want and require people to follow them (within legal bounds) within a voluntary community, whose members adopt those beliefs as matters of private conscience, but

---

[133] Uri Harris, "Wilfrid Laurier and the Creep of Critical Theory," *Quillette*, November 21, 2017, https://quillette.com/2017/11/21/wilfrid-laurier-creep-critical-theory/.

you cannot enforce them on outsiders."[134] A public school, of course, is not a voluntary community: it is compulsory.

In our pluralistic, secularized society, no one has the right or authority to compel a system of belief on another.

Therein lies the rub.

---

[134] Pluckrose and Lindsay, *Cynical Theories*, 263.

16

(Why It's Bad) Pedagogically

A familiar maxim for those in the education profession is that if your students know your political ideology, you're doing a bad job as their teacher. It is sad, indeed, to reflect upon the likelihood that many new entrants to the teaching profession have encountered so much of this kind of "instruction" in their preparation as to be unaware of the proper implementation of better alternatives. Effective instruction requires fair representation of competing views without deletions or distortions.

I've already discussed the inappropriateness of expecting secondary (or younger!) students to apply graduate-level deconstructionism, post-colonialism, or similar critical epistemology to novel material, while they're still struggling with mastering basic academic skills. This is arguably an engaging activity for the teacher, but responsible educators must remember to ask this pertinent question before making a teaching decision: **Whose needs are being met by my course of action: mine or**

the student's?[135] There is only one correct answer here: the needs of the student. You don't serve dessert before dinner. Trendy critiques are for people who have first read the book and can comprehend it on its own merits, before picking it apart.

Excessive leftward tilt in academia likely harms liberal-leaning students as much as, if not more than, conservative-leaning ones; this makes perfect sense when you consider that only the conservative students are being exposed to disconfirmation tests and have to seek out more information in order to back up their views. Studies have, in fact, shown that conservatives understand liberals better than liberals understand conservatives.[136]

This is not a surprising finding when you consider that conservatives are constantly exposed to liberal thought in education, the media, and entertainment whereas liberals can much more easily avoid exposure to conservative thought. Another reason activist teachers might want to reconsider heavy-handed methods is that kids get fed up with this sort of behavior and form negative opinions of any material delivered to them through imperious means. As Dale Carnegie wisely intoned in *How to Win Friends and Influence People*, "A man convinced against his will is of the same opinion still." Another way to state the same message is that power and influence are inversely related. The more you attempt to exert external control over another person, the more s/he will resist you internally. (This is why persuasion is more effective, long-term, than coercion.) That's basic relationship dynamics, which is something everyone in a "people profession" should understand.

Something to think about.

---

[135] Professional Standards and Practices Commission. "Unit 3: The Teacher/Student Relationship." Pennsylvania Department of Education, Accessed March 25, 2021, https://www.pspc.education.pa.gov/Promoting-Ethical-Practices-Resources/Ethics-Toolkit/Unit3/Pages/The-Teacher---Student-Relationship.aspx

[136] Jonathan Haidt, *The Righteous Mind: Why Good People Are Divided by Politics and Religion* (London, UK: Penguin Books, 2013), 334.

Consider what Jonathan Haidt had to say about looking at everything using the same (Marxist) lens. "When I was at Yale in the 1980s, I was given so many tools for understanding the world. By the time I graduated, I could think about things as a Utilitarian or a Kantian, as a Freudian or a behaviorist, as a computer scientist or a humanist. I was given many lenses to apply to any one situation. But nowadays, many students are given just one lens—power—and told to apply it to all situations," he wrote. "Everything is about power. Every situation is to be analyzed in terms of the bad people acting to preserve their power and privilege over the good people. This is not an education. This is induction into a cult, a fundamentalist religion, a paranoid worldview that separates people from each other and sends them down the road to alienation, anxiety, and intellectual impotence."[137]

When all you have is a hammer, everything looks like a nail. So start pounding. There's only so much Marx an American school kid needs. American students should certainly not be exposed more to Marx than they are exposed to the theories underlying capitalism and free enterprise. We are equipping American students to succeed in existing American society—not 1930s Russia or an imaginary unrealized utopia of someone's frustrated longings.

Many teachers seem to imagine that they are the only one presenting this "edgy," "sophisticated," "advanced" critical material in their classes, without awareness that nearly everyone else is now doing the same thing, and kids are marinated in it. There is little doubt that most of these bizarre curricular choices, omissions, deficiencies, and repetitive overinclusions result from a lack of political diversity among the faculty, and from their own inadequate, unbalanced undergraduate educations.

For instance, several years ago, one college held an educational symposium on the war in Iraq, which was underway at the time. Normally, you'd expect that such an event would include people with varying perspectives on the conflict, but instead every single invited speaker shared the exact same position, ensuring that the event operated at the lowest

---

[137] Jonathan Haidt, "The Fine-Tuned Liberal Democracy," Wriston Lecture, delivered at the Manhattan Institute, November 15, 2017.

intellectual level of head-nodding absorption. Rather than being an edu-cational event, as advertised, it functioned instead as an anti-war rally.[138]

Where are the circumspect adults with perspective and maturity to demand balance and fair representation and intellectual challenge in the curriculum for students? Since another way to think of "Marxist" is "anti-capitalist," it's helpful to remember that this means opposition to open markets and competition. In other words: no competing ideas.

Critical Thought before Critical Theory

Before kids can possibly learn about esoteric concepts like critical theory, they first need to master critical thought.

Generally, critical thought refers to the process of collecting evidence and evaluating or analyzing it objectively and impartially in order to form a sound judgment. This would involve looking at the information from a variety of viewpoints to ensure that the evaluation is circum-spect and does not overlook any crucial information or perspectives. The Foundation for Critical Thinking (criticalthinking.org) provides this defi-nition: "Critical thinking is self-directed, self-disciplined, self-monitored, and self-corrective thinking. It presupposes assent to rigorous standards of excellence and mindful command of their use." In *Webster's New World Dictionary*, the relevant entry reads "characterized by careful analysis and judgment" and is followed by the gloss, "critical—in its strictest sense—implies an attempt at objective judgment so as to determine both merits and faults."

This is not at all how the word "critical" is currently used throughout academia, however, and this new modern use tends to preempt the older interpretation. According to David Randall's *Making Citizens* report, we are to understand this when we see the words "critical" and "critique" in an academic context:

---

[138] Ellis, "A Crisis of Competence," 58.

DISMANTLING BELIEF IN THE TRADITIONS OF WESTERN CIVILIZATION AND AMERICAN CULTURE.

To be critical, or to engage in critique, is to attack an established belief on the grounds that it is self-evidently a hypocritical prejudice established by the powerful to reinforce their rule, and believed by poor dupes clinging to their false consciousness. "Critical thought" sees through the deceptive appearance of freedom, justice, and happiness in American life and reveals the underlying structures of oppression—sexism, racism, class dominance, and so on. "Critique" works to dismantle these oppressive structures. "Critical thought" and "critique" [are] also meant to reinforce the ruling progressive prejudices of the universities; it is never to take these prejudices as their object.... The New Civics also draws on Paulo Freire's "empowering" *critical pedagogy*, which was designed to "raise critical consciousness" among the "economically and socially marginalized" so as to enable "students to perceive social, political, and economic contradictions and take action against the oppressive elements of society."[139]

Rather than looking at multiple points of view to form a circumspect analysis or conclusion, we are to look at everything the same way, with this ubiquitous, inescapable "power" lens. This is precisely the way in which oversights, blind spots, and groupthink occur.

---

[139] David Randall, *Making Citizens: How American Universities Teach Civics*, National Association of Scholars, January 2017, https://www.nas.org/storage/app/media/Reports/Making%20Citizens/NAS_makingCitizens_fullReport.pdf.

Sloppy Thinking

Bringing political commitments into class opens the door to all manner of sloppy thinking, in which evidence needs to be retrofitted and uncomfortable information lopped off to conform to a pre-established narrative and overriding aims. Hence, we see the widespread use, allowance, and even encouragement of false Manichean dichotomies, rampant logical fallacies and cognitive distortions, and working backwards from conclusions in courses that operate under these premises. These masquerade as "argument," but are easily picked apart, falsified, and disproven by able thinkers trained in proper dialectical reasoning.

One of the preferred tactics among activist educators is called "motte and the bailey," terminology based upon castle designs to protect positions from attacks. A motte-and-bailey castle is a fortification with a wooden keep on raised ground (the motte) accompanied by a walled courtyard (the bailey). The motte-bailey involves substituting something palatable and seemingly inoffensive to stand in for something far more objectionable; it's pure deception and conflation. Thomas Sowell, senior fellow at Stanford's Hoover Institution, calls this technique "burying controversial specifics in innocuous generalities."[140]

Exaggerated rhetorical example:

The motte: Women are people! (This is the heavily fortified, defensive high-ground position to which to retreat when under fire. No one wants to attack this position.)

The bailey, from which aggressive attacks are launched: Abortions should be allowed in all circumstances! When this position is attacked, the perp pivots swiftly—Return to the motte: You don't believe women are people!

---

[140] Thomas Sowell, *The Vision of the Anointed: Self-Congratulation as a Basis for Social Policy* (New York, NY: Basic Books, 1995) 87.

Upon returning to the motte, the arguer can claim that the extreme bailey has not been refuted because the critic refused to attack the motte, or that the critic is unreasonable by equating an attack on the bailey with an attack on the motte. If you find this confusing, that's by design: the strategy is meant to baffle and disarm opponents. Used knowingly or unknowingly, such false reasoning models and transmits terrible academic bad habits that require correction. Our collective ability to respond to and meet the society challenges of our age will require stronger and more honest cogitation skills than this.

In another example of refutable assertions and shaky reasoning, the *New York Times*'s 1619 Project's stated aims are to "reframe the country's history by placing the consequences of slavery in the contributions of black Americans at the very center of the United States' national narrative." I certainly do not quibble with the idea of making room for competing narratives and opposing views in the classroom (with the crucial caveat that K–12 instructional time is a zero-sum game in which novel or untested views will generally have to yield to well-established ones, when there are time constraints). Of this project, journalist Bret Stephens—in the very paper that promulgated this ambitious project—describes its shortcomings and spells out how it failed to allow and account for a great deal of contradictory evidence.

"Journalists are, most often, in the business of writing the first rough draft of history, not trying to have the last word on it. We are best when we try to tell truths with a lowercase t, following evidence in directions unseen, not the capital-T truth of a pre-established narrative in which inconvenient facts get discarded," Stephens writes. He continues:

> Monocausality—whether it's the clash of economic classes, the hidden hand of the market, or white supremacy and its consequences—has always been a seductive way of looking at the world. It has always been a simplistic one, too. The world is complex. So are people and their motives. The job of journalism is to take account of that complexity, not simplify it out of existence through

the adoption of some ideological orthodoxy.... It should have been enough for the project to serve as *curator* for a range of erudite and interesting voices, with ample room for contrary takes. Instead, virtually every writer in the project seems to sing from the same song sheet.[141]

What an eloquent case for the restoration of our cherished academic ideals of balance, openness, the tentativeness of knowledge, and the shared pursuit of truth.

A central difference between a scholar and an activist is the unwillingness to rethink when fundamentally new evidence comes to light with respect to any social or political question. The mindset of a true academic is one that approaches all knowledge as tentative and subject to revision, pending further information.

Those unwilling to rethink or reconsider are, effectively, trapped in a small structure they should outgrow. The developmental psychologist Jean Piaget describes this as being the difference between assimilation (making new knowledge fit existing mental frameworks) and accommodation (building better mental frameworks to incorporate new information). According to Piaget, accommodation is what leads to mental growth and intellectual advancement.

Opinions Aren't Facts and Assertions Aren't Evidence

Justice Oliver Wendell Holmes Jr. said, "Certitude is not the test of certainty. We have been cocksure of many things that were not so." This sentiment was presaged by Mark Twain, who quipped, "Education is the path from cocky ignorance to miserable uncertainty." In other words, what we don't know far exceeds what we know for sure, and the wise

---

[141] Bret Stephens, "The 1619 Chronicles," *New York Times*, October 9, 2020, https://www.nytimes.com/2020/10/09/opinion/nyt-1619-project-criticisms. html.

will state their convictions tentatively, leaving room open for possible correction.

Let's return to Kemi Badenoch's speech before Parliament as the women and equalities minister for the United Kingdom regarding the encroachment of critical race theory in British schools. "What we are against is the teaching of contested political ideas as if they are accepted fact," she said. "We don't do this with communism. We don't do this with socialism. We don't do this with capitalism."

Indeed. I do not oppose the teaching of varying hypotheses, philosophies, systems, arguments, or assertions. What I oppose is presenting this material in one-sided, unbalanced form, without accurate labeling or appropriate levels of contextualization, and beyond or in defiance of what the official, democratically adopted curriculum dictates should be covered.

In the already omnipresent but amazingly still growing realm of DEI K–12 programming, highly contestable assertions are being promulgated as though they are settled assumptions to be assimilated, memorized, and regurgitated. (Thomas Sowell refers to these as "[m]aking opaque proclamations with an air of certainty and sophistication."[142]) Politicized concepts such as "white privilege," "white complicity," and "systemic oppression," are certainly interesting concepts perhaps worthy of discussion in particular academic contexts (although it is arguable whether they merit K–12 class time consideration, given competing priorities), but they are by no means the final word on any topic, no matter how much proponents might so wish. They are definitely not systems of required belief, but this is how they are being presented and promoted (enforced!) in many classrooms.

Dogmatic belief systems demand unyielding obedience and can lead to the invocation of extreme measures to enforce allegiance. We've already begun to see this in our schools, with callout culture leading to open persecution and "cancellation" of "heretics"—even by adult teachers of minor children—which is chilling indeed. As the poet Robert Frost

---

[142] Sowell, *The Vision of the Anointed*, 87.

once said, "Education is the ability to listen to almost anything without losing your temper or your self-confidence." If this is so, what then is indoctrination? Perhaps it is the inability to listen to almost anything you don't agree with without losing your temper, your perspective, your sense of humor, and your respect for others as fellow imperfect humans.

Justice Oliver Wendell Holmes Jr. also warned us that "Certitude leads to violence. This is a proposition that has an easy application and a difficult one. The easy application is to ideologues, dogmatists, and bullies—people who think that their rightness justifies them in imposing on anyone who does not happen to subscribe to their particular ideology, dogma or notion of turf. If the conviction of rightness is powerful enough, resistance to it will be met, sooner or later by force!"

As frustrating as it can be to hear from people who disagree with us, this is part of the temperament that productive citizens need to develop in order to take their places in our society. In order to achieve this goal, our schools must be populated with educators who model and practice appropriate intellectual forbearance worthy of emulation by the younger generation.

17

(Why It's Bad) Ethically

The preceding hazards of indoctrination describe why teachers have adopted sound principles of professional and ethical conduct which precisely proscribes this behavior. These codes govern the execution of the profession and engagement in certain subjects and disciplines; as such, they should be studied by teachers in training and reviewed regularly by practicing educators, to ensure fidelity. Failure to uphold them would amount to neglect or dereliction of duty that could rise to malpractice and malfeasance.

There is an oath for doctors (first, do no harm) and attorneys (I will conduct myself with integrity and civility), but no universal one for teachers, despite their close contact with our most vulnerable citizens. Perhaps this is because of an uncomfortable history regarding the imposition of loyalty oaths in the United States. The state of Colorado, interestingly, currently maintains a Teacher Oath Requirement, which is as follows:

> State of **Colorado**, County of, I solemnly (swear)(affirm)
> that I will uphold the constitution of the United States
> and the constitution of the state of **Colorado**, and that

I will faithfully perform the duties of the position upon which I am about to enter.[143]

These seem like minimal expectations of an authorized educator in a school run by the government.

There are also statewide codes of ethics or principles of professional conduct that parents or other concerned parties can research and access, to assure themselves that their children's teachers are living up to them. For instance, according to the principles of professional conduct for the education profession in the Sunshine State, Florida educators:

1. Shall make reasonable effort to protect the student from conditions harmful to learning and/or to the student's mental and/or physical health and/or safety.
2. Shall not unreasonably restrain a student from independent action in pursuit of learning.
3. Shall not unreasonably deny a student access to diverse points of view.
4. Shall not intentionally suppress or distort subject matter relevant to a student's academic program.[144]

In New Jersey, the Professional Standards for Teachers spell out (among others) the following expectations:

The teacher brings multiple perspectives to the discussion of content, including attention to learners' personal, family, and community experiences and cultural norms.... The teacher appreciates multiple perspectives within the

---

[143] "Teacher Oath Requirement (per Senate Bill 17-296)," Colorado Department of Education, accessed November 26, 2020, https://www.cde.state.co.us/cdeprof/teacheroath.

[144] "Principles of Professional Conduct for the Education Profession in Florida," Florida Department of Education, accessed November 24, 2020, http://www.fldoe.org/teaching/professional-practices/code-of-ethics-principles-of-professio.stml.

discipline and facilitates learners' critical analysis of these perspectives.... The teacher recognizes the potential of bias in his or her representation of the discipline and seeks to appropriately address problems of bias.[145]

What are the state teaching expectations where you live? These are easily locatable via an internet search. Are your child's teachers living up to them?

Similarly, long-established disciplinary and union ethical codes stipulate the conduct expected of practitioners of the profession of education. I have collected these ethical codes, along with existing legal precedents, at undoctrinate.org.

Beyond the laws, which we'll cover shortly, and in concert with them, we have guiding principles for teachers from organizations such as teachers' unions and the national groups representing different fields of study (such as history/social studies or English). These also indicate that teachers must not use the classroom to indoctrinate their students by imposing their own viewpoints without giving a fair, innuendo-free analysis of opposing ideas and positions. For instance, here are some relevant, excerpted portions from the Code of Ethics for Educators by the Association of American Educators (bolding emphasis mine):

PRINCIPLE I: Ethical Conduct toward Students

The professional educator accepts personal responsibility for teaching students character qualities that will help them evaluate the consequences of and accept the responsibility for their actions and choices. **We strongly affirm parents as the primary moral educators of their children**. Nevertheless, we believe all educators are obligated to help foster civic virtues such as integrity,

---

[145] "N.J.A.C. 6A:9, Professional Standards," New Jersey Department of Education, accessed November 26, 2020, https://www.nj.gov/education/code/current/title6a/chap9.pdf.

diligence, responsibility, cooperation, loyalty, fidelity, and respect–for the law, for human life, for others, and for self.

4. The professional educator makes a constructive effort to protect the student from conditions detrimental to learning, health, or safety.

5. The professional educator endeavors to present facts without distortion, bias, or personal prejudice.[146]

The **National Education Association's Code of Ethics**, in its preamble, states that an educator, "believing in the worth and dignity of each human being, recognizes the supreme importance of the pursuit of truth, devotion to excellence, and the nurture of the democratic principles. Essential to these goals is the protection of freedom to learn and to teach and the guarantee of equal educational opportunity for all." In terms of the educator's presumed commitment to the student [bolding, again, mine], the code states that the educator will work to "stimulate the spirit of inquiry" while the fulfillment of their obligation to students requires that educators:

1. Shall not unreasonably restrain the student from independent action in the pursuit of learning.

2. Shall not unreasonably deny the student's access to varying points of view.

3. Shall not deliberately suppress or distort subject matter relevant to the student's progress.

---

[146] "AAE Code of Ethics for Educators," Association of American Educators, accessed November 26, 2020, http://ethics.iit.edu/ecodes/sites/default/files/Association%20of%20American%20Educators%20Code%20of%20Ethics.pdf.

14. Shall make reasonable effort to protect the student from conditions harmful to learning or to health and safety.[147]

When it comes to specific academic disciplines, the **National Council for the Social Studies Revised Code of Ethics for the Social Studies Profession** issued a clarifying **position statement** that explains:

> The social studies professional should acknowledge the worth and tentativeness of knowledge. He or she should engage in a continuous search for new knowledge, retaining both the right and the obligation as a student scholar to doubt, to inquire freely, and to raise searching questions. The social studies professional has an obligation to distinguish between personal opinion and beliefs that can be supported by verified facts and to impart the knowledge of these differences to his or her students.

> Social studies professionals have an obligation to establish classroom climates that support student rights to know, to doubt, to inquire freely, to think critically, and to express openly.

> Social studies professionals should not develop or use materials that oversimplify, distort, or otherwise manipulate the truth, except as these materials may be used to illustrate distortions, propaganda, inadequate logic, and the like. It is unethical for any social studies professional to foster the use of materials in ways that do not meet accepted standards of scholarship.

> Freedom to learn and freedom to teach are dependent on the unrestricted access to works of knowledge. Social

---

[147] "Code of Ethics for Educators," National Education Association, September 14, 2020, https://www.nea.org/resource-library/code-ethics.

studies professionals have an obligation to defend the rights of students and colleagues to such access and should strive to make available a balanced variety of educationally significant materials from which students of all ages and backgrounds can learn.[148]

At the college level, the **American Association of University Professors** made a very famous **Declaration of Principles** in 1915 that still stands as the measure of quality teaching. I'm including it here since it speaks directly to the sensitive subject of student immaturity. Let me quote the most relevant portions from that:

> **There is one case in which the academic teacher is under an obligation to observe certain special restraints—namely, the instruction of immature students. In many of our American colleges, and especially in the first two years of the course, the student's character is not yet fully formed, his mind is still relatively immature.** In these circumstances it may reasonably be expected that the instructor will present scientific truth with discretion, that he will introduce the student to new conceptions gradually, with some consideration for the student's preconceptions and traditions, and with due regard to character-building. **The teacher ought also to be especially on his guard against taking unfair advantage of the student's immaturity by indoctrinating him with the teacher's own opinions before the student has had an opportunity fairly to examine other opinions upon the matters in question, and before he has sufficient knowledge and ripeness of judgment to be entitled to form any definitive opinion of**

---

[148] "Revised Code of Ethics for the Social Studies Profession," National Council for the Social Studies, accessed November 26, 2020, https://www.socialstudies. org/position-statements/revised-code-ethics-social-studies-profession.

his own. It is not the least service which a college or university may render to those under its instruction, to habituate them to looking not only patiently but methodically on both sides, before adopting any conclusion upon controverted issues.[149]

And, finally, the **American Council on Education** had this to say in its "**Statement on Academic Rights and Responsibilities**":

Colleges and universities should welcome intellectual pluralism and the free exchange of ideas. Such a commitment will inevitably encourage debate over complex and difficult issues about which individuals will disagree. Such discussions should be held in an environment characterized by openness, tolerance and civility.[150]

Additionally, freedom of thought is recognized as a fundamental right of individuals, worldwide. It is explicitly mentioned in the Universal Declaration of Human Rights 1948, Article 18, which declares, "Everyone has the right to freedom of thought, conscience, and religion." The European Convention on Human Rights likewise includes freedom of thought among the basic rights of every citizen. Both these texts make it clear that free thought is a basic right of "everyone"; there is no age limit at which a human being begins to enjoy such a legal right.[151]

Most K–12 teachers and administrators are unaware of these existing commonsense standards, by which they are already expected to comport themselves. It's time to change that. Responsible adults must step up to

---

[149] "1915 Declaration of Principles on Academic Freedom and Tenure," American Association of University Professors, 1915, https://www.aaup.org/NR/rdonlyres/A6520A9D-0A9A-47B3-B550-C006B5B224E7/0/1915Declaration.pdf.

[150] "Statement on Academic Rights and Responsibilities," American Council on Education, accessed November 26, 2020, https://www.acenet.edu/Documents/Statement-on-Academic-Rights-and-Responsibilities-2005.pdf.

[151] Desmond Clarke, "Freedom of Thought in Schools: A Comparative Study," *International and Comparative Law Quarterly* 35, no. 2 (April, 1986): 271–301.

protect the integrity of American education by familiarizing themselves with these established conduct codes and by ensuring that today's K–12 educators adhere to them by holding them accountable.

Sanctity of Thought in the Classroom

In the process of forming our opinions, our minds wander, we experiment, we think out loud, we make mistakes, and sometimes we make happy discoveries. This is the process of thought and the function of education. In fact, the word education comes from the prefix "ex" meaning "out" and the root "ducere" meaning to "lead" or to "draw out." In other words, an educator merely draws out from a student the potential that is inside. An indoctrinator, conversely, attempts to put something inside the student that wasn't there before.

According to Harvey Silverglate and Jordan Lorence, writing on the problems of thought reform programs within education, there is an "indispensable right to private conscience." They argue that "[b]efore one can have the freedom to express ideas in open debate…one must have freedom of conscience: the right to arrive at one's private beliefs, without being coerced into an artificial unity by those who wield power over us. After all, the freedom to speak is a dead letter if one lacks the freedom to think, to believe, or to disbelieve. At the heart of American liberty lies a recognition of individual rights, individual responsibility, and individual dignity. Over one's inner mind, conscience, and self, no one has coercive power." They go on to assert that the "freedom to disagree, to state one's beliefs and values, and to discuss and argue peacefully makes democratic deliberation possible and allows us to pursue truth unfettered by the demands of any one ideology or orthodox point of view."[152]

Students who are not allowed to think or speak freely will go unchallenged, intellectual muscles will go untested and undeveloped, and

---

[152] Silverglate and Lorence, *FIRE's Guide to First-Year Orientation and Thought Reform on Campus*, 1–2.

pupils will never be allowed or enabled to achieve their potentials. This is the antithesis of an education.

Silverglate and Lorence go on to explain:

> Censorship is generally a dreadful thing, but coercing belief and conscience is yet more pernicious and evil, because it invades the inner being of an individual's life. Sometimes tyrannical power seeks to force individuals under its sway to speak or utter things that the speaker does not believe. In our moral tradition, that is a frightful assault upon the innermost sanctum of human privacy and dignity. This form of censorship goes beyond prohibiting "bad" speech and ideas. It instead seeks to impose on a student, and coerce the student to adopt, and to believe in, the "approved" point of view advanced by the authorities. Official acts that invade this private sphere of thought and conscience—what we call, in its starkest form, "thought reform"—are related to the more familiar concept of censorship of public speech, but reach far deeper. Instead of preventing students from expressing their views and beliefs, thought reform seeks to coerce students into contradicting those views and beliefs by saying things that they do not believe and that may, in fact, violate their most deeply held beliefs, with the ultimate goal of forcing change in those beliefs themselves. This act reaches deep into the mind and heart of a human being and seeks to force him not only to abandon his own beliefs, but also to mouth and indeed adopt the beliefs of those in positions of power and authority over him. Censoring speech is bad enough, but requiring people to adhere to, and even to believe (or at least to proclaim belief) in an official, orthodox ideology

is completely incompatible with a free society and is the hallmark of totalitarian social control.[153]

They additionally point out:

> Of course, those who endeavor to force others to believe in an official ideology and who punish the expression of dissent frequently do so under the guise of enforcing "good," "moral," and "ethical" values and social goals. When a government or administration seeks to force those under its authority to believe and to mouth certain views, that authority claims to be implementing positive values—"politically correct," as the phrase goes—leading to the good society. For those who would coerce thought, belief, and conscience, dissent from their own point of view is evil or immoral or antisocial, and not simply the expression of a different point of view. History should have taught us to hold in horror the violation of conscience and private belief. The "peat bog soldiers," Nazi prisoners sent to work in the fields until they died, sang the song, *"Die Gedanken sind frei,"* "Thoughts Are Free." Inward thoughts and convictions truly are the final atoms of human liberty. No decent institution, civilization, or person pursues an unwilling fellow creature there.[154]

Yet educational institutions do so routinely.

Forgotten, Ignored Wisdom

There are several moral and legal objections to leveraging a public educational institution to advance a political purpose. First of all, public schools

---

[153] Ibid, 4–5.
[154] Ibid.

are agencies of the government. As such, when they use their position and resources to keep themselves in power, they injure democracy and undermine their own integrity. The school, itself, is also obviously constructed, equipped, and maintained with funding extracted from all members of the community. Public school teachers, as government actors, are paid for their classroom time with public funds. The building, the lights, the custodian's time, and the furnace are all public property. Using classroom time, money, and other resources to achieve partisan goals that advantage themselves is self-evidently improper. When funds are appropriated for achieving certain public aims, such as transmitting state-adopted learning objectives, but are then diverted towards achieving a personal, private purpose, such as furthering an educator's particular political objectives, those funds are patently misused. A state legislature would never approve public funding to promote one party over another without immediate outcry, and a school would never put up with a teacher taking home an overhead projector (I realize I'm dating myself here, but you get the point) and claiming it is now their personal private property. Public funds are for public purposes, and public school teachers are hired to serve the public, not themselves, at public expense.

What Responsible, Ethical Education Looks Like

So what does good education look like?

This is a broad topic which could fill a book of its own, but I'll share some concise thoughts on the matter. Responsible, ethical education respects the sanctity of the student's individual, private conscience and adheres to long-established codes of professional and ethical conduct for teachers. Responsible educators do not overstep the boundaries of their course syllabi or their own training.

As stated in the ACTA *Intellectual Diversity* report, "faculty members are hired for their expertise and are expected to instruct students on the subject of their expertise. If they are teaching biology, they should be talking about biology. If they are teaching Medieval English literature, we expect them to be lecturing on Chaucer, not Condoleezza Rice."[155]

Attitudes and Dispositions in Teacher Education

Even more brazen than surreptitiously embedding social justice in a student's high school career track have been attempts to program it into their teachers' mental "dispositions" as a pre-requisite to earning their teacher certification. These attempts go back at least a decade, but were successfully defeated on grounds that they improperly interfered with individual private conscience.

Will Creeley, legal director of the Foundation for Individual Rights in Education, explained this: "Dispositions assessment opens virtually all of a candidate's thoughts and actions to scrutiny...[and] brings under the examiner's purview a key element of the candidate's very personality."[156] FIRE led victorious campaigns against the inclusion of a "social justice" disposition by the National Council for the Accreditation of Teacher Education (NCATE), a governmentally authorized accreditor of education schools, as well as at Columbia University's Teachers College after concluding that the "use of 'dispositions,' and the use of a 'social justice' disposition in particular, leads directly to the adoption of ideological litmus tests for teacher candidates at education schools. If NCATE wants to remain an authorized accreditor, it needs to wield its power responsibly and not appear to endorse a standard that leads to the establishment of a political orthodoxy within schools of education."[157]

---

[155] *Intellectual Diversity: Time for Action*, American Council of Trustees and Alumni, December 1, 2005, 6, https://www.goacta.org/resource/intellectual_diversity/.

[156] Will Creeley, "Dispositions in Teacher Education: Old Tricks, New Name," FIRE Newsdesk, March 14, 2007, https://www.thefire.org/dispositions-in-teacher-education-old-tricks-new-name/.

[157] "FIRE Statement on NCATE's Encouragement of Political Litmus Tests in Higher Education," Foundation for Individual Rights in Education, June 5, 2006, https://www.thefire.org/fire-statement-on-ncates-encouragement-of-political-litmus-tests-in-higher-education/.

What is a "social justice disposition" exactly?

Another FIRE blog post explains: "Columbia University's Teachers College requires students to demonstrate a 'commitment to social justice' and employs 'dispositions,' which it defines as 'observable behaviors that fall within the law and involve the use of certain skills,' to evaluate students. These dispositions, 'expected of Teachers College candidates and graduates' and 'assessed at each transition point,' include 'Respect for Diversity and Commitment to Social Justice.'"[158]

However, "evaluating students according to their commitment to an officially defined ideal is a violation of a student's right to decide for himself or herself what is and is not socially just," FIRE pointed out in a letter to the school. "These 'dispositions' require students to adopt fundamental outlooks with which they might not agree in order to conform to the 'present consensus vision' on campus."

This is the opposite of how most parents raise their children to be. Peer pressure is never the way to establish one's belief systems. And probably almost every parent has uttered some iteration of these words: "If everyone else was jumping off a bridge, would you follow?" Something as personal as establishing one's beliefs should not be left to committee.

"Judging students against ill-defined, politically loaded standards is simply incompatible with the core intellectual precepts of a modern liberal education," the FIRE letter continued. Then the author, Greg Lukianoff, made a salient point: "Would an applicant with conservative Muslim beliefs risk attending Teachers College if he suspected that his religious beliefs might not be considered "socially just"? What about Orthodox Jewish applicants, anarchists, evangelical Christians, or Randian atheists? Many potential applicants have internal beliefs that are inconsistent with the worldview laid out by Teachers College's Conceptual Framework. Does this mean they would not make good teachers? Does it mean that Teachers College does not want them?"

And you wonder why there is such an ideological imbalance in the teaching profession?

---

[158] Ibid.

Of course, this isn't about "social justice." Lukianoff pointed out that he "would oppose with equal effort a 'disposition' purporting to grade students according to their demonstrated commitments to 'capitalism,' 'patriotism,' or 'individualism.' Indeed, the crux of our objection is that by so defining and evaluating a student's possible understanding of a concept as amorphous and personal as 'social justice,' Teachers College is substituting its own conclusions for those of its students. Education demands that students analyze, critique, reason, argue, and research on their own; what Teachers College encourages here is instead rote recital, a kind of conceptual spoon-feeding."[159]

Likewise, FIRE was also concerned that the National Council for Accreditation of Teacher Education (NCATE) used its power as a federally authorized accreditor of education schools to promote vague standards that facilitate discrimination against students based on their political views. They, too, put themselves in the position of evaluating a candidate's commitment to "social justice" and "diversity." This puts a "federal imprimatur to a pernicious form of viewpoint discrimination," FIRE wrote.[160]

Happily, this challenge succeeded, proving that those opposed to tendentious tendencies in academia can prevail when they know their rights and stand firmly on principle. "The standards essentially resulted in a political litmus test for teachers, as it was virtually impossible to evaluate a student's commitment to 'social justice' without evaluating his or her politics," admitted the agency as they reversed the policy.[161]

While formal graduation disposition requirements for aspiring teachers were successfully challenged and defeated in this case, pressure to internalize and promote the social aims contained under the amorphous

---

[159] "FIRE Letter to Columbia University Teachers College Trustees, March 12, 2008," Foundation for Individual Rights in Education, March 12, 2008, https://www.thefire.org/fire-letter-to-columbia-university-teachers-college-trustees-march-12-2008/.

[160] "FIRE Statement on NCATE's Encouragement of Political Litmus Tests in Higher Education."

[161] Ibid.

umbrella term "social justice" and the newer "anti-racism" persist informally throughout academia and K–12 education, and pop up regularly. They will need to be regularly re-confronted.

As I'm writing this, the Illinois State Board of Education is considering a set of new standards for teachers and administrators that include calling on educators to "[e]mbrace and encourage progressive viewpoints and perspectives that leverage asset thinking toward traditionally marginalized populations," as well as to "understand and value the notion... that there is not one 'correct' way of doing or understanding something, and that what is seen as 'correct' is most often based on our lived experiences." According to representatives of an alliance opposing these new proposed standards, "This requirement will create potential conflicts with the deeply held religious convictions of teachers, parents, and students in the state of Illinois. Not all teachers would be able to comply with the new standards without violating their consciences."[162] People should get to decide for themselves what "notions" they will "value," while the idea that there is not a correct way of understanding something takes direct aim at the concept of objective reality and personal belief systems.

Discouragement and Minimization of Opportunities

Many educators are so good at critically pointing out all the flaws they perceive with this country and its systems that their students wind up discouraged and with a failure to appreciate the many positive benefits that our way of life provides and the many advantages and tremendous opportunities available to them. This is a terrible disservice to them.

Modern activist teachers are filling kids' heads with boundless criticism of the systems in which these children will need to operate as adults. Charged with upholding and transmitting the great history and traditions

---

[162] Peter Hancock, "Proposed New Teacher Standards Spark Controversy," *Capitol News Illinois*, November 10, 2020, https://capitolnewsillinois.com/NEWS/proposed-new-teacher-standards-spark-controversy.

of Western civilization that led to the formation of our government and its founding documents and operating principles, some educators feel instead that they have the unlimited right—and even *obligation*—to pass harsh negative judgment on this system and then inculcate this worldview in young people in their classrooms. I call this putting "carts before horses," because they are training kids to criticize a system before they even fully understand it, before they have been properly instructed in it, and before they have fully experienced it.

This is like being given a movie review and then being asked to explain or take a test on the movie. Or, worse: being given a movie review and being asked to speak on the book on which the movie was based, without having read it.

Activist teachers are attempting to preempt this natural ordering process by substituting a mere critique for a great deal of foundational knowledge that can only be gained through a lot of hard work, background reading, and contextual knowledge. In order to understand our system and why it was established that way it was, one needs a thorough grounding in the philosophy and history behind it and the previous systems it opposes; these challenging endeavors are being skipped over at many schools in favor of "engagement in the community" and other activities that are beside the point. Current levels of civic knowledge among young people are woeful indeed. It's hardly surprising, given the distracting political preoccupations of many activist educators. The endless criticism of America in education suffers from a boring, depressing, and predictable sameness. Students can easily anticipate and ape the repetitive narrative, rather than thinking spontaneously and originally. In other words: it's *easy* and requires little to no original thought. Mouthing slogans is effortless, fast, and instantly gratifying: What could be simpler than reciting a bumper sticker staying?

A little bit of appropriate criticism is one thing—like salt or spice in a recipe—but hyper-focus on anything begins to seem like an obsession. I've heard the term "ideological fetish" used to describe some educators' attachment to a single theory or idea. Unrelenting negativity and hyper-focus on examining faults and shortcomings are hard for anyone to take in large doses without respite. It's cheerless, somber, and lacking in proportionality or perspective. It's also very dispiriting to a young person looking for something positive and hopeful to believe in, and hence, a disservice to them at the outset of their lives. It's fundamentally age-inappropriate.

How about balancing all of this incessant criticism with some appreciation? As I reviewed story after story of America-bashing in the classroom, I thought of the Monty Python skit in *Life of Brian* in which a rebel band plots a coup, justifying it with the lament "What have the Romans ever given us?!" To which the timid, awkward replies come— the aqueduct, sanitation, the roads, irrigation, medicine, safety in the streets—with grudging acknowledgments, leading to the punchline "All right, all right…but apart from better sanitation, the medicine, education, wine, public order, irrigation, roads, a fresh water system, and public health…what have the Romans ever done for us?"

Perhaps a bit more reflection and tempered proportion are called for in the classroom.

I happen to believe this is a great country, and I'm pretty sure K–12 teachers are not certified in "country-ranking" or "economic system evaluation." No, the United States is not perfect, but it does hold a special place in world history. Teachers should not try to completely dismantle this notion in American schoolchildren.

Young People Need and Deserve Encouragement and Optimism

Rather than engaging in fault-finding and blame-fixing, how much better we would all be if we learned to count blessings and to cultivate a garden of gratitude rather than grievances? A classic bit of parenting and teacher-disciplinary advice is to "notice the good and ignore the bad." This is because of the idea that "what we focus on expands." Where your attention goes, energy flows. If it flows in a positive direction, this is more likely to lead to a positive upward spiral.

Kids need optimism, confidence, and hope. They need to be filled with constant encouragement that builds them up. Here's an all-purpose empowering message I wish all teachers and parents would try to transmit to young people: "I can succeed in spite of obstacles in my life." It's a message most adults need too.

Teachers serve students well when they focus their pedagogical energy on transmitting solid knowledge and building undeniable skills to equip students to be able to take advantage of life's opportunities and to overcome the inevitable hardships. That's what comprises real confidence and is the source from which honest self-esteem derives. Young people with academic competence, knowledge, and understanding will have the confidence to face the challenges in life successfully and to bounce back from setbacks. Couple that with a positive, hopeful mindset and they will go far. When we help kids learn to regulate their emotions, cultivate a positive attitude, channel their efforts, set goals, and work diligently towards their attainment, we give them the best chances of success in life.

18

(Why It's Bad) Emotionally

"I told him to keep his mouth shut," a college classmate told me of her advice to her son when he was in high school at a notable New England boarding school. "These people control your college options and your career chances! Just go along with whatever the majority says and stay safe."

This is the inevitable result of what happens when teachers and schools assert, openly or implicitly, an acceptable view on open questions. Either students "go along to get along" or they stand out and suffer the consequences. Not surprisingly, surveys show that a majority of students now self-censor and self-silence in school.[163] Young people, like everyone else, are inclined to say what they think other people want to hear. Sometimes, that's what they think their teacher wants to hear in order to give them a good grade. Other times, it's what they think will make them more popular with their peers.

---

[163] Greta Anderson, "Survey Identifies 'Dangerous' Student Self-Censorship," *Inside Higher Ed*, April 29, 2020, https://www.insidehighered.com/quick-takes/2020/04/29/survey-identifies-%E2%80%98dangerous%E2%80%99-student-self-censorship.

Strategic self-censorship may seem like a prudent move in school, but what is the cost of a student's learning to hide his or her true self, just to fit in or to please an authority figure? What is the psychic toll?

The current psychology literature on self-silencing and self-censorship states the obvious. When people feel fear, a sense of vulnerability, or conditional approval, they might protect or defend themselves by masking, suppressing, or otherwise altering their self-expressions. To the extent that people find themselves regularly engaging in interpersonal strategies that involve self-obscuring, self-distortion, or self-muting, they are likely to experience psychological ill-being.[164]

On the contrary, when humans experience themselves as possessing individual autonomy and genuinely connected to other persons through meaningful relatedness, development will progress optimally. Because autonomy and relatedness are basic human psychological needs, the loss associated with self-silencing represents a serious threat to well-being and healthy development. To the extent that organizations, such as a school, undermine these positive attributes, they impede and compromise student development and well-being.

Relying on a self-silencing strategy can result in reduced self-esteem and feelings of loss of self. When people predisposed to self-silencing find themselves operating in social or institutional contexts with particularly strong demands for self-silencing, they are likely to be especially vulnerable to depression.[165] Numerous empirical studies have established

---

[164] Brian Patrick, et al., "Self-Silencing in School: Failures in Student Autonomy and Teacher-Student Relatedness," *Social Psychology of Education* 22 (2019): 943–967, Carl R. Rogers, *On Becoming a Person: A Therapist's View of Psychotherapy* (Boston, MA: Houghton Mifflin, 1961), Dana Crowley Jack, *Silencing the Self: Women and Depression* (Cambridge, MA: Harvard University Press, 1991), and D. C. Jack and A. Ali, "Introduction: Culture, Self-Silencing, and Depression: A Contextual-Relational Perspective," in D. Jack and A. Ali, eds., *Silencing the Self across Cultures: Depression and Gender in the Social World* (New York, NY: Oxford University Press, 2010) 3–18.

[165] D. C. Jack and D. Dill, "The Silencing the Self Scale: Schemas of Intimacy Associated with Depression in Women," *Psychology of Women Quarterly* 16 (1992): 97–106.

a relationship between self-silencing and depression.[166] Self-silencing has also been shown to relate to a wide variety of other negative psychological and behavioral outcomes, including insecure attachment,[167] poor dyadic relationship adjustment,[168] risky sexual behaviors (difficulty saying "no"),[169] and low achievement motivation.[170] Other results suggest that self-silencing is related to low behavioral engagement, negative emotions, and a lack of school belongingness, to the extent that self-silencing is associated with feelings of reduced autonomy and/or poor relationships with teachers.[171]

Growing evidence shows the effects of both autonomy and teacher-student relationship quality on a variety of valued academic and socio-emotional outcomes for students. For example, autonomous self-regulation and/or student perceptions of autonomy in school have been shown to be associated with intrinsic motivation to learn,[172] engage-

---

[166] J. G. Carr, F. D. Gilroy, and M. F. Sherman, "Silencing the Self and Depression among Women: The Moderating Effects of Race," *Psychology of Women Quarterly* 20(3) (July 2006) 375–392, G. L. Flett et al., "Perfectionism, Silencing the Self, and Depression," *Personality and Individual Differences* 43 (2007): 1211–1222, and J. M. Thompson, "Silencing the Self: Depressive Symptomatology and Close Relationships," *Psychology of Women Quarterly* 19 (1995): 337–353.

[167] J. M. Thompson and B. I. Hart, "Attachment Dimensions Associated with Silencing the Self," poster presented at the American Psychological Association Annual Convention, Toronto, Ontario, Canada, 1996.

[168] Thompson, "Silencing the Self," 337–353.

[169] R. J. Jacobs and B. Thomlison, "Self-Silencing and Age as Risk Factors for Sexually Acquired HIV in Midlife and Older Women," *Journal of Aging and Health* 21 (2009): 102–128.

[170] C. L. Spratt, M. F. Sherman and F. D. Gilroy, "Silencing the Self and Sex as Predictors of Achievement Motivation," *Psychological Reports* 82 (1998): 259–263.

[171] B. Patrick et al., "Self-Silencing in School: Failures in Student Autonomy and Teacher-Student Relatedness," *Social Psychology of Education* 22 (2019): 943–967.

[172] T. Garcia and P. R. Pintrich, "The Effects of Autonomy on Motivation and Performance in the College Classroom," *Contemporary Educational Psychology* 21 (1996): 477–486.

ment,[173] academic achievement,[174] school adjustment,[175] positive emotions,[176] and staying in school versus dropping out.[177]

The self-silencing problem in school begins early: previous studies suggest that students may be particularly vulnerable to developing motivational and engagement difficulties in school in the mid- to late elementary school years, and that these difficulties may be related to decreases in opportunities to satisfy needs for autonomy and relatedness. Intrinsic motivation in school declines from the ages of eleven to sixteen, and this decline is related to insufficient satisfaction of the needs for autonomy, competence, and relatedness.[178] The years between the ages of nine and eleven may be particularly sensitive when it comes to the effects of autonomy and relatedness on school engagement.[179]

[173] R. M. Ryan and J. P. Connell, "Perceived Locus of Causality and Internalization: Examining Reasons for Acting in Two Domains," *Journal of Personality and Social Psychology* 57 (1989): 749–761.

[174] W. S. Grolnick, R. M. Ryan and E. L. Deci, "The Inner Resources for School Performance: Motivational Mediators of Children's Perceptions of their Parents," *Journal of Educational Psychology* 83 (1991): 508–517 and M. Vansteenkiste et al., "Examining the Motivational Impact of Intrinsic versus Extrinsic Goal Framing and Autonomy-Supportive versus Internally Controlling Communication Style on Early Adolescents' Academic Achievement," *Child Development* 86 (2005): 483–501.

[175] B. Soenens and M. Vansteenkiste, "Antecedents and Outcomes of Self-Determination in 3 Life Domains: The Role of Parents' and Teachers' Autonomy Support," *Journal of Youth and Adolescence* 34 (2005): 589–604.

[176] A. E. Black and E. L. Deci, "The Effects of Instructors' Autonomy Support and Students' Autonomous Motivation on Learning Organic Chemistry: A Self-Determination Theory Perspective, *Science Education* 84 (2000): 740–756.

[177] R.J Vallerand and R. Bissonnette, "Intrinsic, Extrinsic, and Amotivational Styles as Predictors of Behavior: A Prospective Study," *Journal of Personality* 60 (1992): 599–620.

[178] T. Gnambs and B. Hanfstingl, "The Decline of Academic Motivation During Adolescence: An Accelerated Longitudinal Cohort Analysis on the Effect of Psychological Need Satisfaction," *Journal of Educational Psychology* 36 (2016): 1691–1705.

[179] Patrick et al., "Self-Silencing in School."

The quality of teacher-student relatedness has also been linked with outcomes such as academic attitudes and feelings of school belongingness,[180] social and emotional adjustment,[181] positive coping strategies,[182] engagement,[183] and school completion.[184] Conversely, student perceptions of autonomy in school have been shown to be associated with intrinsic

---

[180] F. G. Lopez, "Student-Professor Relationship Styles, Childhood Attachment Bonds and Current Academic Orientations," *Journal of Social and Personal Relationships* 14 (1997): 271–282.

[181] K. A. Arbeau, R. J. Coplan, and M. Weeks, "Shyness, Teacher-Child Relationships, and Socio-Emotional Adjustment in Grade 1," *International Journal of Behavioral Development* 34 (2010): 259–269, J. A. Baker, "Contributions of Teacher-Child Relationships to Positive School Adjustment During Elementary School," *Journal of School Psychology* 44 (2006): 211–229, and C. Murray and M. T. Greenberg, "Children's Relationship with Teachers and Bonds with School: An Investigation of Patterns and Correlates in Middle Childhood," *Journal of School Psychology* 38 (2000): 423–445.

[182] R. M. Ryan, J. D. Stiller, and J. H. Lynch, "Representations of Relationships to Teachers, Parents, and Friends as Predictors of Academic Motivation and Self-Esteem," *Journal of Early Adolescence* 14 (1994): 226–249.

[183] C. Furrer and E. Skinner, "Sense of Relatedness as a Factor in Children's Academic Engagement and Performance," *Journal of Educational Psychology* 95 (2003): 148–162, D. L. Roorda, et al. "The Influence of Affective Teacher-Student Relationships on Students' School Engagement and Achievement: A Meta-Analytic Approach," *Review of Educational Research* 81 (2011): 493–529, and M.J. Zimmer-Gembeck, et al., "Relationships at School and Stage-Environment Fit as Resources for Adolescent Engagement and Achievement," *Journal of Adolescence* 29 (2006): 911–933.

[184] T. G. Reio, R. F. Marcus, and J. Sanders-Reio, "Contribution of Student and Instructor Relationships and Attachment Style to School Completion," *Journal of Genetic Psychology: Research and Theory on Human Development* 170 (2009): 53–71.

motivation to learn,[185] self-regulated learning strategies,[186] academic achievement,[187] school adjustment,[188] positive emotions,[189] and staying in school versus dropping out.[190]

Previous studies also demonstrate connections between self-silencing and maladaptive coping[191] and poor interpersonal relationship quality.[192] School self-silencing is strongly associated with internalizing and denial strategies as well as feelings of disconnection from teachers and reluctance to seek teachers' support in times of distress. Self-silencing in school was also related to feelings of emotional distress and low levels of behavioral engagement consistent with feeling depressed in school. This result is in keeping with previous studies showing the relationship between self-silencing and depression.[193]

---

[185] T. Garcia and P. R. Pintrich, "The Effects of Autonomy on Motivation and Performance in the College Classroom," *Contemporary Educational Psychology* 21 (1996): 477–486.

[186] M. Vansteenkiste et al., "Identifying Configurations of Perceived Teacher Autonomy Support and Structure: Associations with Self-Regulated Learning, Motivation and Problem Behavior," *Learning and Instruction* 22 (2012): 431–439.

[187] Grolnick, Ryan, and Deci, "The Inner Resources for School Performance," 508–517 and Vansteenkiste, et al., "Examining the Motivational Impact of Intrinsic versus Extrinsic Goal Framing."

[188] Soenens and Vansteenkiste, "Antecedents and Outcomes of Self-Determination in 3 Life Domains."

[189] Black and Deci, "The Effects of Instructors' Autonomy Support and Students' Autonomous Motivation on Learning Organic Chemistry, 740–756.

[190] R. J. Vallerand and R. Bissonnette, "Intrinsic, Extrinsic, and Amotivational Styles as Predictors of Behavior: A Prospective Study," *Journal of Personality* 60 (1992): 599–620.

[191] K. Kayser and C. Acquati, "Dyadic Coping across the Lifespan: A Comparison Between Younger and Middle-Aged Couples with Breast Cancer," *Frontiers in Psychology*, March 19, 2019.

[192] Thompson and Hart, "Attachment Dimensions Associated with Silencing the Self."

[193] Carr, Gilroy, and Sherman, "Silencing the Self and Depression among Women."

Dana Crowley Jack, in her book *Silencing the Self,* describes a no-win, either/or tension between sacrificing personal needs and preserving an important relationship. This bind involves dependence, pleasing, anger, accommodation, self-censorship, low self-esteem, and depression. When a particular school context heightens students' awareness of their lack of empowerment and the need to subjugate their own needs to those of teachers and other school authorities, those who are predisposed to self-silencing would be especially vulnerable to negative outcomes.[194]

Other relevant studies, classic and poignant in stature, highlight the unfortunate tendency of people to conform to majority opinions, even when it means disregarding the ample evidence of their own eyes.[195] For an enhanced understanding of the potentially deleterious effects of this effect, see Irving Janis' explanations of the phenomenon of groupthink and its role in various lamentable but preventable disasters.[196] The confidence of those in the majority does not, of course, make them right, nor does the reticence of those who perceive themselves to be in the minority make them wrong. Review the fable of "The Emperor's New Clothes" for a colloquial demonstration of this familiar and once well-understood concept. Other compelling literary demonstrations of the same principle include *The Captive Mind* and *Private Truth, Public Lies: The Social Consequences of Preference Falsification*, and the European movie about Stasi invasion of privacy, *The Lives of Others.*

Similarly, the research on concealed stigma—socially devalued identities that can be hidden from others—also indicates that the feeling of being unable to reveal facets of one's authentic self in interaction with important others can carry a heavy psychic toll. These can include increased anxiety and intrusive thoughts related to the suppression of a

---

[194] Crowley Jack, *Silencing the Self.*

[195] Solomon Asch, "Effects of Group Pressure upon the Modification and Distortion of Judgment," in H. Guetzkow, ed., *Groups, Leadership and Men* (Pittsburgh, PA: Carnegie Press, 1951).

[196] Irving Janis, *Victims of Groupthink: A Psychological Study of Foreign-Policy Decisions and Fiascoes* (Boston, MA: Houghton Mifflin, 1972).

"secret,"[197] heightened subjective feelings of psychological distress, such as depression,[198] and raised perceived stress.[199]

The theory of the spiral of silence states that one's perception of the distribution of public opinion motivates one's willingness to express opinions.[200] Individuals who feel they are in the majority become louder, more confident, and dominant over time, while those in the minority become increasingly silent.

According to D. Garth Taylor in "Pluralistic Ignorance and the Spiral of Silence," "The appearance of strength becomes a self-fulfilling prophecy; those who think they are in the majority are more willing to speak out, those who think they are in the minority have an extra incentive to remain silent. The description of the plight of those who believe they are in the minority gives the name to this theory: the spiral of silence."[201]

Taylor goes on to explain:

> The Spiral of Silence begins with the premise that the individual assesses the distribution of opinions in the social environment by evaluating the strength, commitment, urgency, and the chances of success of certain proposals and viewpoints.... If the individual discovers he agrees with the prevailing view it boosts his self-confidence and enables self-expression without the danger of social

---

[197] L. Smart and D. Wegner, "Covering Up What Can't Be Seen: Concealable Stigma and Mental Control," *Journal of Personality and Social Psychology* 77, no. 3 (1999): 474–486.

[198] Quinn, et al., " Examining Effects of Anticipated Stigma" and Quinn and Chaudoir, "Living with a Concealable Stigmatized Identity."

[199] A. Sedlovskaya, "Concealable Stigma and the Distinction between Public and Private Selves: Implications for Psychological Well-Being," *Dissertation Abstracts International* 72 (2016): 10-B.

[200] E. Noelle-Neumann, "Turbulences in the Climate of Opinion: Methodological Applications of the Spiral of Silence Theory," *Public Opinion Quarterly* 41, no. 2 (1977): 143–158.

[201] D. G. Taylor, "Pluralistic Ignorance and the Spiral of Silence," *Public Opinion Quarterly* 46 (1982), 311.

isolation. If he finds his views are losing ground he will become more uncertain and therefore less inclined to express his opinion to others.... [T]he self-interest that people protect by monitoring the environment and shaping their expression of opinions is their fear of social isolation.[202]

Numerous scholars and critics have remarked the student-teacher relationship is typically characterized by a considerable power differential, with clear role demands that can enforce a dynamic of social inequality.[203] Recalling her own educational experiences in her book, *Teaching to Transgress*, bell hooks (intentional lowercase usage) comments, "During [school], the primary lesson was reinforced: we were to learn obedience to authority.... The vast majority of our [teachers]...used the classroom to enact rituals of control that were about domination and the unjust exercise of power."[204] Similarly, Ira Shor argues, "Power in society is like power in schools, colleges, and classrooms—unilateral, unelected, top-down, hierarchical, patriarchal, not democratic."[205]

According to Dana Crowley Jack, when relationships are defined by such social inequality, this enhances the likelihood that persons who are characterologically predisposed to self-silencing will, in fact, use self-silencing strategies.[206] If we extrapolate this logic to the student-teacher relationship, when people who are predisposed to self-silencing find themselves enacting the role of "student" in a school context in which teachers hold power over them, they would be expected to be especially

---

[202] Ibid, 314.
[203] bell hooks, *Teaching to Transgress: Education as the Practice of Freedom* (New York, NY: Routledge, 2017), Alfie Kohn, *Punished by Rewards* (Boston, MA: Houghton Mifflin, 1993), Ira Shor, *When Students Have Power: Negotiating Authority in a Critical Pedagogy* (Chicago, IL: University of Chicago Press, 1996), and Paulo Freire, *Pedagogy of the Oppressed* (New York, NY: Bloomsbury Academic, 2013).
[204] hooks, *Teaching to Transgress*, 4–5.
[205] Shor, *When Students Have Power*.
[206] Crowley Jack, *Silencing the Self*.

susceptible to silencing themselves in school. In self-determination theory terms, it would be predicted that students faced with the perception of threatening power relationships might be especially likely to be willing to sacrifice autonomy as an ill-fated strategy for preserving relatedness with the powerful other, the teacher.[207]

What about the public shaming, manipulated guilt confessions, scoldings, and humiliation associated with today's high-handed instructional methods? According to articles published in *Scientific American*[208] and The *Journal of Psychology*,[209] these are associated with rising rates of anxiety, depression, and incapacitating feelings of inferiority, hopelessness, and helplessness.

The implications of this assembled research are as stark as they are clear. Without the opportunity to speak authentically, think independently, and question received wisdom, our students will not develop the internal capacity to reason thoroughly and to trust their own considered judgment. Their developing self-confidence is undermined. They will not practice and develop the internal capacity to stand up for themselves, even when they sense that something is wrong or that their rights are being violated. This is concerning enough on an individual level, but what does it mean for our society writ large?

---

[207] B. Patrick, et al., "Self-Silencing in School," 946.

[208] Annette Kammerer. "The Scientific Underpinnings and Impacts of Shame." *Scientific American*, August 9, 2019.

[209] Patrizia Velotti, et al., "Faces of Shame: Implications for Self-Esteem, Emotion Regulation, Aggression, and Well-Being. The Journal of Psychology 151: 2 (2017), 174-184, https://www.tandfonline.com/doi/full/10.1080/00223980.2016.1248809.

19

(Why It's Bad) Democratically

Public schools function as democratic institutions within their communities. As such, they teach and should be modeling civic practices in their organization and operation. This implies transparency in all of their proceedings, including school board meetings, curriculum adoption and changes, proper handling of grievances and questions from the community or from their constituents, and adherence to sunshine laws, FOIA, open records, and right-to-know requests.

In many important ways, public schools are like police departments. Their employees are trained public servants, paid with taxpayer dollars and expected and required to deal with all members of the public, regardless of their background. In doing so, it is essential for the institution to treat citizens across the board equally and fairly, because when the perception of partiality or bias arises, the institution risks losing the community support upon which it depends. School districts cannot afford this.

Since 1925, public school employees have been considered to be so-called state or government actors,[210] which means that they are bound by the First, Fifth, and Fourteenth Amendments to the U.S. Constitution and obligated to follow some civil rights laws.[211] Since 1969,[212] U.S. courts have recognized that public school students have rights that state actors (like public school employees) must respect. And ultimately, the government, under the Tenth Amendment, is beholden to the people. School districts operate democratically, and follow state guidelines as laid out by state boards of education.

The school board embodies the "public" side of public education. They are the principal democratic body representing citizens in local education decisions. Since the U.S. Constitution does not mention education, those rights are held by the states. Power over public education derives from the state's power to tax and to provide for the general welfare of the state's citizens. State boards of education establish graduation and teacher certification requirements, and accountability and assessment standards. By state law, local school boards are delegated broad and nearly

---

[210] Gitlow v. New York, 268 U.S. 562 (1925). Gitlow "incorporated" the First Amendment's protection of speech into the Fourteenth Amendment's due process protection, converting the speech clause from a prohibition on the federal Congress to a limitation on all government actors. So the next time someone says the First Amendment doesn't apply in schools because it says "Congress shall make no law," cite Gitlow.

[211] Some civil rights laws, like Title VII of the Civil Rights Act of 1964, bind more than just government actors. Some, like Title III of the Civil Rights Act of 1964, target government actors specifically. And still others are conditional upon receipt of certain government funding, like funding under Title III of the Elementary and Secondary Education Act of 1965 or "E-rate discounts" on internet services. Which laws will be applicable in a given case will depend on the circumstances.

[212] See, e.g., Tinker v. Des Moines Independent Community School District, 393 U.S. 503 (1969) (finding public school teachers are limited by the First Amendment); New Jersey v. T.L.O., 469 U.S. 325 (1985) (finding public school teachers are limited by the Fourth Amendment); and Goss v. Lopez, 419 U. S. 565 (1975) (holding public school teachers are limited by the Fourteenth Amendment's due process clause).

unquestioned power to control the operation of the schools, including power to set curriculum and define what is and is not permissible teacher speech in classrooms. As such, K–12 classroom teaching, particularly in a publicly funded public school, is emphatically not an impromptu, unilateral, improvised free-for-all.

According to University of Wisconsin-Madison Professor Julie Underwood, "School boards set the curriculum for schools, and they have the legal right to decide what materials and speech are appropriate for the classroom.... Teachers face particular challenges when they are teaching political or controversial topics in classrooms. They must navigate a narrow passage between delivering the curriculum as required by their local board of education and sharing their own personal views and other information, while also abiding by board regulations regarding content and delivery. In addition, they must deliver the curriculum without attempting to indoctrinate students with their own personal beliefs, particularly on religious, political, and controversial topics."

Regarding teachers' personal views, Underwood states, "Teachers cannot let their personal beliefs interfere with their obligation to deliver the school's curriculum, and they may not hijack the curriculum or use their position as teacher as an opportunity to inculcate students to their personal beliefs.... In K-12 public schools, the local school board has the authority to set the curriculum, and teachers must adhere to it, as well as following all state and school board regulations."[213]

In one settled case, an Ohio school teacher's contract was not renewed because she used books in class that some parents found objectionable and chose pedagogical approaches that her school principal disfavored. She argued that the school district violated her First Amendment right to "select books and methods of instruction for use in the classroom without interference from public officials." The school district argued that her speech did not qualify for First Amendment protection since public employees do not enjoy that right when they communicate pursuant to their official employment duties. The court sided with school authorities and

---

[213] Underwood, "School Districts Control Teachers' Classroom Speech."

her contract was not renewed. In its decision, the court pointed out that school boards are legally responsible for implementing the curriculum and classroom content (speech) and they "hire" that speech (in the form of teachers) and must, therefore, regulate what is or is not expressed."[214]

Similarly, political science Professor Joshua Dunn, in an essay titled "Free Speech Accountability and Public Trust," points out that:

> An additional reason for teachers to practice neutrality is that support for public education depends on it. If the public believes that only certain viewpoints are allowed, or their classrooms are ideologically one-sided, support for public schools will erode.… When officials allow their teachers to be openly partisan in school, they risk doing even more to alienate 1/3 to 1/2 of the electorate. Even ideologically homogeneous districts could undermine financial support for public education, since some school funding comes from the state rather than just from local taxes. Why, legislators may reasonably ask, should public dollars go to support those who will use those resources to push their Partisan agendas on students? Some state legislatures have already targeted universities for these reasons, and K-12 education only makes itself a similar target when teachers can depart from the norm of neutrality during the school day.[215]

Regarding the necessity of political accountability, Dunn continues:

> At some point, public employees must be accountable to the people who pay their salary. In public education, the obvious place to locate that accountability is with elected school boards who must respond to taxpayer and particularly, parental concerns. The school board's decision

---

[214] Evans-Marshall v. Board of Ed. of Tipp City, 624 F. 3d 332 (Sixth Cir. 2010).
[215] Dunn, "Free Speech Accountability and Public Trust," 255–257.

can be debated and discussed and ultimately overturned through the political process. If teachers take offense at the idea that they are nothing more than "hired" speech, they are free to choose another career that they find less insulting. Teachers may view it as part of their job to evangelize for their political preferences, but if the people who hired them disagree, they should proselytize on their own time.

The messaging of much of this wayward programming that is finding its way into our schools seeks to tear our system apart without teaching uninformed and inexperienced young people why it is worth preserving. To the extent that it is Marxist, it is also anti-democratic, in that it is both totalitarian and authoritarian, in its aims and in its implementation. Because we, fortunately, have local control of our school districts, it can and must be confronted and defeated locally, teacher by teacher, school by school, district by district, and state by state.

Another important part of teaching involves modeling behavior for younger citizens. As democratically run and operated institutions charged with preparing and educating the next generation of American citizens to enter democratic, civil society, public schools can reasonably be expected to model and uphold appropriate, healthy civic norms in their ordinary operation. These would, of course, include First Amendment values and principles such as respect for competing opinions, open discourse, and rigorous free debate. The operation of the schools provides a model that serves as preparation for participatory democracy. They must be democratic in order to teach democracy through examples worthy of emulation and avoid, therefore, the top-down imposition of unquestionable so-called dogma. Teachers who impose or allow censorship and restricting student consideration of competing ideas in the classroom fail to model civic virtues and fall short of these expectations.

Professor David Moshman writes that "public education in a democratic society must provide for the transmission of knowledge and values across generations without undermining the democratic ideals of government by the will of the governed. For democracy to continue, the next generation must develop a will of its own. Non-indoctrination protects not only the moral rights of individual students but also the moral and constitutional legitimacy of public education."

He also points out that "[d]emocracy entails a commitment not to indoctrinate each other's children. Academic freedom is particularly important in safeguarding the Democratic legitimacy of public education in a multicultural society."[216] Is it any wonder that school systems are already seeing an exodus in favor of charter, private, and homeschooling alternatives? Homeschooling numbers have surged dramatically, recently, to nearly 10 percent of U.S. students.[217] This should be of great concern to every public school educator and administrator.

---

[216] David Moshman, *Liberty and Learning: Academic Freedom for Teachers and Students* (Portsmouth, NH: Heinemann, 2009), 47.

[217] Kerry McDonald, "Homeschooling More Than Doubles during the Pandemic," Foundation for Economic Education, December 4, 2020, https://fee.org/articles/homeschooling-more-than-doubles-during-the-pandemic/.

20

(Why It's Bad) Developmentally

Tendentious, activist teaching isn't merely a political or pedagogical problem. It is also developmentally damaging, from a number of well-established perspectives. One of the giants of educational thought is the humanistic psychologist Carl Rogers who believed in the capacity of every human being to thrive and reach his or her potential if allowed to develop under proper conditions. Much like a seed, each individual carries within him or herself all that is needed to develop correctly, as long as s/he is provided with the necessary conditions essential for growth.

According to Rogers, unconditional positive regard, meaning genuine acceptance, is foundational to any helping relationship, including education. Unfortunately, all too often these days, activist-minded educators are only offering conditional acceptance to students in school: "I will accept you on the condition that you believe the things I want you to believe and share the same opinions as me."

Many students today instead experience rejection in the classroom and are therefore learning to be guarded and inauthentic in their classroom interactions. They say things they do not believe in order to win phony acceptance and avoid open conflict with a person who carries direct authority over them. This is the essence of a dysfunctional relationship—where one person's rights are not respected and they are expected to adapt themselves (play a role, be ungenuine) to remain in an unhealthy relationship. This is what sends people to therapy later in life and is completely non-conducive to their intellectual or emotional development.

Perry's Stages of Cognitive Development and the Limits of "Dualism"

Another way that dogmatic teaching falls short is when comparing it to our understanding of the different stages of intellectual development. William Perry's theory of cognitive development teaches us that there are levels of understanding the world. Perry was a professor in education at Harvard and he observed different stages through which students pass on their way to the highest level of understanding of complex issues. At the lowest level is dualism. This is where people simplistically believe that everything is binary, which means there is an absolute right or wrong answer to everything. People who think dualistically tend to believe there is a correct list of answers engraved on golden tablets in the sky, and that these are known by authority figures. The role of the student is to learn (memorize) the right answers, so that then s/he will know them too. Other ways to describe dualistic/binary thinking: either-or, black-white, good-bad (evil), all-or-nothing, with-us or against-us thinking. This type of low-level thinking can lead to tribalism, an us-them mentality that sees an in-group/out-group dichotomy and can lead to the persecution of those not in the "right" group.

Unfortunately, this seems to be the type of thinking being promoted widely in education now. The role of a responsible educator, then, would be to break through this lower-order thought and prod students to higher levels of intellectual functioning.

The next level of Perry's theory involves recognition of multiplicity (different points of view each with some merit and encountering con-flicting ideas). Next, we learn that there are reasoning methods that can be used to determine which answers have the most support and how to evaluate the relative merits of competing solutions.

Ideally, students should be moving from believing that there are categorically right answers that we can be told to understanding there are ways we can be taught to find the right answers for ourselves. The point is clear: dualistic/binary thinking is not indicative of lofty intellectualism; this is a low-order and even damaging habit of thought to be overcome through the process of education—not inculcated through it.

Jean Piaget's Theory of Cognitive Development and the Need for Circumspection

Similarly, psychologist Jean Piaget has developed a well-regarded theory of cognitive development that posits that young people grow from concrete, inductive (based on personal experiences and feelings) reasoning to abstract, and deductive, abilities. He proposes four levels of intellectual development, but we'll just look at the school-aged ones here. They are:

Preconventional—ages 2–6
Concrete Operations—7–11
Formal Operations—12–18

Preconventional reasoning is inductive and based on personal experiences. Preconventional children are egocentric: perceiving the world only through their own personal point of view, and unable to consider others' perspectives and different vantage points. This is why, for instance, a very young child talking on the phone may ask you to look at something in front of her, which you can't see. They're unable to conceptualize your viewpoint. Being able to look at situations from another person's angle requires a level of abstraction that takes time to develop, but ideally, we want students to develop the scholarly skill of circumspection: the ability to look all the way around a problem from every perspective. This is the only way to understand a situation fully.

The stage of concrete operations, beginning around age seven, corrects the errors of the preconventional stage, but only relative to things that can be perceived or experienced directly by the child. Children at this level tend to describe themselves, and others, in external terms, such as "I am a boy. I have brown hair. I am tall." It is not until the child reaches formal operations that s/he becomes capable of hypothetical (abstract)-deductive (logical) thought. At higher levels, people move beyond describing themselves according to simplistic concrete terms to more abstracted, internal ones: "I am a hard worker, talented in music, and a good friend." In other words, the assessment moves deeper than the mere surface level.

The difference between inductive and deductive reasoning matters. Deduction is a form of valid reasoning. It is considered to be top-down (or big to little), where you start with a general premise and then follow logical steps to collect evidence and reach a specific conclusion. The scientific method, for example, uses deduction to test hypotheses or theories. Deductive reasoning generally follows the steps you can learn in classes on logic: the syllogism, for example, where certain premises determine whether resulting conclusions are valid. For example: if A = B and B = C, then it is logical to conclude that A = C. Inductive reasoning is the opposite: making broad generalizations from specific examples. For example: I have curly hair, and my brother has curly hair; therefore, all my relatives have curly hair. A child may reasonably reach this kind of inductive conclusion before learning that the laws of genetics can produce some surprising physical traits among family members. Inductive reasoning allows for the conclusion to be false, whereas proper deductive reasoning does not. Inductive reasoning can be a way to begin to uncover questions worth investigating, but it is insufficient to settle arguments because it is potentially flawed; deductive reasoning is considered to be the standard for scientific research and empirical proof or evidence. Not surprisingly, then, Piaget lists the development of our cognition as proceeding from childhood induction to adult deduction. This is certainly the goal to strive for in academia. Inductive reasoning comes naturally and intuitively, but deductive capacities must be developed, taught, and practiced.

Erik Erikson and the Damage of Identity "Foreclosure"

Another way in which dogmatic instruction undermines healthy development is in the realm of identity development. According to developmental psychologist Erik Erikson, people pass through different predictable stages as they develop and mature. At each stage, there is a developmental crisis—a fork in the road—where you have to make a (subconscious) choice over which way to go. At each stage, when the crisis is resolved in a positive way, a core ego strength emerges.

The most famous Eriksonian developmental stage (and the one most relevant to the topic of this book) is the adolescent stage of identity versus confusion. This is the stage of life when a young person attempts to answer the important question "Who am I?" This stage starts around age twelve and is normally resolved by around ages eighteen to twenty-four. During this stage, a young person is naturally expected to undergo a period of exploration, questioning, and testing in order to determine which of his family's and culture's values and beliefs he will accept, and which he will not. This is a natural and important process, and is part of the nature of the rebellious characteristic of this stage. A person has different components of identity: political commitment would be one, religious views would be another, and so on.

According to Erikson, and psychologist James Marcia, who elaborated in more detail on this stage, there are four possible outcomes or phases of identity development. A person who is not committed to any particular identity and is not actively testing or exploring would be considered *diffuse* (low commitment and low exploration). Many young people start off adolescence with this "who cares" attitude before moving on to questioning, as they mature. A person who is in the process of testing and exploring but who has not yet committed to an identity is said to be in *moratorium* (which means they are taking a break, while working it out). This is the healthy, expected process on the path to identity *achievement*, which is the ultimate resolution of this stage. A person who has achieved his or her identity has gone through a lot of questioning, testing, exploration, and possibly even rebellion and has settled on a consistent sense of who they are and what they believe.

But what about a young person who is dedicated to something but never went through a period of appropriate testing, exploration, or questioning? Marcia calls this outcome *foreclosure*, and it is marked by high commitment with low exploration. This is a person who is committed to a certain identity or ideology without having considered any others. In extreme cases, this would include cult members who are effectively shielded from other views and required to profess adherence to a particular way of life without knowing about any others. This is a very negative outcome, with corresponding pathologies. When authority figures impose irresistible acceptance pressure, the young person is fearful to question, to think out loud, and to test ideas, and hence may wind up adopting a false identity to please or to suit others. This is precisely why most legitimate religious groups recognize the role of free will in agreeing to become a member of the church; in most denominations, this is called "confirmation." Most churches expect a person to be of a reasonably adult age and able to make independent decisions before formal confirmation. Even closed religious communities like the Amish encourage their young people to take a period of moratorium and exploration (they call it *rumspringa* for "running around in the springtime"), to try out other ways of life before committing to the heavily restricted Amish lifestyle. To know what you are, after all, you must first know what you are not.

21

(Why It's Bad) Legally

Seven-year-old Camille attended school next to Philadelphia's Independence Hall, where the Declaration of Independence was signed in 1776.

"I got in trouble for bad language," she told her dad one day after school. "I said the Pledge of Allegiance." Camille's dad was confused as, I'm sure, you are. Is it really possible to get in trouble for saying the Pledge of Allegiance in America?

Yep.

Every morning, a student led the pledge over the intercom. Because the school didn't like the words agreed upon by a bipartisan Congress in 1954, they decided to omit "under God." Since Camille learned the pledge at another school, she didn't realize she was expected to know a new version. The other students didn't know they'd been taught a doctored version. When Camille confidently said, "one nation, under God," her friends said, "one nation, indivisible." Her classmates laughed, but the teachers didn't think it was funny at all.

The principal explained to Camille's dad (David French, president of FIRE at the time) "God" could make her atheist classmates feel uncomfortable and was "hate speech." In America, no one can be forced to pledge allegiance to anything. People can stand while it's being led without joining in or can turn their back to the intercom. But the school wanted to protect any student from even having to *hear* the word "God."

The principal revoked Camille's privilege of leading the pledge and told her the language could harm her fellow students. And that's how—in the shadow of the Liberty Bell—a kid in Philly could easily grow up believing the word "God" was hate speech, while older generations are left scratching their heads at what's become of young people these days... and what's become of our nation.

This, of course, is not the way things should be.

The Supreme Court has ruled that students do not shed their constitutional rights at the schoolhouse gate. Numerous case decisions over the years have established the boundaries of speech rights and other legal protections for citizens, in general, and for minor K–12 pupils in school, particularly. These include our First Amendment rights, such as freedom of conscience and religion, the right to privacy, and Fifth Amendment rights not to self-incriminate, among others.

The foundations for freedom of conscience in schools were laid in two Supreme Court cases: *Minersville School District v. Gobitis* and *West Virginia State Board of Education v. Barnette*. Both cases involved the Pledge of Allegiance in schools. At its core, the pledge is an oath of loyalty to the flag and the "republic for which it stands"; some Christian denominations, including Jehovah's Witnesses and some Quakers, object to taking oaths to anything except God.

At the same time, schools in the 1920s to 1950s were experiencing a moment of nationalistic fervor. Rising immigration after the First World War led to a concern that shared American values (such as patriotism and liberty) might be diluted. To make the observance of American values shared, uniform, and constant, some legislatures made it mandatory for children to recite the pledge in school.

In 1935, twelve-year-old Lillian Gobitis and her ten-year-old brother William refused to salute the flag in their Minersville, Pennsylvania, classroom. The administration called their father, Walter, who informed the school that he had directed them not to salute, as the family were Jehovah's Witnesses. The administration responded by expelling the children.

The *Gobitis* case came before the Supreme Court in 1940, and by a vote of eight to one, the court upheld the expulsion, reasoning that the government's interest in preserving national identity outweighed the religious objections of the Gobitis family. The court observed that, in the effort to preserve national unity, some of the methods "may seem harsh and others no doubt are foolish. Surely, however, the end is legitimate."[218]

Gobitis did not increase national unity, however.

Instead, the children of Jehovah's Witnesses were routinely expelled from schools, and Jehovah's Witnesses suffered as many as 2,500 acts of violence in the two years after the decision.[219] Others saw a connection between forcing children to recite a pledge and Germany's forcing children to join the Hitler Youth. A Yale professor said the Supreme Court had "in effect [...] ordered the children to 'Heil.'"[220] Similarly, Solicitor General Francis Biddle spoke out against the violence in terms that seemed to encompass the ruling itself: "We shall not defeat the Nazi evil by emulating its methods."[221]

Three years later, the Supreme Court would reverse itself in *West Virginia State Board of Education v. Barnette*. That case began in 1942, and involved two girls, nine-year-old Gathie Barnett (the *e* in the case name was a clerical error that stuck) and her eight-year-old sister Marie. Like the Gobitis family, the Barnett family were Jehovah's Witnesses. With the benefit of seeing the country after *Gobitis*, the Supreme Court

---

[218] Minersville School District v. Gobitis, 310 U.S. 586, 597-98 (1940).

[219] David T. Smith, "Mass Violence against Jehovah's Witnesses, 1940–1942" in *Religious Persecution and Political Order in the United States* (New York, NY: Cambridge University Press, 2015), 119–150, DOI: 10.1017/CBO9781316338216.006.

[220] Justin Driver, *The Schoolhouse Gate: Public Education, the Supreme Court, and the Battle for the American Mind* (New York, NY: Pantheon Books, 2018), 63–64.

[221] Robert Tsai, "Reconsidering *Gobitis*: An Exercise in Presidential Leadership," *Washington University Law Review* 86, no. 2 (2008): 406–07, https://digital-commons.wcl.american.edu/facsch_lawrev/1330.

ruled that children could not be required to recite the pledge. The court's reasoning set the precedent that still guides questions of conscience in schools today:

> Those who begin coercive elimination of dissent soon find themselves exterminating dissenters. Compulsory unification of opinion achieves only the unanimity of the graveyard. It seems trite but necessary to say that the First Amendment to our Constitution was designed to avoid these ends by avoiding these beginnings.
>
> [...]
>
> [F]reedom to differ is not limited to things that do not matter much. That would be a mere shadow of freedom. The test of its substance is the right to differ as to things that touch the heart of the existing order. If there is any fixed star in our constitutional constellation, it is that no official, high or petty, can prescribe what shall be orthodox in politics, nationalism, religion, or other matters of opinion or force citizens to confess by word or act their faith therein.

Teachers also have expressive rights, but they are constrained when acting in their "official capacity"—that is, when teaching or otherwise acting as a representative or employee of the institution, such as during field trips or when coaching events.[222] A teacher who is speaking as

---

[222] See Pickering v. Bd. of Educ., 391 U.S. 563 (1968) (finding teacher writing letter to newspaper about bond issue protected from retaliation by the First Amendment) and Connick v. Myers, 461 U.S. 138 (1982) (upholding termination of public employee who circulated an internal list of grievances, finding the list not relevant to the public and potentially harmful to the operation of the office). Taken together, these cases form the "Pickering-Connick test": If speech is on a matter of public concern, the interest of the employee to the speech in question is weighed against the burden to the employer.

a "citizen" about a matter of public concern generally enjoys the full benefit of the First Amendment; for example, a teacher who goes on Facebook to advocate for gun control could not be retaliated against by their institution. (However, teachers *can be*, and *have been*, fired when their "citizen" speech is unprofessional, interferes with their ability to do their job, or is otherwise unprotected, including when it discloses private student information.)[223]

If the same teacher who called for gun control on Facebook decided to read their Facebook post about gun control out loud during instructional time, that would generally not be protected by the First Amendment. When teachers speak in their "official capacity" as employed educators inside publicly funded classrooms, they enjoy less freedom to speak their minds. And where teachers have deviated from the proscribed curriculum, courts have defended the right of school administrators to discipline or terminate them.[224] The key question is not the substance of the teacher's speech or lesson plan, but whether they fulfill the goals and expectations of the institution paying them to deliver it.

---

[223] Matthew Christian, "Florence One Teacher Removed Following 'Inexcusable' Facebook Post," SCNow, September 17, 2020, https://scnow.com/news/local/florence-one-teacher-removed-following-inexcusable-facebook-post/article_f3011cf8-f91f-11ea-a31c-d712ec8f5d28.html#:~:text=FLORENCE%2C%20S.C.%20%E2%80%94%20A%20teacher%20is,Schools%20following%20a%20Facebook%20post.&text=O'Malley%20added%20that%20the,any%20kind%20within%20the%20community.

[224] See, e.g., Burns v. Rovaldi 477 F. Supp. 270 (D. Conn. 1979) (finding fifth-grade "penpal" exercise in penmanship class, where students wrote letters to teacher's girlfriend, who discussed her membership in a Communist political party, a valid basis for termination); Boring v. Buncombe County Bd. of Educ, 136 F.3d 364 (Fourth Cir. 1998) (upholding transfer of a teacher who selected controversial play, as play was curricular speech of the institution, not First Amendment protected speech of the teacher); and Kirkland v. Northside Independent School Dist., 890 F.2d 794 (Fifth Cir. 1989) (upholding non-renewal of teacher who substituted his own reading list instead of using the district's mandatory list).

At the core of this dichotomy is the "Pickering-Connick test,"[225] which asks two questions. First, is the teacher speaking about a matter of public concern, or does this only implicate private or internal grievances? Only matters of public concern enjoy First Amendment protection, in this context; if this is not a matter of public concern, there is no First Amendment right involved, and the test ends. For example, if a teacher feels they were unfairly excluded from a meeting, that is not a matter of public concern; the teacher is constrained to making their complaints through official channels. Assuming this is a matter of public concern, then, the second part of the Pickering-Connick test applies: Does the teacher's interest in the expression outweigh the burden it puts on the institution? Some speech, such as a pro-gun control bumper sticker on a car parked in a school parking lot, would seem to impose a minimal burden on the school's curricular goals. On the other hand, hijacking a math class to rant about the "true meaning of the Second Amendment" would completely eliminate the value of that class to the school and its students alike.

Student Speech More Free, but Not Unrestrained

The final overlay to teacher speech rules is the easiest: how teachers must treat the speech of their pupils. According to numerous Supreme Court precedents, teachers in public schools are considered to be government actors; hence, their actions are constrained by the responsibility to respect

---

[225] Pickering v. Bd. of Educ., 391 U.S. 563 (1968); Connick v. Myers, 461 U.S. 138 (1982); Boring v. Buncombe County Bd. of Educ, 136 F.3d 364, 372 (Fourth Cir. 1998) (J. Luttig, concurring) (discussing the application of Pickering and Connick to secondary education teachers).

students' First Amendment and other constitutional rights.[226] Political science Professor Joshua Dunn notes that, when a conflict arises between teacher and student speech, students generally win. "Students are compelled to attend school but no one is forced to be a teacher. As well, no one has a right to be a teacher, and, therefore, no one has a right to teach a certain way," Dunn states. "Teachers might want to openly declare their political preferences in class because they think it is either their moral or educational duty, but they do not have a right to do so." He concludes, "The prudent [decision] for teachers and school boards is to follow a principle of neutrality, not endorsing one political side or the other in the school or classroom."[227]

This isn't to say that students have unlimited speech rights; they do not, of course. Speech can be limited during instructional time and in curricular publications for any legitimate pedagogical reason.[228] Additionally, it can be restrained if it creates a substantial risk of a material disruption of the orderly operation of school[229] or could be understood to promote illegal drug use.[230] These are all court-recognized carve-outs of the First Amendment. The Supreme Court, however, has not created any exception

---

[226] See, e.g., Tinker v. Des Moines Independent Community School District, 393 U.S. 503 (1969) (finding public school teachers are limited by the First Amendment); New Jersey v. T.L.O., 469 U.S. 325 (1985) (finding public school teachers are limited by the Fourth Amendment); and Goss v. Lopez, 419 U.S. 565 (1975) (holding public school teachers are limited by the Fourteenth Amendment's due process clause).

[227] Dunn, "Free Speech Accountability and Public Trust," 254.

[228] Hazelwood v. Kuhlmeier, 484 U.S. 260 (1988). Be aware, however, that *Hazelwood* gives greater rights to student publications that have been, by policy or practice, opened as a forum for student expression. In addition, several states have laws preventing the *Hazelwood* rule from applying to student publications, or in some cases—such as in California's case—at all. See California Education Code sections 48907 and 47950.

[229] Tinker v. Des Moines, 393 U.S. 503 (1969). Note that the disruption cannot be metaphysical; there must be specific, articulable evidence that it is reasonable to expect a disruption.

[230] Morse v. Frederick, 551 U.S. 393 (2007).

to student expression rights on the basis of a teacher's individual desire to express something other than what the school has directed them to teach.

Even in those areas where schools have the authority to restrain speech, there are limitations in how they do it. Schools are prevented from engaging in what is known as "viewpoint discrimination," which means that they cannot shut down speech simply because they dislike the views that are being expressed, or target one side of a debate for suppression and not the other. For example, a school is not obligated to permit students to make the gun control debate the subject of a classroom session, but if it chooses to do so, it would be unconstitutional for the school to permit arguments in favor of gun control but not those arguments against it.

A related issue of "disparate impact" says that rules must be applied evenhandedly, so that one group is not unfairly targeted. For instance, according to an article by the American Civil Liberties Union (ACLU), some school administrators may be "surveilling students on social media and unjustly disciplining them for what they say on it," and "experience shows that discipline for student expression is not always applied evenhandedly."[231] Blind spots and biases can lead to this sort of uneven enforcement of existing school policies. Many schools get in trouble when they permit employees to engage in ad hoc, do-what-you-think-is-right regulation of student speech—because when the employee is a government actor, it is unlawful to impose their individual, subjective concept of right or wrong on student speech.

Examples of Conflicts

Senior Fellow and civics teacher Robert Pondiscio, writing for the Thomas Fordham Institute in "Teachers, Curb Your Activism," points out that American courts are likely to assume that "as the adult in the room, the

[231] Vera Eidelman and Sarah Hinger, "Some Schools Need a Lesson on Students' Free Speech Rights," American Civil Liberties Union, September 18, 2018, https://www.aclu.org/blog/free-speech/student-speech-and-privacy/some-schools-need-lesson-students-free-speech-rights.

teacher has an obligation *not* to air his or her views in front of children."[232] Specifically, in *Mayer v. Monroe County Community School Corp.* (2007), the U.S. Court of Appeals in Chicago ruled against an elementary school teacher who lost her job after criticizing the U.S. war on Iraq during class.[233] She sued the school district on First Amendment grounds and lost. In its decision, the unanimous judges wrote, "The First Amendment does not entitle primary and secondary teachers, when conducting the education of captive audiences, to cover topics, or advocate viewpoints, that depart from the curriculum adopted by the school system."[234] The captive audience, additionally and notably, comprises minors.

Professor of education law, policy, and practice of the University of Wisconsin-Madison Julie Underwood, writing in *Phi Delta Kappan*, comments on this case: "[T]he teacher claimed she was dismissed because she expressed her disapproval of the Iraq war to students during a current events session in her elementary classroom. Administrators told her she could teach about the controversy but had to keep her opinions on the subject to herself. The Seventh Circuit Court of Appeals upheld her dismissal, finding that teachers do not have a constitutional right of expression within their classrooms. The court stated:

> [T]he school system does not 'regulate' teachers' speech as much as it hires that speech. Expression is a teacher's stock in trade, the commodity she sells to her employer in exchange for a salary. A teacher hired to lead a social studies class can't use it as a platform for a revisionist perspective that Benedict Arnold wasn't really a traitor, when the approved program calls him one; a high school teacher hired to explicate *Moby Dick* in a literature class can't use *Cry, The Beloved Country* instead, even if Paton's book better suits the instructor's style and

---

[232] Pondiscio, "Teachers, Curb Your Activism."

[233] Mayer v. Monroe County Community School Corp., 474 F.3d 477 (Seventh Cir. 2007).

[234] Ibid, 479.

point of view; a math teacher can't decide that calculus is more important than trigonometry and decide to let Hipparchus and Ptolemy slide in favor of Newton and Leibniz."[235]

A court held similarly in a case involving a math teacher told by administrators to remove banners displaying religious beliefs from his classroom. The teacher challenged the district in court, asserting a violation of free speech and establishment of religion under the First Amendment. In *Johnson v. Poway Unified School District*, the court ruled against the teacher, finding that inserting his religious views into the curriculum was not protected speech, stating:

> Just as the Constitution would not protect Johnson were he to decide that he no longer wished to teach math at all, preferring to discuss Shakespeare rather than Newton, it does not permit him to speak as freely at work in his role as a teacher about his views on God, our nation's history, or God's role in our nation's history as he might on a sidewalk, in a park, at his dinner table, or in countless other locations.[236]

Again, the courts affirmed that school districts have the right and responsibility to set the curriculum and, within the delivery of that curriculum, teacher speech can be regulated. Public school teachers can, however, generally wear religious clothing or jewelry as long as it is not "proselytizing" and "disruptive."

Says Robert Pondiscio, "In sum, a math teacher who decides to stop teaching math because he wants to lead a discussion on Kavanaugh [i.e., controversial Supreme Court Justice appointments] is not merely on thin

---

[235] Ibid.
[236] Johnson v. Poway Unified Sch. Dist., 658 F.3d 954, 957 (Ninth Cir. 2011).

ice. There is no ice under his feet at all…as a teacher, *my* politics has no place in the classroom."[237]

In other exemplary cases, a long-term substitute teacher was permanently banned from a high school in California after wearing a Black Lives Matter pin at school on Election Day in 2016. The high school has a clear policy prohibiting employees from engaging in "political activities" during the workday, which the teacher was judged to be directly violating. He responded with surprise and asserted that the BLM pin was not a political statement. According to professors of education Meira Levinson and Jacob Fay, this "interpretation of Black Lives Matter BLM as apolitical may seem quirky or even disingenuous, given that BLM's guiding principles described BLM as 'as [sic] ideological and political intervention in a world where black lives are systematically and intentionally targeted for demise.'"[238]

At roughly the same time, a fifth-grade teacher in Michigan was fired for informing a group of students that "on that particular day she felt less safe than ever, because our country had just elected a president who had openly spoken out against women, people of color, the LGBTQ plus community, and other people he felt were different than him."[239]

The 2016 election season was, of course, not the first time teachers have been fired or threatened with termination for expressing political perspectives that were out of sync with the surrounding community, Levinson and Fay point out. In 2009, a Kansas high school history teacher claimed his contract was not renewed because he criticized Barack Obama in class, charging that after a student complained, his assistant principal told him to stop "picking on Obama in class."[240] In their analysis of these incidents, the authors explain that:

> Deborah Mayer…found herself on the wrong side of community consensus while teaching current events

---

[237] Pondiscio, "Teachers, Curb Your Activism."
[238] Levinson and Fay, *Democratic Discord in Schools*, 241.
[239] Ibid., 242.
[240] Ibid.

in her fifth-grade social studies class in Bloomington Indiana.… [O]nce Mayer signed her contract with the district, the contact of her expression in the classroom was wholly subject to the authority of the school administration. This does not mean that teachers have no First Amendment rights – but those rights are entirely outside of the classroom walls, and they are in practice increasingly limited.[241]

The Cost of Polarization

Dunn believes that the conduct of the teachers implicated in the aforementioned cases raises questions about their judgment and fitness for the profession and that the teacher's claim that the Black Lives Matter button was not a political statement and that he just wanted to show solidarity with "the kids" is "beyond fatuous." Dunn asks:

Would he have called a button with "blue lives matter" merely a "peaceful call to end this violence" against the police? And did he give any consideration to how children of police officers in his class would feel about that button? He claimed he wanted to show solidarity with "the kids" but apparently only some kids. Similarly, would students supporting Barack Obama have felt more or less free to speak up in…class after [the teacher] negatively compared Obama's professional experience to McCain[']s? It was clear that he was endorsing McCain and questioning the judgment of those supporting Obama. As well, Deborah Mayer broadcasting that she thinks it is important to look for peaceful solutions before going to war expressed a position so banal that it

---

[241] Ellis Reid, Meira Levinson, and Jacob Fay, "Talking Out of Turn: Teacher Speech for Hire" in *Democratic Discord in Schools*, 244.

dripped with condescension and trivialized a matter of immense political and moral importance. Who would disagree with her except the congenitally bellicose? Does it not apply to anyone who disagreed with her [that they] must not want to find a peaceful solution and would that not discourage students who disagreed with President Bush from speaking up?[242]

Professor Dunn argues that these examples illustrate the risk of moral grandstanding in education, which philosophers Justin Tosi and Brandon Warmke define as "participation in moral discourse for self-promotion." Of its inherent perils, Dunn writes that:

[The] perniciousness of moral grandstanding comes from the desire to appear morally superior. This corrodes public discourse by increasing cynicism and promoting even greater polarization. Cynicism increases because people suspect that moral discourse is about "showing that you are on the side of the angels" rather than honest deliberation. It increases polarization, since speakers engage in a "moral arms race" and make "increasingly strong claims" which "signal that one is more attuned to matters of justice and that others simply do not understand or appreciate the nuance or gravity of the situation."

These problems are heightened in education precisely because students are supposed to be learning how to honestly deliberate across lines of difference. Instead of teaching students to critically evaluate and discuss complex and contentious areas of political disagreement, the grandstanding teacher instead models dogmatism and self-righteousness. Good people like me, they imply, simply want to stop the violence, or want qualified leaders,

---

[242] Dunn, "Free Speech Accountability and Public Trust," 254-255.

or want peace rather than war, while those who do not support them must want the opposite.[243]

This mindset is why, as one guide suggests, teachers use "interrupter phrases" to stop students from speaking: *What you said is harmful; I'm going to stop you there; We don't say things like that here.*[244] One can imagine that teachers might need to rein in profanity, slurs, or generally maintain classroom order. However, these "interrupter phrases" are intended to shame "wrong thinking." For example, this is precisely almost verbatim what the Philadelphia teacher said to Camille as she reprimanded her for saying the Pledge of Allegiance. "We don't say the word 'God' here." This sentiment was echoed in a sign on the wall of the school declaring "At this school, we use school-approved language."

This is chillingly Orwellian, and more to the point, undermines the purpose behind having compulsory, state-funded education to begin with. Our education system is meant to educate future citizens and get them engaged in the deliberative process, not to silence their voices and leave them disenchanted with it. If public education produces citizens who only repeat orthodoxy and view dissent as an attack, it not only fails to serve its purpose, but actively undermines it.

But it doesn't have to be that way.

The Better Way

Helpfully, Dunn explains the ways that principles of impartiality can protect teachers instead of hindering them. Rather than discouraging the introduction of controversial subjects in class, practicing neutrality can "liberate them to take on those topics in the classroom by inoculating them from accusations of indoctrination. A teacher can tell his students that the conditions of his contract forbid him from revealing his political preferences and, thus, students should not assume that any

---

[243] Ibid.
[244] Hadley Dunn, "Teaching on Days After."

arguments he advances represent his position. The only way that students would know their teacher's politics is if he always took the conservative or liberal side."[245]

Other ways Professor Dunn suggests of making sure that challenging topics are thoroughly discussed in a balanced fashion in school include assigning classroom debates and requiring students to defend the position they oppose, thereby satisfying the rule of neutrality. "Surely it would be useful for Trump supporters to have to advance arguments for why he should not be president, and for his opponents to explain why someone would support him. These kinds of exercises are not difficult to implement, and the only thing preventing teachers from doing so is not wanting their students to think through opposing viewpoints," he says.[246] Without this sort of challenge, our mental faculties rust through disuse.

Compelled Student Speech Still Prohibited

We saw above that students can't be silenced in every case. But can they be made to agree? What if the topic is really uncontroversial?

According to the landmark 1943 case *West Virginia State Board of Education v. Barnette*—the one where the Supreme Court decided students cannot be forced to salute the flag—no, they emphatically cannot. In fact, this rule is the "oldest standing precedent" about curricular speech, and it is a fundamental assumption of public education. In Supreme Court Justice Robert Jackson's words, "If there is any fixed star in our constitutional constellation, it is that no official, high or petty, can prescribe what shall be orthodox in politics, nationalism, religion, or other matters of opinion or force citizens to confess by word or act their faith therein."[247]

Jackson noted that the school board's flag salute requirement was different than teaching a student math or science, because it compelled

---

[245] Dunn, "Free Speech Accountability and Public Trust," 255–256.
[246] Ibid, 256.
[247] West Virginia State Bd. of Educ. v. Barnette, 319 U.S. 624, 642 (1943).

a student "to declare a belief [and]...to utter what is not in his mind."[248] In matters of belief, the court saw human beings as essentially distinct; each was free to find "jest and scorn" where another found "comfort and inspiration."[249] Hence, in the United States of America, others—even adult teachers with authority over minor schoolchildren—do NOT get to put words in your mouth or compel you to perform actions you do not volitionally choose. The *Tinker* case reaffirmed this freedom, concluding that students "may not be confined to the expression of those sentiments that are officially approved."[250]

According to Justice Jackson, "The purpose of the First Amendment to our Constitution" was precisely to protect "from all official control" the domain that was "the sphere of intellect and spirit."[251] Enforced conformity, far from teaching the value of liberty, would "strangle the free mind at its source." He concluded, "It seems trite but necessary to say that the First Amendment to our Constitution was designed to avoid these ends by avoiding these beginnings." In other words, let's not go down this road!

Ultimately, what this tells us is that public schools, as government actors, must refrain from attempts to enforce belief systems upon students. And yet, schools continue to attempt to do this. Recently, some schools have used "anti-racist" training materials that would require students to confess guilt for such things as "white complicity," "violent silence," or other imagined sins. But it is unconstitutional and a violation of civil rights to require a student to agree. In fact, silence is itself a way of speaking and expressing oneself, and students have a right to use it.

Unfortunately, we've also seen situations where innocent students have been presumed guilty of offensive acts in sweeping statements issued by groups of educators, in which students were singled out by race by the school district and/or held presumptively responsible for acts they hadn't committed. For instance, one mother wrote to a school administrator

---

[248] *Barnette*, 319 U.S. at 634.
[249] *Barnette*, 319 U.S. at 633.
[250] *Tinker*, 393 U.S. at 511.
[251] *Barnette*, 319 U.S. at 642.

claiming that, "in my tenth grader's AP World class, [the teacher] called out any Trump supporters and asked them to assure the class that they weren't racist." In response, in a letter dated August 24, 2017, Peter Kirsanow of the U.S. Commission on Civil Rights wrote directly to the chairman of the school board, reminding them that "[s]uch behavior, if it occurred, would be discriminatory and unprofessional." He expressed his support for disciplining students who had engaged in repugnant acts, but reminded the district "that does not free teachers from their obligations of professionalism and nondiscrimination toward those students who had nothing to do with those incidents." In his letter, he explained:

> Title VI prohibits discrimination on the basis of race, period. That means that it also prohibits discrimination against white students. With a new school year about to start, I hope that you will remind the teachers, administrators, and students of this fact. I also hope that you will remind teachers that they serve as role models for how citizens should comport themselves, regardless of race, and that bullying students of different races or with different political beliefs is not how adults should behave.[252]

Surely, the people charged with teaching young people about the proper understanding and exercise of their constitutional protections should not have to be reprimanded for failing to follow it themselves!

Private schools do, of course, have greater latitude to attempt to impose belief systems (and some of these are religious schools) but should surely only do so with good faith, full disclosure, and transparency of their belief systems and ideological aims, so that potential parents and students are not misled or deceived in making a choice to enroll there. Anything else would risk falling into false advertising or breach of implied contract territory.

---

[252] Peter Kirsanow, letter to Edina High School, August 24, 2017, United States Commission on Civil Rights, http://www.newamericancivilrightsproject.org/wp-content/uploads/2014/03/Edina-High-School-letter-8.24.2017-final.pdf.

Here are some other key court cases that have established the importance and protection of freedom of expression for citizens in America:

Whitney v. California (1927): "If there be time to expose through discussion the falsehood and fallacies, to avert the evil by the process of education, the remedy to be applied is more speech, not enforced silence." —Justice Louis Brandeis[253]

United States v. Schwimmer (1929): "[I]f there is any principle of the Constitution that more imperatively calls for attachment than any other it is the principle of free thought, not free thought for those who agree with us but freedom for the thought that we hate." —Oliver Wendell Holmes Jr.[254]

Police Department of Chicago v. Mosley (1972): "[A]bove all else, the First Amendment means that government has no power to restrict expression because of its message, its ideas, its subject matter, or its content." —Justice Thurgood Marshall[255]

Texas v. Johnson (1989): "If there is a bedrock principle underlying the First Amendment, it is that the government may not prohibit the expression of an idea simply because society finds the idea itself offensive or disagreeable."—Justice Brennan[256]

---

[253] Whitney v. Cal., 274 U.S. 357, 377 (1927) (J. Brandeis concurring).
[254] United States v. Schwimmer, 279 U.S. 644, 654-55 (J. Holmes dissenting).
[255] Police Dep't of Chicago v. Mosley, 408 U.S. 92, 95 (1972).
[256] Texas v. Johnson, 491 U.S. 397, 414 (1989).

When Have Teachers Gone Too Far?

Legally speaking, if you want to determine when a K–12 teacher has exceeded the boundaries of professional pedagogical discretion in the classroom, you might refer to the following four-way test of evaluation:

> Is it aligned with the curriculum?
> Is it even-handed?
> Is it inflammatory?
> Is it age-appropriate?

According to education professors Maxwell, McDonough, and Waddington, judges have returned "consistently to four rights and interests that need to be balanced with teachers' constitutional right to free expression—namely, the State's interest in determining the content taught in schools, the rights of pupils as a captive audience, the right of students to benefit from a stable learning environment, and the interest of maintaining public confidence in the public school system."

They see these four principles as "reasonable limits" on teachers' right to curricular free speech which, "when taken together, seem helpful for delineating the reasonable and responsible exercise of curricular free speech, especially with regard to the scope of teachers' professional autonomy when it comes to introducing and having their students work with politically controversial or socially sensitive topics."[257] Let's take a closer look at each of these principles:

1. **Curricular alignment**
   The first principle, which links primarily to the State's interest in prescribing the knowledge and skills taught in public schools, is that teacher speech must be clearly aligned with the curriculum.... [I]t must be possible

---

[257] Bruce Maxwell, Kevin McDonough, and David I. Waddington, "Broaching the Subject: Developing Law-Based Principles for Teacher Free Speech in the Classroom," *Teaching and Teacher Education* 70 (February 2018): 196–203.

to show that the particular material or topic used, and the approach to dealing with that content in class, was intentionally chosen to further a pedagogical purpose explicitly sanctioned by the curriculum.

2. **Even-handedness**

   Teachers must not be seen as using their position of authority to promote their own personal views on contested or sensitive issues. This condition links to the importance of maintaining public trust in teachers and the public school system and providing protection for students as a recognized captive audience. Respecting this criterion does not require teachers to avoid exposing their personal views in class and it does not mean asking teachers to feign strict pedagogical neutrality. What it does require is for teachers to take a reasonably even-handed approach to teaching about sensitive topics so as to avoid giving the impression that they are teaching with the intent of imposing their perspective about sensitive topics on their students. There is no simple recipe for avoiding a perception of abuse of authority in this sense but doing so would seem to entail, among other things, adhering to the principle of curricular alignment discussed above, encouraging students to consider several competing viewpoints, treating students who adhere to views one disagrees [with] respectfully, and generally conducting oneself in a way in class that models honest intellectual inquiry.

3. **Avoiding foreseeably inflammatory speech**

   A third aspect of the legally-informed conception of reasonable and responsible curricular free speech relates to the school's interest in maintaining an environment conducive to learning. It is reasonable to ask teachers to avoid making comments, dealing with topics, or using material that could foreseeably cause significant disruption to the normal operation of the school.

4. **Age appropriateness**
   The courts widely recognize that the school system has a duty to make sure that young people are not exposed to "inappropriate" content at school.... [I]nappropriate content is content that a pupil could reasonably be expected to find traumatizing given their age or developmental level or that that depicts extreme violence or graphic sexuality. The principle of age-appropriateness is based primarily in the public interest maintaining confidence in the public school system. Failing to respect this principle would likely lead to a "poisoned" school environment in the sense that parents would reasonably be reluctant to entrust their children to the school and children uncomfortable about attending.[258]

Beyond these, school authority extends over classroom displays such as posters, blackboard writing, stickers on laptops, and teacher clothing with messaging on it. Are your child's teachers adhering to these basic standards in class?

Parental Rights Supersede All

The question of who is in charge and who has final authority over the education of children has long been settled: it is the parents—not the schools or the teachers. (That might, on occasion, end up in a take-it-or-leave-it deal, where the parental right boils down to the right to withdraw the child from the class. But that's still a right.) This is clearly stated in existing law. Furthermore, national educational organizations readily

---

[258] Ibid.

concede this long-established legal fact, even if they don't always appear to be following it.

The U.S. Supreme Court has a long history of decisions upholding parental rights as fundamental. For instance, in *Troxel v. Granville* (2000), the court ruled that "the interest of parents in the care, custody, and control of their children—is perhaps the oldest of the fundamental liberty interests recognized by this Court. More than 75 years ago, in *Meyer v. Nebraska* (1923), we held that the 'liberty' protected by the Due Process Clause includes the right of parents to 'establish a home and bring up children' and 'to control the education of their own.' Two years later, in *Pierce v. Society of Sisters* (1925), we again held that the 'liberty of parents and guardians' includes the right 'to direct the upbringing and education of children under their control.'"[259]

Perhaps because this fundamental point is so well established, activist educators inclined to opposing parental wishes or to teaching outside the established curricular guardrails appear to be resorting to covert means and dissembled terminology to accomplish their aims without going through open, democratic channels where they have to face and overcome opposition. This is obviously unacceptable and must be actively exposed and opposed by those who know and understand their rights and natural authority.

According to attorney Christopher Klicka, "The Supreme Court of the United States has traditionally and continuously upheld the principle that parents have the fundamental right to direct the education and upbringing of their children. A review of cases taking up the issue shows that the Supreme Court has unwaveringly given parental rights the highest respect and protection possible." As Chief Justice Burger stated in the opinion of *Wisconsin v. Yoder* in 1972:

> [T]his case involves the fundamental interest of parents, as contrasted with that of the state, to guide the religious

---

[259] Troxel v. Granville, 530 U.S. 57, 65 (2000), *citing* Meyer v. Nebraska, 262 U.S. 390, 399, 401 (1923) *and* Pierce v. Society of Sisters, 268 U.S. 510, 534-535 (1925), https://supreme.justia.com/cases/federal/us/530/57/.

future and education of their children. The history and culture of Western civilization reflect a strong tradition of parental concern for the nurture and upbringing of their children. This primary role of the parents in the upbringing of their children is now established beyond debate as an enduring tradition.[260]

A group of prominent education groups, including the National Education Association, the Association for Supervision and Curriculum Development, and National School Boards Association joined with several national religious organizations to affirm a public statement of principles regarding "Religious Liberty, Public Education, and the Future of American Democracy." Here is part of that statement:

3. **Public Schools Belong to All Citizens**
   Public schools must model the democratic process and constitutional principles in the development of policies and curricula.

   Policy decisions by officials or governing bodies should be made only after appropriate involvement of those affected by the decision and with due consideration for the rights of those holding dissenting views.

4. **Religious Liberty and Public Schools**
   Public schools may not inculcate nor inhibit religion. They must be places where religion and religious conviction are treated with fairness and respect.

---

[260] Christopher J. Klicka, "Decisions of the United States Supreme Court Upholding Parental Rights as 'Fundamental,'" *Connecting with the Community and the World of Work* 52, no. 8 (May 1995): 92–93; Wisconsin v. Yoder, 406 U.S. 205, 232 (1972).

Public schools uphold the First Amendment when they protect the religious liberty rights of students of all faiths or none. Schools demonstrate fairness when they ensure that the curriculum includes study *about* religion, where appropriate, as an important part of a complete education.

5. **The Relationship between Parents and Schools**
Parents are recognized as having the primary responsibility for the upbringing of their children, including education.

Parents who send their children to public schools delegate to public school educators some of the responsibility for their children's education.

6. **Conduct of Public Disputes**
Civil debate, the cornerstone of a true democracy, is vital to the success of any effort to improve and reform America's public schools.

Personal attacks, name-calling, ridicule, and similar tactics destroy the fabric of our society and undermine the educational mission of our schools. Even when our differences are deep, all parties engaged in public disputes should treat one another with civility and respect, and should strive to be accurate and fair. Through constructive dialogue we have much to learn from one another.[261]

This Statement of Principles is not an attempt to ignore or minimize differences that are important and abiding, but rather a reaffirmation of

---

[261] "Religious Liberty, Public Education, and the Future of American Democracy: A Statement of Principles," *Connecting with the Community and the World of Work* 52, no. 8 (May 1995): 92–93.

what we share as American citizens across our differences. Democratic citizenship does not require a compromise of our deepest convictions. We invite all men and women of good will to join us in affirming these principles and putting them into action. The time has come for us to work together for academic excellence, fairness, and shared civic values in our nation's schools.[262]

The National PTA has produced a pamphlet called *A Parent's Guide to Religion in Public Schools*, in which they clearly state that:

> Parents are recognized as having the primary responsibility for the upbringing of their children, including education.
>
> Public schools may not inculcate nor inhibit religion.
>
> Teaching about Religion
> Is it constitutional to teach about religion in public schools? Yes.
> The Supreme Court has indicated many times that teaching about religion, as distinguished from religious indoctrination, is an important part of a complete education. The public school's approach to religion in the curriculum must be academic, not devotional.
>
> Student Religious Expression
> No student should be allowed to harass or pressure others in a public school setting.
>
> Commit to Civil Debate
> Conflict and debate are vital in a democracy. Yet, if we are going to live with our differences, then how we debate, and not only what we debate, is critical. Personal attacks, name-calling, ridicule, and similar tactics destroy

---

[262] Ibid.

the fabric of our society and undermine the educational mission of our schools. All parties should treat one another with civility and respect and should strive to be accurate and fair. Through constructive dialogue, we have much to learn from one another.[263]

Regarding the admonition that "No student should be allowed to harass or pressure others in a public school setting,"[264] it is reasonable to conclude that this includes value systems that take the place of religion in a student or teacher's life. Allowing vituperative talk in school is one of the ways in which minority views and speech are being chilled and intimidated in American schools. FIRE maintains additional free resources for educators on healthy discourse in the classroom at thefire.org/k12.

It's possible, if you're reading this book, that you are wondering whether you can sue your child's school. In order to do so, you would need to be able to prove that the school broke the law or violated your child's rights. To find out if you have a case, you would need to consult an attorney licensed in your state. You could also contact a public interest group, like the ACLU, or a religious liberty nonprofit. There are many other effective ways of addressing your dissatisfaction, disappointment, and frustration with your child's school, however, which we are about to discuss.

---

[263] "A Parent's Guide to Religion in the Public Schools," National PTA, First Amendment Center, https://www.religiousfreedomcenter.org/wp-content/uploads/2015/01/Parents-Guide-to-Religion-in-the-Public-Schools.pdf.

[264] Charles C. Haynes and Oliver Thomas, "Finding Common Ground: A First Amendment Guide to Religion and Public Schools," First Amendment Center, 2007, https://www.religiousfreedomcenter.org/wp-content/uploads/2015/01/Religion-in-the-Public-School-Curriculum-Questions-and-Answers.pdf.

PART

FOUR

What to Do about It

22

A Note to Parents

First, to Parents Who Have Students in Private Schools

Parents with students in private schools have special considerations, since private schools have different rights under the law. It's true that private schools have less curricular oversight, which enables them much more leeway in what is taught. Their teachers are also not licensed by the state, which removes a layer of supervision. However, the schools rely on the tuition dollars of the parents, which gives parents power.

Use it.

Caveat emptor (let the buyer beware) is always good advice when making large expenditures. Parents have the responsibility to do their due diligence in seeking a school, but schools also have a responsibility to engage in truthful advertising and faithful representation of their offerings and programming in presenting themselves to the public. Beware of the use of harmless platitudes and "sounds nice" language being used deceptively at the institutional level to paper over blatant activist aims pursued below the surface.

Sometimes, these practices are going on without administrator knowledge; other times, the administration is actively pursuing ideological ends while claiming otherwise. Private school parents must, of course, exercise their right to take the money elsewhere when school practices do not match school promises or when there is a misalignment between the parents' educational goals for his/her children and what the school is delivering.

Public schools provide several layers of oversight and public disclosure of proposed changes in curricula; some private schools have a way to go in offering sufficient transparency for prospective parents to be able to make informed decisions. Schools that advertise themselves merely as "college preparatory" when, in fact, they are deeply progressive are falsely representing themselves and hiding their true intentions. This is unacceptable. Certainly, private schools can choose to have whatever mission or ideology they want, but they don't get to disguise this in their marketing and descriptive materials.

It is time to develop high-school-level watch groups, to be on the lookout for, and to help expose and hold accountable, worrisome programming and activist pedagogy. There are a few college-level watch groups that monitor and expose silly and partisan course offerings and overreach at the college level. We need to do the same thing at the K–12 level to ensure fairness to all students, and especially considering that these are minors with more need of protection than adult college students.

Also, withhold donations and explain why. This hits the school where it hurts and will give you great leverage when stating your complaints.

Vote with your feet when schools fail to deliver a quality education as promised. Private schools are subject to the constraints of supply and demand. A note on leaving a school: fortunately, there are more alternative options for schooling children than ever before, and schools that fail to live up to parent expectations risk losing financial support. From charter schools to cyberschools to emerging homeschooling arrangements, parents can now more easily reclaim appropriate control over their children's educations. Those choosing to leave a wayward school can assist others still remaining by speaking openly and frankly about the reasons why they felt compelled to make this major decision.

A Note to Parents Who Have Kids in Public Schools

Beyond these systems that determine our government, laws, and economy, there are certain cultural values that unite a group of people and grease the skids of their interaction. We have certain unspoken "agreements" that make daily life easier. Part of these could be considered to be "manners," but they are also ways of looking at life that may make one group of people distinct or different from another group. For instance, for many generations, the prevailing American ethos on matters of opinion has been "We can agree to disagree," or "People of goodwill can disagree and part friends." Many of us still believe in and comport ourselves according to this familiar guideline: Do your child's teachers?

Traditionally, secular schools only taught what could be called "lowest-common-denominator (LCD)" or "community consensus" values. These are secular values on which pretty much everyone agrees: "Wait your turn," "Don't cut in line," and "The Golden Rule." The Golden Rule, "Treat others the way you want to be treated," is, of course, derived from the biblical teaching "Do unto others as you would have them do unto you," so you can see that our Judeo-Christian heritage is indelibly a foundational part of our way of life, even though it becomes secularized in community practice. Much of this is distilled knowledge, passed down through the ages, derived from faith traditions but ultimately absorbed into our common culture for the betterment of our society.

When straying beyond these LCD values, teachers run up against parental prerogatives regarding the inculcation of children's values and it's HANDS OFF. Schools have no greater wisdom and less authority than parents in these matters.

If you read the news, you may have seen these headlines that indicate teachers are going beyond the LCD: "Georgia Teacher Pulled from

Classroom for Anti-Obama Rant"; "Witness: Teacher Caught Telling Students to Attend Anti-Second Amendment Rally"; "San Francisco Teacher's Union Offers Anti-Trump Lesson Plan"; "Georgia Teacher Allegedly Tells Students Their Parents Are Evil If They Voted for Obama"; "Anti-Obama Teacher Is Placed on Leave in Alabama"; "Teacher Delivers Anti-Military Rant in Class"; "Teacher Caught in Bush 'Rant'"; "Ohio Student Suspended for Refusing to Leave Classroom during Gun Control Walkout"; "Philadelphia Elementary School Displays Anti-NRA and Anti-GOP Signs"; "Witness: Teacher Caught Telling Parkland Students to Attend Anti-Second Amendment Rally"; "Teacher Who Reportedly Gave Pro-Obama Homework Crossed Line"; "Teacher Under Fire for Slipping Anti-Trump Question into Homework"; "Assistant Principal Placed on Leave after Saying F the Police at Protest"; "Local School District Speaks Out after Presentation Compares President Trump to Hitler"; "Even Students Are Ashamed of This Teacher for Flipping Off the White House"; "Teacher Used Class Time to Call Trump a Racist and a Dictator"; "Middle School Students Taught That Islam Is the True Faith"; and "Georgia Seventh Graders Required to Write Letters to Lawmakers Demanding Gun Control."

Most of these embarrassing headlines are self-explanatory. A bit of historical distance makes it easy to see how inappropriate most of the past incidents are. The ones involving former presidents and past controversies obviously look more preposterous than the ones involving current politicians and recent events. Such a retrospective makes clear why wise teachers have long eschewed weighing in on cultural squabbles. Doing so only makes you look foolish, immature, impetuous, unprofessional, and untrustworthy. Timeless ethical and professional guidelines exist precisely to guide us when our emotions threaten to override our rational capacities.

Parents have decided to organize, forming multiple organizations across the country as they become more aware of school indoctrination. They've had the courage to share with me their pain and sense of injustice and betrayal. "These parents are rising up because the school has pivoted and sold them a bill of goods. And these are mostly liberal parents objecting, not conservatives," one parent explained to me of his involvement. A common theme among these parent coalitions is frustration at school opacity (or, in some cases, outright deception) and exasperation at the dismissive, cursory "brush-offs" parents are receiving from administrators in response to their earnest concerns.

Oregonians for Liberty in Education, one of the parent groups, explained what was going on in their state: "Children are being told in class they are racist from birth and have inherited racial guilt. Teachers delegitimize the Founding Fathers and the Constitution, and undermine our law enforcement."

Do these teachings support ODE's mission, to promote "educational practices that lead directly to the educational and life success of all Oregon PK-12 students"?

Martin Luther King Jr. would be appalled. In fact, many black scholars are speaking out against teaching these ideas to young people, especially in heavy-handed, shame-based ways. These lessons could be potentially harmful for all children, resulting in polarization, hopelessness, guilt, and permanent victim status.

One social justice program—called Deep Equity—supposedly trains teachers in eliminating racial disparities and instructs them how to treat individuals who disagree with the program's ideas. They teach to "explicitly reject and resist" parents and other outsiders who take issue with the curriculum's content and to align against anyone who objects.

The slides in the program help teachers deal with resistance. "Doing this work with your colleagues, what might be some resistance BEHAVIORS you will encounter? What might be some of the different SOURCES of this resistance? What are some possible RESPONSES that you and your team could make to deal with these types of resistance? How might some of the activities we have done here be used to either prevent resistance, or limit its impact?"[265]

---

[265] Chase Watkins. "Social Justice Program Says Teachers Should 'Reject and Resist' Parents Who Disagree with It." *College Fix*, November 29, 2019. https://www.thecollegefix.com/social-justice-program-says-teachers-should-reject-and-resist-parents-who-disagree-with-it/.

One parent tweeted, "It's happened to my school. A private school, no less. They're segregating the kids by race."[266] One highly involved parent and former donor to an exclusive private school on the West Coast wrote an exasperated letter to the head of the school. The school, he claimed, had "grown hostile to patriotism and parental feedback. It has become an intolerant institution where facts are less important than attitude." He wrote that the "intolerance of political/viewpoint diversity has been deepening, but it has clearly gone off the rails this year.... The school has abdicated its fiduciary duty of political neutrality and quest for intellectual diversity of viewpoints and exploration in favor of a self-appointed mandate to be a leftist, progressive indoctrination camp."

Another concerned parent letter reads:

> We want the trustees and administration to rectify the grave [injustices] to our children by the recent repositioning of the curriculum. As stakeholders in [the school], we cannot stress enough the need to present a non-politicized, anti-racist, diverse and equitable education. This requires the immediate abandonment of all... unproven and unvetted concepts you seem so intent on proselytizing in order to indoctrinate our community.

> The lack of transparency and rapidity in which you have pivoted is unnerving; what is next? The pernicious epistemological opinions of so few, which maligns the viewpoints of so many, are being instituted without our consults and consideration. We have been told by the administration to seek the assistance of the board, and the board has declared the issue of the curriculum is solely in the hands of the administration. This

---

[266] Libby Emmons, "Parents—It's Time to Speak Out against Critical Race Theory Indoctrination in Schools," *Post Millennial*, September 10, 2020, https://the-postmillennial.com/parents-it-is-time-to-speak-out-against-critical-race-theory-indoctrination.

diversionary technique and intentional opaqueness, is not professional, nor does it respect the growing majority of parents who disagree with the systemic misdirection of [the school].

Dozens of Minnesota parents, students, and residents responded to instances of improper politicization of one of their state's most prominent school districts. "We're tired of our kids coming home feeling defeated because their beliefs are forbidden at school and they will be ostracized if they speak out," one parent wrote. "We're tired of our kids [hearing] white people, especially white men, are bad, over and over. We're absolutely sickened when our son tells us that he is labeled a racist, sexist and rapist—yes, a RAPIST—because he is a white male."[267]

One northern Virginia mother removed her children from public school as they implemented a new curriculum. "My kids are not going to receive a rigorous academic education anymore," she wrote. "I'm done." She objected to the school encouraging children to form a racial identity and to classify each other by their appearance. "You'll never actually fully attain the level of an anti-racist. You're just always going to be working for it. It breaks down interpersonal trust because every single interaction that you have with somebody who doesn't look like you, there is a power dynamic. You wonder where they are on the power pyramid and am I pressing them? Am I causing micro aggressions? Or is that a micro aggression against me? You feel like you're walking on eggshells."[268]

Parents in a district in eastern Pennsylvania have also complained. They say the school district "has gone off the deep end with an aggressive

---

[267] Tom Steward, "Edina Parents and Students Rebel against Politics in Classroom," Center of the American Experiment, July 11, 2017, https://www.americanexperiment.org/2017/07/edina-parents-and-students-rebel-against-politics-in-classroom/.

[268] Juliette Fairley, "Loudoun County Mother Homeschools Kids to Avoid Critical-Race Education," West Nova News, October 26, 2020, https://westnovanews.com/stories/559352192-loudoun-county-mother-homeschools-kids-to-avoid-critical-race-education.

indoctrination campaign, spending loads of money on resources created by the most radical and bigoted organizations to force feed the students with poisonous lies! Teachers and Administrators have enthusiastically jumped in up to their necks in promoting this racist and partisan agenda. They are intently brainwashing children to be stormtroopers to their partisan causes."

Another parent described it as institutional intimidation:

> Right about the time [the school district] began [their training], our district's national standing began to fall. That, along with Covid's virtual teaching push, really opened so many parents' eyes to the decay of education and the flourishing of indoctrination in our school system. We are angry that the District has taken such a focused stance on bringing undeniable biased learning into our classrooms. We are angry by the fact that students who speak up against this bias are deliberately and systemically called out by teachers and bullied by their peers – to the point that many kids are refusing to turn on their sound and cameras as not to be "recognized as the problem". She went on to say that this caused many students to feel humiliated and isolated.

In one district in central Pennsylvania, hundreds of letters were sent to be read aloud by the school board (but only a few were). Here are selections from some:

"I support the board members who stood against dragging the group identity politics...into our schools. The day either of my children come home discussing these topics is the day my tax dollars begin going to homeschooling."

"It's important that we as a district are taking steps to help our staff and students to understand and cope with the issues of our trying times. It's also important that we seek to unite, not divide, ourselves as a community. To understand and respect each other requires mutual transparency," wrote a parent who also is a certified public school teacher. "This is why I feel strongly that all curriculum relating to the defining of feelings, beliefs, culture, and the political characteristics of others be available for a full review process by the public before implementation is approved by the school board. We live in turbulent times and it's the parents role to impart knowledge, teach character, and share spiritual guidance to students with questions or concerns. As a district, it's our job to support parents and their different choices in raising our future citizens."

Another wrote, "I'm not going away and I will continue to ask questions. If you look at my immediate family picture you will see many races represented. You're only showing what kind of fool and bully you are if you call me a 'Racist' for asking questions.... Is it even occurring to you to talk to parents about what they want? If there is extra time in the day to teach a new curriculum (your teachers are telling me there isn't extra time), why not put that extra time into getting the children back on grade level?"

"We no longer trust you to educate our children," another wrote. "We want you to do your jobs. Get the test scores up."

"Our forefathers bravely stood against injustice and for right," another wrote. "It is now our time to stand against this mob mentality. They will only get away with it if we cower. I choose not to be governed by fear. We will get what we put up with!"

"We are their parents and we are the ones who oversee their moral development," another wrote. "Your job is to make sure that they practice kindness, empathy, and respect. It is obvious this committee is misguided in its mission by using such one-sided political agenda-based curriculum talking points. These materials are not meant to bring together but to tear apart."

You'll notice a difference in tone and content.

However, the same theme runs throughout all of these letters. Parents are fed up, and they are not being quiet about it.

You don't have to be quiet either.

23

A Note to Teachers and Administrators

Dear teachers and administrators: In this book, I've been talking a great deal about you. Now, I'm going to speak directly to you. First, thank you for your service to our families and communities. You have been given a holy charge: the formation of young minds.

You do not want to lose the good faith of parents and students in your school community. Do not squander it with short-sightedness. If this tendency to abuse and misuse this opportunity continues, for personal or political gain, you will find your reputations and corresponding influence virtually irretrievable. You will be micromanaged endlessly when this is lost, and move from being professionals to mere functionaries—a huge diminishment in your prestige and individual-intellectual authority/autonomy/discretion. Already, we have seen a drastic decline in respect for higher education.

A recent Pew poll found that, when asked whether "colleges and universities have a positive/negative effect on the way things are going in the country," 58 percent of Republicans said "negative," while a *Wall Street Journal*/NBC News poll found that 47 percent of Americans don't believe college is worth the cost.[269] Declining respect means declining support. With it will go all manner of cultural respect and deference long enjoyed by educational professionals. We're already seeing increasing numbers of parents choosing charter schools, cyberschools, and alternative K–12 educational options, while homeschooling rates have doubled nationwide and tripled in some states.[270] This results in loss of funding and reduced staffing for the schools driving these students away. The growing availability and comfort with remote learning alternatives is already accelerating this trend.

This is what happens when educators squander the traditional faith that communities have placed in them:

"Two Arizona legislators introduce a bill that would prohibit state institutions from offering any class or activity that promotes 'division, resentment or social justice toward a race, gender, religion, political affiliation, social class or other class of people.'" The bill failed, but it is a sign of the times. (Arizona has already banned the teaching of ethnic studies in grades K–12.) In Arkansas, a bill seeks to prohibit any writing by or about Howard Zinn from school curricula. In Iowa, a state senator introduced a bill to use political party affiliation as a test for faculty appointments: "A person shall not be hired as a member of the faculty… if the person's political party affiliation…would cause the percentage of faculty belonging to one political party to exceed by ten percent the percentage of the faculty belonging to the other political party."[271] Teachers must exercise their classroom prerogatives responsibly or risk losing them legislatively. Restore trust or run the risk of losing the authority and operating discretion to exercise professional judgment in your classrooms.

---

[269] Josh Mitchell and Douglas Belkin, "Americans Losing Faith in College Degrees, Poll Finds," *Wall Street Journal*, September 7, 2017, https://www.wsj.com/articles/americans-losing-faith-in-college-degrees-poll-finds-1504776601.

[270] McDonald, "Homeschooling More Than Doubles during the Pandemic."

[271] Jen Hayden, "Iowa Legislature Introduces Bill to Require University Faculty Applicants to State Party Affiliation, *Daily Kos* (blog), February 20, 2017, https://www.dailykos.com/stories/2017/2/20/1635991/-Iowa-legislature-introduces-bill-to-require-university-faculty-applicants-to-state-party-affiliation.

However, if you are a teacher who is concerned about the indoctrination happening all around you, then thank you for having the best interests of the children at heart. Teachers are the first ones to see the effects on students of biased initiatives and curricula. The feel-good and usually well-meaning school-wide statements of belief and diversity initiatives exist in the abstract until the effects manifest within the walls of classrooms, often in disastrous ways.

First, educate yourself and others on the ideologies behind curriculum changes. Don't take seemingly innocuous terminology like "equity," "anti-racism" or "ethnic studies," at face value, but instead take a dive into the literature which unpacks enthusiastically promoted concepts so that you can equip yourself with the knowledge required to understand and discuss these topics circumspectly.

Volunteer for all relevant school committees—and show up! Attend school board meetings. Talk to parents and other teachers about their legitimate concerns and make sure that the administration is aware of the full range of opinion and the true extent of concerned opposition. Be active in discussions related to curriculum changes and ask questions to help you better understand others' motivations and perceptions of the issues at hand.

Second, speak up. If you are a tenured teacher, now is not the time to sit back and shut up. Do what you can to help and defend the untenured, who may find they have much more on the line than you do.

Third, be hypervigilant about diversity consultants. Unpacking deceptive terminology will provide you valuable insight into the minds and motivation of those who work to narrow the opinion corridor. Oftentimes, questionable ideology is smuggled into schools through diversity, equity, and inclusion consultants who use such concealing terminology. Once you are well versed in the ambiguous language they use, you will realize the tremendous amount of baggage that comes with accepting many of the recommended ideas and programs. "Equity" sounds like equality, but isn't. It's sometimes said to be a synonym for fairness, but how do you determine what is fair, and to whom? And where does meritocracy fit into the equation? These discussions are never as straightforward as consultants make them out to be.

Ask what values are being promoted with DEI programs or initiatives. Do they reflect yours? The parents'? The school's? Insist on clarity by asking exactly what the problem is (if one exists at all), and how it should be addressed (if at all). Ask to see all materials and learning objectives planned for school use, as well as the evidence of the effectiveness of the content and programming. How a consultant answers such a simple question can be quite telling. Also, ask to see the credentials of all outside personnel brought into the schools to interact with students. If you find yourself thinking your values conflict with those of a DEI program or initiative, unapologetically opt out.

Fifth, be aware of complicit administrators.

Insist that administrators uphold and enforce existing ethical standards among staff. Insist that teachers refrain from teaching outside their area of training/competence or in the private realm of values or dispositions. Reject the notion that a short training seminar by an outside consulting group qualifies teachers to be instructing on complex and values-laden topics such as "justice," "equity," or "social justice."

24

How to Prevent School Indoctrination

The solution to classroom indoctrination, as the title of this book implies, is to "undoctrinate" our schools. If there has, indeed, been a sustained "long march through the institutions," then we must have a long, relentless countermarch to defend our rights, our children, our history, and our cherished way of life. This must be led by determined parents, grandparents, principled educators, concerned citizens, and legislators prepared to oppose unhealthy school degradation with sufficient energy and necessary stamina. Addressing the current problem requires transparency, organization, determination, and effort, but it can—and must—be done.

While some iterations of this problem are clearly being organized and disseminated at a national (and international) level through partisan organizations, facilitated by teachers' unions and other existing educator groups, our schools are organized and run locally. Therefore, it will need to be confronted, defeated, and overcome locally—teacher by teacher, school by school, school board by school board, district by district, and state by state.

First and foremost, we need clear and open transparency and full disclosure of aims and methods between schools, communities, teachers, and parents. Since some activist educators are aware parents may not share their ideological aims, they operate covertly. This is unacceptable. Good faith must be restored and bad operators opposed and removed if they fail to adhere to minimal expectations of competence and ethical comportment. No hidden or disguised agendas, unstated assumptions, or undisclosed philosophical commitments can lurk beneath the surface.

Along the same lines, all terminology must be clearly defined. No confusion should exist about what anyone is talking about. (I recommend the Social Justice Encyclopedia at NewDiscourses.com for help with this.) The terminology evolves swiftly, in an apparent attempt to elude careful analysis, so constant vigilance is essential. Already, "social justice" has shifted to "critical race theory," and "anti-racism" is being overtaken by "ethnic studies" and "culturally responsive" teaching. Each of these examples includes cloaked sunk premises that deserve thorough examination and exposition before acceptance. Exert due diligence and appropriate skepticism with all novel terms. The more schools attempt to glide past neologisms, the more carefully they must be scrutinized. If you're unsure or concerned about hidden aims, ask directly: Is it Marxist? You have a right and a duty to know. Even in a private school, truthful advertising of institutional aims and ideological commitments must be used so that potential "customers" may make fully informed decisions about whether or not to enroll a child there.

Given the state of higher education and the even more improbably leftist slant of ed schools within them, you probably can't underestimate how little some activist educators may understand about perspectives other than their own. It may fall to your student to have to point out obvious omissions or misrepresentations in class, as difficult as it is for a child to correct the teacher. Yes, it's a high hurdle for a youngster, but successfully accomplished, it's a tremendous (if unintended) learning opportunity and a great role model for the rest of the class.

Other admittedly bold suggestions for dealing with blatant abuses of authority in the classroom include having a student raise his/her hand and say, "I feel like I'm being indoctrinated" or "I don't feel comfortable answering questions in this class, given the bias that exists." (When repeated over and over, this is called the "broken record" technique of self-defense.) This is likely to get the school authorities involved as would taking the same statements to the school counselor.

It's pretty easy to predict what sort of material your child is going to be overly exposed to at school, so a wise parent will counterbalance this at home. One of the ways to strengthen our students is by supplementing and counteracting what is missing or going wrong in the schools. You can find suggested supplemental resources for parents, teachers, and students in the appendix of this book, at thefire.org/k12, and at undoctrinate.org.

Remember, it's an imperfect world and we are all imperfect people: practice forgiveness and give others the benefit of the doubt whenever possible. Please teach your kids to stand up for the isolated target of Alinsky-style ridicule, name-calling tactics ("racist!" "homophobe!"), and associated mobbing taking place in schools today—often with no intervention or, worse and *almost* unbelievably, with indefensible participation by an activist teacher. This is utterly terrorizing to a young person. It's ironic, indeed, that as anti-bullying programs have increased in the schools, public shaming has increased. Standing up to it defuses its power; even one ally punctures the power of the mobbing effect. You don't even have to agree with the stated premise to stand against this tactic on principle.

Remember that nature abhors a vacuum. If you do not instill values in your child at home, the schools will choose for you, and these values are likely to be based in secular humanism, postmodernism, progressivism, and neo-Marxism. Give your child values to consider before the schools do and model the intellectual skills you want your child to develop. Values are a guiding star by which to evaluate competing ideas and ideologies.

Review the Speech Policies at Your Child's School and Consider Proposing a Free Speech Statement

Does your child's school protect free speech and respect viewpoint diversity? Review the student handbook and other published materials to see what its stated commitments are. At the college level, FIRE encourages schools to consider adopting the so-called "Chicago Statement,"[272] which is an exemplary defense of free expression on campus. Some concerned parents in the Chicago area, dealing with speech suppression, succeeded in convincing their children's school district to adopt a similar statement, adapted for K–12 purposes. This exemplary statement recognized that a fundamental aspect of the school's mission is to "develop critical thinkers who can navigate a complex world through civil discourse, respectful inquiry, engaged listening and open consideration of multiple perspectives" and affirmed that "the open exchange of ideas lies at the core of a democratic society."[273]

Create Clubs That Celebrate Free Thought

Some enterprising students are starting "discourse" and "dialogue" clubs in their schools, which welcome everyone. Having a community of people helps students feel less isolated and lonely when they feel their rights are being violated.

"I want to start a new club, where all voices, regardless of opinion or political stance, are welcomed. I want people to obtain a deeper understanding of other people's views, rather than to categorize them as 'right' or 'wrong.' I want people to be able to widen their paradigm," said one Alabama high school student. "Most importantly, I want students to be able to form their opinions from knowledge, and what is really happening in the world. I feel as though a lot of opinions are being formed from

---

[272] *Report of the Committee on Freedom of Expression*, University of Chicago, https://provost.uchicago.edu/sites/default/files/documents/reports/FOECommitteeReport.pdf and "Adopting the Chicago Statement," Foundation for Individual Rights in Education, https://www.thefire.org/get-involved/student-network/take-action/adopting-the-chicago-statement/.

[273] "New Trier School Board Adopts Statement Promoting Civil, Diverse Discourse," New Trier Neighbors, https://myemail.constantcontact.com/New-Trier-Adopts-Statement-promoting--Civil-Discourse-and-Critical-Thinking.html?soid=1127160807981&aid=YPtxp2OWA6k.

ignorance and labels. If my generation holds the future of America in their hands, I would want them to be understanding, knowledgeable, and respectful of one another."

If this doesn't exist at your child's school, consider encouraging them to start their own. Founding a new club is a great way for ambitious students to show the kind of initiative that is favorably viewed by both college admissions committees and potential employers. FIRE has materials to help students do this at thefire.org/k12 or write to highschooloutreach@thefire.org for more information.

Suggest the Use of Nonpartisan Curricula That Encourage Free Thought and Open Discourse

To combat declining respect for civil norms and diminished understanding of basic civics, encourage your child's teachers and schools to research and consider adopting some of the many fine, nonpartisan resources available from organizations such as the Civics Renewal Network (whose tagline is "A Republic, If We Can Teach It") and other quality supplemental resources listed in the appendix of this book. At FIRE, we have developed an array of standards-aligned curriculum-enrichment modules designed to educate students on the philosophy, history, and law surrounding their free speech and other First Amendment rights. You can find these, available for free download by teachers, parents, or students, at thefire.org/curriculum.

Inoculate Your Kids against Indoctrination

Families can practice and rehearse argumentation skills at home. We want our kids to be able to cope with a certain appropriate amount of intellectual challenge, so adapting to a reasonable amount of substandard or tilted pedagogy can be a learning opportunity. It can spur them to question things they are being told and do independent research. We don't need to shield our kids from every form of adversity in life, and hearing opposing points of view, within reason, is healthy.

You are going to have to "inoculate" your kids against indoctrination, and, when your child does encounter it (they will), you're going to have to conduct a debriefing, so that your kids can understand the missing perspectives unsupplied via formal education. This means you will need to do some of the work that schools are failing to do.

Holding Teachers and Schools Accountable

Some of this is out of the parents' hands. Department chairs, curriculum supervisors, principals, and district administrators must insist on balance, proportion, and fair representation in their curriculum selections. They must demand teachers adhere to existing public codes of ethics for educators and remain in alignment with established learning standards, adopted through democratic, open means. Teacher education programs must stress these codes of ethics. Overreaching educators—exceeding the boundaries of their professional roles or training competence—must be called to account and reined in by their supervisors.

Accreditation agencies, such as NCATE, can help increase viewpoint diversity among teacher education programs. FIRE was very successful in holding NCATE accountable when they tried to insert "social justice dispositions" as part of their accreditation expectations.

However, you as parents can be helpful watchdogs. You can demand that teachers be certified in their areas of competence and not exceed them. Be particularly demanding on qualifications when teachers are delving into the areas of values, dispositions, attitudes, or opinions. Remember there are NO teaching certifications or degrees on these topics. Do not accept attendance at seminars (often run by ideologically driven, highly paid consulting firms) as a "qualification" to instruct on matters of private conscience. It isn't.

A lot of what these teachers are doing in the realm of "attitude adjustment" is closer to "unlicensed therapy." Classroom teachers have absolutely no business engaging in such unethical practices—for which they are not even professionally qualified—with others' minor children. Insist that teachers stick to established learning objectives in their area of certification and not exceed them. Teachers are not priests and are not tasked with instructing on moral values or character beyond "lowest-common-denominator" values, such as the Golden Rule.

Assess Your Child's School Climate of Indoctrination

To assess whether students feel silenced at your child's school, or if a classroom has a "chilly climate" for expression of minority viewpoints, you may ask the school to administer an anonymous survey. This will detect any particular ideological lean in their schools, and help them correct for any overrepresentation or deficiencies. (Heterodox Academy has an adaptable example called a "Campus Expression Survey."[274]) Here's an example of a course evaluation that could be used with students:

Student End-of-Course Faculty Evaluation Questions

1 = Strongly agree, 2 = Somewhat agree, 3 = Neutral, 4 = Somewhat disagree, 5 = Strongly disagree

Instructor's presentation of social and political issues

Balanced and fair   1   2   3   4   5   Biased and unfair

---

[274] "Campus Expression Survey," Heterodox Academy, accessed November 27, 2020, https://heterodoxacademy.org/campus-expression-survey/.

Course readings on controversial issues

Multiple perspectives   1   2   3   4   5   One-sided

Classroom environment with respect to student expression of political or social views

Tolerant   1   2   3   4   5   Hostile

Treatment of students who express political or social views

Tolerant   1   2   3   4   5   Hostile

Use of classroom to present instructor's personal political views

Rare or infrequent   1   2   3   4   5   Frequent

Instructor comments on politics unrelated to the course

Rare or infrequent   1   2   3   4   5   Frequent[275]

When Dealing with Authorities, Be Polite and Respectful

In Rockingham, North Carolina, the system worked as it was intended to. Children reported to parents concerning incidents at their school, teachers sought assistance from political organizations when pushed to attend and promote programming that violated their values and beliefs, and parents showed up at the public school board meeting where they voiced their concerns, passionately, but civilly. School board members listened attentively and respectfully, and promised to address the situation. Here is some of what the board members had to say:

---

[275] Adapted from *Intellectual Diversity: Time for Action*, 34.

"I want to thank everybody who came tonight and spoke and participated. It's important that the board hear from people in the community about things that are going on. If we don't know about problems and perceptions, then we can't work on them, we can't fix them. So I thank you very much for coming, and sharing your views."

"I want to thank all of you for being here tonight and [I want all of you] to know that we do listen, we see you, we hear you. We feel you, sometimes…. [I]t's not falling on deaf ears. We are trying. If you do anything, there are gonna come times that you are gonna make a mistake. I appreciate you all, so let's talk and let's listen, and let's talk and let's listen. Thank you."

"I also want to thank everyone. I've been in that position [the position of the parents bringing their complaints to the school board] and I know—at least for me—it took a lot of courage to prepare a speech and come up there, so I do thank you for that and I'll try and be as available as I can be. My phone number's on the website, if anybody has any questions for me."[276]

Even though there were some extremely frustrated parents at the meeting who had reached the point of threatening to remove their children from the public school system, everyone remained respectful throughout this exchange. Parents were active, engaged, and vocal, and local officials were responsive.

And another! Burlington High School in Wisconsin had a couple of incidents of classroom bias—from both sides. First, a teacher taught

---

[276] Victor Skinner, "White Middle Schoolers Forced to Stand in Front of Classmates, Apologize for 'Privilege,'" EAGNews.org, June 21, 2017, https://www.eagnews. org/2017/06/parents-teachers-slam-nc-school-districts-mandatory-white-privilege-training/.

about Black Lives Matter in a way that caused concern amongst some parents. The school held a special meeting to discuss it in public and acknowledged it was not an approved part of the curriculum.

Later, at the same school, a teacher assigned a one-sided video about election integrity to his students, raising eyebrows. After parents complained to the school district about this one, the district first suspended the teacher. Then, they responded beautifully to the concerned parents.

"In a time that has no precedent, we recognize that within our district, we have varying perspectives," they wrote. "We feel urgency in embracing our entire community of learners as we seek to explore diverse ideas without bias."[277] Moving forward, the district pledged to thoroughly review proposed curricular changes through consultation with a cross-representation of city representatives, pointing out that "[t]his is a highly charged and emotional topic. There are varied perspectives and we know there is plenty of work to do—work that should be done collaboratively, with the whole community."[278]

This is what ALL school districts should be doing in order to live up to their responsibility to appropriately and impartially serve all of their constituents.

Have Courage

It took courage for these parents to come forward—but they did. You might need to show similar courage, persistence, and determination. (And, as the saying goes, "One man with courage is a majority.") The forces behind these ideologies are powerful, yes…but they are not indomitable. Like most bullies, if you stand up to them, they will cave. They rest

---

[277] Williams, "Burlington High School Teacher Suspended."

[278] Dave Fidlin, "Black Lives Matter Debate Takes Center Stage at Burlington Area School District Meeting," *Journal Times*, September 17, 2020, https://journaltimes.com/news/local/black-lives-matter-debate-takes-center-stage-at-burlington-area-school-district-meeting/article_294fdaac-09aa-5297-a95f-1c9f3612ec24.html.

on an extremely shaky intellectual foundation as well, and will quickly topple under intelligent cross-examination. They thrive using fear, intimidation, and the expectation of appeasement in the face of those tactics.

You're going to have to look the fear and intimidation directly in the face and say, "I'm not afraid of you." To embolden you, read the lovely piece written about the same phenomenon encroaching within the legal profession in Canada, titled "They Can't Cancel All of Us: How We Fought the Woke Thought Police and Won."

Canadian lawyer Lisa Bilby explains how a few principled and determined lawyers and paralegals risked their careers, relationships, and reputations to stand up to a professional regulator who'd taken it upon himself to tell members what to think and believe to practice law. Bilby points out that courage is contagious and it only takes one or two people to stand up and say "This is wrong" for others to find their voices and spines too. "Yes, we were called some names," she writes, but "the world doesn't end" and "there is something remarkably freeing about standing up for something you believe in, and withstanding the slings and arrows."[279]

Take heart: we didn't choose this battle, but now that we're in it, we have to win it.

We will.

---

[279] Lisa Bildy, "They Can't Cancel All of Us: How We Fought the Woke Thought Police and Won," New Discourses, June 11, 2020, https://newdiscourses. com/2020/06/how-we-fought-woke-thought-police-won/.

25

How to Fight School Indoctrination When It Happens

Even if you've done all you can to prevent indoctrination, it might happen anyway. Here are some tips on what to do.

Figure Out What You're Dealing With

There are two types of wayward, indoctrinating teachers: the misguided and the true believer. A sincere but misguided teacher may simply be unaware and uninformed about hidden motives and political ideologies embedded in skillfully packaged materials helpfully offered by partisan actors. Such a teacher may be willing and able to correct errors and oversights when they're pointed out, but a true believer never will.[280] A "good faith" educator may suffer an occasional lapse and let a partisan, ill-advised statement slip on occasion. But when good faith exists, they will respond to objections and seek to amend their ways (assuming that they are able to recognize what the problem is, depending on the

---

[280] [For more on the nature of a true believer, see Eric Hoffer's book, *The True Believer*.]

depth of their own self-awareness and the quality of their preparation). Admittedly, classroom teaching is an ongoing live performance during which a well-intentioned individual can have an accidental, unintentional bad moment or slip-up, so please make allowances for human frailty and imperfection.

A "bad faith" educator, however, sees nothing wrong with what s/he is doing, believes it is his/her right and duty to appropriate the classroom for personal partisan ends, and is unrepentant and unremorseful. They will lie, dissemble, double down, and persist proudly. For their protection, children must be removed from such teachers' classrooms, and for the protection of others, such educators must be publicly exposed for the interested, partisan actors they are.

You have to figure out what kind you're dealing with. However, begin with the presumption of good faith, unless proven otherwise.

Teach Your Kids to Disengage

Because ordinary "discussions" have become terribly unpleasant in the current hyper-partisan climate, equip students on how to disengage from poorly handled "debates" that are really bad-faith harangues or disguised insults. They don't have to attend every argument to which they are invited. They can simply walk away. Everyone needs solid "exit strategies" for pointless, baiting political discussions (which is, of course, why inflicting them on a captive audience of students is so pernicious). Teach kids defensive statements and safe exit phrases for baiting, take-no-prisoners, "bad faith" "conversations."

Remind your kids they do not need to justify all their opinions—or lack of opinions—to their peers or any authority figure. They're allowed to be in "identity moratorium" (which psychologist James Marcia defines as questioning different possibilities before making commitments)—as long as it takes them to reach their own conclusions without undue influence or unfair pressure tactics.

It's perfectly fine for them to say, "I'm not sure how I feel about that. I need some time to think about it." They must be allowed to leave it at that. Pursuing them after such a final statement constitutes harassment.

Even though adults seem to be talking about politics all the time, kids also need to be given the right not to care about politics. I certainly didn't care at all about politics when I was in high school. It was so boring! I wanted to talk about sports, and records, and boys (mostly sports and records). Now we have elementary school children being exposed to upsetting, acrimonious news events with no escape even on the playground. They're expected to take ideological stands and participate in activism, which is woefully misguided. It's also very, very selfish. Developmentally, kids still deserve to be shielded from upsetting, age-inappropriate material, even if the teacher finds the outrage du jour captivating and engrossing.

Teach Your Kids to Document

Instruct your child to write concerning incidents or interactions down, word for word, with the date. Tell a counselor or an administrator. Some students are filming errant teachers in the classroom, which is a sad state of affairs indeed, but which has revealed clear abuses. Every teacher has a bad day once in a while, or gets off topic accidentally. If the teacher is not characterized by such behavior, don't sweat it. However, do notice and document persistent patterns of tendentious behavior.

But when there's no way to avoid the indoctrination, document everything. Keep records of inappropriate or unbalanced assignments; photocopy if necessary.

Appeal to Authorities

Follow the chain of command: appeal first to the teacher, and give him or her a chance to address the problem directly. If that doesn't work, you would appeal to the department chair, then the curriculum head, then to the principal. Next would be the school board and the district's administrative office. You could also report incidents to the relevant teachers' unions. Following the chain of command without jumping anyone's rank is partly a matter of respect, but it also alerts everyone up and down the chain that there is a problem, so that all the internal stakeholders are fully informed and to increase the likelihood of documentation. Then would come the state board of education, and finally, the federal Department of Education. In fact, the states and the Department of Education may need to establish a reporting portal to collect information on educational indoctrination to document the extent of the problem and determine how to correct the situation. This would also provide concrete data for holding teachers' unions accountable for living up to their profession's responsibility to serve the public well.

What to Do If You Are Ignored

Sometimes, even if you document faithfully and go through proper channels, the authorities ignore complaints about indoctrination. This happened at Columbia University, where students' complaints about Middle East studies professors were ignored or mishandled. As a result, complaints festered, and the department became infected by suspicion, incivility, and a highly politicized atmosphere.

"As one of the nation's most prestigious liberal-arts universities, Columbia has a responsibility to respect the freedom of students to protest what they feel is ideological bias by their professors," remarked David French, the former president of FIRE. "Columbia also has a responsibility to students, donors, and the public to be open and honest about a department's political agenda, if any, and to let them decide whether to continue to attend or support the institution."[281] In response to concerns from this

---

[281] "Columbia Embroiled in Academic Freedom Controversy; FIRE Defends Student Expression," Foundation for Individual Rights in Education, January 11, 2005, https://www.thefire.org/columbia-embroiled-in-academic-freedom-controversy-fire-defends-student-expression/.

pressure, Bollinger reaffirmed his strong commitments to free expression, professional teaching, and academic freedom: "Maintaining the proper atmosphere of free and open inquiry in the classroom is an essential and special responsibility of the faculty."[282] He established a method of formal complaint and encouraged students to file formal grievances against professors who pressured them "into supporting a political or social cause."[283]

Clear reporting mechanisms protect and empower students and parents while putting faculty and administrators on notice that the classroom climate must be monitored and protected from corruption by political or other biasing influences.

Equip Your Kid to Use Humor and Other Deflection Techniques

Humor is a very effective defensive/deflection technique and is considered a "healthy" ego defense mechanism. While school has always involved a certain amount of verbal tussling, the heat has intensified and it's increasingly difficult for the average kid to get through the day without being drawn into an emotionally loaded and often politically charged situation. As if being a teenager wasn't already challenging enough!

When my kids were in school, *The Daily Show with Jon Stewart* was at peak popularity, and their classmates frequently watched it to memorize zingers that they would then use to try to "one-up" other students the next day. It was tedious, predictable, and frustrating. It was also mean-spirited and eye roll-inducing. After listening to them complain about this same issue one too many times, we came up with the mildly

---

[282] "Letter from Columbia President Lee Bollinger to FIRE," Foundation for Individual Rights in Education, January 18, 2005, https://www.thefire.org/letter-from-columbia-president-lee-bollinger-to-fire/.

[283] James Romoser, "Middle East Studies: University Response to Controversy Focuses on Systemic Failures," *Columbia Spectator*, March 27, 2013, https://www.columbiaspectator.com/2005/05/09/middle-east-studies-university-response-controversy-focuses-systemic-failures/.

saucy comeback line "Sounds like YOU watched *The Daily Show* last night!" which worked like a charm at deflating their pretensions. No, it's not the funniest one-liner ever, but it was pretty harmless yet effective. They got the message.

For more effective communication deflection devices, head to thefire. org/curriculum for our free, downloadable "Handling Offensive Speech" lesson plans. This module includes a subunit on "Healthy Discourse" that is based on sound counseling theory and includes numerous resources for instructing kids on how to disengage from unproductive conversations. For example, it's very helpful to pre-equip kids with prepared but unprovocative phrases that they can pull out when someone (teachers included!) attempts to bait them into a manipulative pre-planned interaction with the potential to turn toxic.

The trick is to be non-confrontational and to say vague, noncommittal things that sound like agreement, but actually aren't. Examples include simply nodding or saying something vaguely insipid, such as "I see," "Oh," "I didn't know that," "Uh huh," "I never heard that before," "Thanks for letting me know," or "Got it." We're also starting discourse clubs and will be offering free starter kits for interested faculty advisors, in order to help improve the level of conversation in schools. Ultimately, our goal (and the club's tagline) is to help students to "Keep Your Views and Keep Your Friends."

Certainly, any true friendship needs to be built on a foundation of mutual respect and interpersonal authenticity. Real friends don't require each other to pretend to be someone else or to falsify their views in order to be accepted.

Ask for Reasonable Alternatives for Unacceptable Lesson Plans

If any unusual readings violate your values, religious beliefs, or personal convictions, did you know that you can request alternative assignments? I'm not recommending this for ordinary controversial classics, but for blatantly politically infused books and lessons. You wouldn't want to do this without a good reason, but when warranted, by all means do so. A reasonable alternative assignment is exactly that; it's not sending your kid into the hallway to sit and stare at the wall as though he's being punished. I've done this on behalf of my children on occasion and was always successfully accommodated. Be polite, clear, and firm. When enough parents insist upon alternatives for extreme lesson plans, schools will get the message as the extra workload will become its own problem. This is not a technique to abuse and should only be used for sincere concerns.

Teachers can't be expected to make individualized lesson plans for every student regularly. Knowing to make this request implies that you have pre-notification of upcoming lessons and that the teacher is being fully transparent and keeping you apprised of what's going on in class. In today's climate, neither of these is assured, but this is all the more reason to pay close attention, to communicate with your child about exactly what's happening in class, and to write to the teacher directly and ask to be informed about what's being planned.

Repeat offenders can legitimately be asked for ongoing pre-notification of upcoming lessons, which ensures oversight and accountability. Also: be alert for attempts to bait and switch lesson content. When you have suspicions, follow up to ensure that planned lessons are actually presented as they are represented to you. Anything else is a violation of your trust, which is its own problem, requiring a separate discussion involving both the wayward teacher and appropriate administrators.

Go Public

Though it's best to handle issues on a person-to-person basis, it's sometimes helpful to publicize errant assignments and teaching online via social media. Post ridiculous assignments and initiatives online for exposure.

Though this possibly will anger the school administrators, public schools—which are funded by taxpayers—should not want to hide what they are doing from a curious public. Sunshine, after all, is sometimes the best disinfectant.

Lawsuits

Sometimes, playing nice just doesn't work. Thankfully, in America, we have the opportunity to use the courts to make things right. In order to sue a school successfully, you need to be able to prove that it broke a law. To find out if you might have a case, you would need to consult an attorney licensed to practice in your state.

Talk to Other Parents and Share Stories

In years past, parents used to mingle after walking children to school in their communities. But now, with busing and car drop-off lines, parents don't naturally come into contact with each other as frequently. It's important for many reasons to know the parents of your children's friends, especially as it pertains to keeping an eye out for indoctrination. As you discuss instances of bias and unprofessional intolerance by school staff, patterns can be recognized.

Cultivating relationships with other parents will allow you to share stories of what's going on in the classroom with others. You'll be able to ask which teachers to avoid and warn other parents which teachers to avoid. You can also more easily recognize and support the teachers who refuse to yield to classroom activism. They need help, because the pressure is so strong to conform. I've heard from several of these who are tired of having so many fed-up students transferring into their classrooms, which reduces the workload on errant teachers while increasing their own. As this "supply-and-demand" problem becomes more apparent, school administrators will be forced to respond.

Also, in a more formal setting, you can use the PTA/PTO as a forum to expose and confront classroom orthodoxy and activism. It's important for parents to stand together and support others who speak up in opposition. Remember: they can't cancel us all. It's also important to support the teachers who oppose classroom indoctrination. There are more of them than you might think!

Make the Most of Evaluations

Schools sometimes give students evaluations at the end of the year. Make sure your student provides honest and kind feedback on the forms. Also, have your child take advantage of the Rate My Teachers website to share information about biased teachers with others.

Demand Transparency

Demand full disclosure of ideological commitments and biases by teachers. If the school is embedding "social justice" or other intentions throughout the entire curriculum, insist on knowing precisely what that means and how it will be implemented, so the community of stakeholders can discuss and respond as needed. Refuse to have your child placed in classrooms with teachers known for politicizing the discussions and make sure that the administration understands why. Be alert for biased grading and bring it to the attention of department chairs.

Dig More Deeply

If a lesson seems "off" to you, insist to see which statewide learning standards concerning lessons meet. Review all statewide learning standards and ask which lessons will cover them. In this way, all omission and commission will be noticed.

Know Your Rights and Use Them

As an American, you have strong First Amendment rights. However, they don't mean anything unless you use them.

Also, if you see problematic signs in your school or are concerned about outside lessons being used in the classroom, you can use the Freedom of Information Act to uncover the sources of these materials and associated costs.

Insist upon Recognition of the Basic Principle of the Separation of Church and State

Public schools are not churches and do not get to impose belief or faith systems on students. While schools may cover theories in class, they cannot insist that your child must believe in them. Firmly invoke the separation of church and state when resisting thought reform efforts in your child's school.

Recognize Potential Allies

School counselors are responsible for the social and emotional needs of students in schools. If your child is feeling silenced, unwelcome, targeted, or otherwise uncomfortable in class, take the issue to the school counselor, who should be able to be an effective sounding board and a potential mediator between parents, teachers, and administrators, on behalf of the student's needs.

Make Teachers Accountable, Statewide

Educators are awarded licenses and expected to be both competent and accountable in adhering to the professional practices outlined by the state board of education. Teacher education programs can often be improved so that teachers in training have a balanced understanding of relevant topics and can fairly present multiple viewpoints on issues they will be responsible for covering under their licensure.

Improve your familiarity with statewide learning standards and encourage other concerned parents to do the same so as many people as possible are fully informed on the scope of teachers' instructional responsibilities and the limits on what they're supposed to be covering in each class in each grade. Familiarize yourself as well with any applicable statewide educator professional expectations and disciplinary procedures, by reviewing the information available at your state's Department of Education website. Since states issue educator licenses, they are the ones charged with maintaining the standards and revoking licensure when educators fail to live up to them. This is another reason why local and statewide elections matter, so don't blithely pass over these "small-time" elections without fully investigating the candidates and their positions and making your voice heard at the ballot box.

Consider lobbying legislators for school choice options and creating state and national Department of Education reporting mechanisms for non-aligned instruction (indoctrination) in the classroom. Also, pay much closer attention to what's going on in your state legislature; some states are now pushing for learning standards that practically *require* the indoctrination of students. This must be actively opposed by alert citizens.

Support Organizations Promoting Classical Liberal Education and Fighting Biased Indoctrination

Donate to organizations promoting classical liberal education and opposing school indoctrination. You can find a list of reputable organizations under "Recommended Resources" at the end of this book.

26

In Conclusion

At the beginning of this book, I told you about William—the son of a black mother named Gabrielle and a deceased white father—whose dreams of studying music at college were jeopardized because he was unable to accept the lessons he was being taught about the evil of his skin color.

Now, William is receiving therapy and, hopefully, the family is well on their way to healing and justice. Maybe. Maybe not. The suit was just filed as I'm writing this book. No matter the outcome, William is learning invaluable lessons of life—that we do not have to compromise our values, even if it comes at a significant cost.

You've also read of countless other students who have experienced a similar fate. Perhaps your own children are going through this nightmare too. However, all Americans, regardless of political persuasion or direct personal experience, should be alarmed at the path on which our nation is careening.

We're at a crossroads.

It's a good time—a necessary time—to see what is going on and to fight for the ideals our founders envisioned for us. We cannot allow freedom to die in the classroom. When fear, intimidation, and censorship hold sway in American classrooms, our children are shortchanged, our schools bankrupted, and our culture is increasingly impoverished.

In 1961, President John F. Kennedy addressed the Canadian Parliament. "The free world's cause is strengthened because it is just. But it is strengthened even more by the dedicated efforts of free men and free nations," he said. "The only thing necessary for the triumph of evil is for good men to do nothing."

These words are even truer today, except I'd amend this quote to include "good men and women." Be inspired by the tenacity and advocacy of mothers like Gabrielle.

Educators, act now to protect your institutions from the loss of trust and integrity that will prove irretrievable. Parents, act now to protect your children from harm that can be irreparable.

The hour is already late and the stakes are immeasurable.

It's time to fight for our children and for our nation.

APPENDICES

I.

Five Warning Signs of K–12 Indoctrination

1. Your school uses ambiguous language signifying values commitments to ill-defined ("slippery") concepts such as "justice," "equity," and "accountability." (Another sign is rapidly shifting language.)
2. Your school issues a collective "We Believe" statement of values containing politically loaded terms.
3. Outside consultants are brought in to "reeducate" or "sensitize" staff and/or students.
4. Curriculum from partisan organizations is being adopted by your school or teacher.
5. Your child is pressured or expected to participate in a march or rally for a political cause organized by the class or school.

*BONUS—The only stated lesson objective/learning standard is "Social-Emotional Learning" (SEL).

II.

10 Principles for Opposing Thought Reform in K-12

By Greg Lukianoff, President and CEO of the
Foundation for Individual Rights in Education

1. No compelled speech, thought, or belief.
2. Respect for individuality, dissent, and the sanctity of conscience.
3. K-12 teachers & administrators must demonstrate epistemic humility.
4. Foster the broadest possible curiosity, critical thinking skills, and discomfort with certainty.
5. Foster independence, not moral dependency.
6. Do not teach children to think in cognitive distortions.
7. Do not teach the 'Three Great Untruths.'
8. Take student mental health *more* seriously.
9. Resist the temptation to reduce complex students to limiting labels.
10. If it's broke, fix it. Be willing to form new institutions that empower students and educate them with principles of free, diverse, and pluralistic society.

If you would like to read the full article, please use the following link: thefire.org/opposing-thought-reform

III.

Parental Transparency Protocol (PTP)

Good Faith Statement

Parents have ultimate legal authority over the education of their children. The law is quite clear on this. Schools and teachers have an obligation to uphold the existing and long-established professional and ethical codes that govern K–12 education and schools, and teachers have a moral and ethical responsibility to engage in full disclosure and truth in advertising in the conduct of their professional (teaching) affairs. Parents have a legal right and parental duty to insist on this. These codes call for neutrality and impartiality when dealing with matters of contention in the classroom.

Teachers or schools with hidden agendas or ideological commitments beyond providing high-quality education have a moral and ethical duty to operate in good faith and disclose them, so that parents can make fully informed decisions about how best to educate their children. Schools that fail to do so breach their fiduciary responsibilities.

Teachers and schools are responsible for "maintaining the highest professional standards of accuracy, honesty, and appropriate disclosure of information when representing the school or district within the community and in public communications." (Model Code of Ethics for Educators, National Association of State Directors of Teacher Education and Certification.) There is a general understanding that teachers act *in loco parentis* (in place of the parents) and thus may not undermine the parents in interactions with their children who are legally entrusted to their professional care.

States have rules that govern the conduct of educational institutions. In Pennsylvania, for example, there is a code of professional practice and conduct to which teachers must adhere: "In Pennsylvania, school attendance is compulsory and thus parents are mandated to entrust their children to our education system. As a result of this mandate, 'trust' has evolved into the operative foundation of the relationship of students with their teachers. It is from this foundation that the duty of teachers to act as a fiduciary in their students' best interest and to create and maintain a safe environment for their students derives."[284] Once trust is broken, it is almost impossible to repair.

Therefore, parents have a perfect right and due diligence duty to ask the following sorts of questions when searching for a school or dealing with dubious teaching practices:

Transparency Questions:

Are there any unstated ideological premises or biases at this school? (Has this school embraced commitments to any aims other than excellent teaching, such as to a particular political ideology or social aim?) If so, what are they? This same question could be asked of individual teachers.

How do teachers and administrators handle students with opposing viewpoints?

Are the readings assigned in classrooms balanced in terms of viewpoint or ideology? For instance, if you assign something by Marx or on communism, do you balance it with a commensurate reading on capitalism?

---

[284] Pennsylvania Professional Standards and Practices Division. "The Teacher/Student Relationship." https://www.pspc.education.pa.gov/Promoting-Ethical-Practices-Resources/Ethics-Toolkit/Unit3/Pages/The-Teacher---Student-Relationship.aspx, Accessed February 4, 2021.

What sort of representation do you have on your faculty of teachers from different sides of the political spectrum? (Does the school know what the balance/imbalance is?)

What is your philosophy on free speech in this school? Have you adopted any statements on free speech at this school?

Do you attempt to instill particular values, beliefs, attitudes, or dispositions in this school? If so, what are they, and what professional credentials do the teachers possess that qualify them to be instructing on these particular values, beliefs, attitudes, or dispositions? (FYI: There are *no* professional teaching credentials in values, beliefs, attitudes, or dispositions—not even school counselors, who deal with emotions but are expected to remain value-neutral. Also, a short "training" program, often offered by an outside consulting firm to a school district, is not a "credential.")

Do you ever have teachers teaching "out of area" (outside the area of their certification/expertise)? Under what circumstances?

Do your classroom curricula and daily lesson plans align with established, published learning standards? May I see those?

Will I receive syllabi of the planned coursework and assigned readings?

Outside Curricula:

Does any outside curricular material that you use align with established learning standards?

Do you ever incorporate curricular materials from outside organizations with partisan aims? Which ones? Why?

Why is your school choosing to implement a program/curriculum that comes from this source? What do you know about this source?

What other curricula did you consider before choosing this one?

Do you consider this curriculum to be neutral, balanced, and/or unbiased? (If no, what bias does it have?)

Are there any problems you can anticipate from implementing this curriculum?

Is there space in this curriculum for a variety of viewpoints and potential dissent? How would such diversion be handled?

Where does this lesson fit in the curriculum? With which established standards and learning objectives does it align?

What research exists to demonstrate that this curriculum is effective?

What safeguards/discussion mechanisms are in place if problems with this curriculum, or its implementation, arise?

Collecting Info on Children:

Do you ever conduct surveys on children? If you do, do you notify parents beforehand? Do students have a choice of whether or not to participate?

All this is required by the ethical guidelines that govern academic research.

Do you ever monitor your classrooms or collect anonymous data on whether certain groups of students feel "silenced" in your classrooms?

Do you ever survey students on their attitudes or dispositions without parental consent?

Supervision:

Do your teachers adhere to ethical teaching practices and follow existing codes of professional ethics? If so, which one(s) and may I see it/them? If not, why not? What constrains their behavior otherwise?

How do you hold teachers accountable when they violate ethical teaching practices?

How do you supervise teachers to ensure they do not insert political material into their instructional activities?

IV.

Flowchart for Dealing with Bias in K-12

Steps for parents dealing with classroom bias in K-12

Get your facts straight
- Document everything
- Educate yourself on your rights

Contact the teacher
- Ask for the other perspective before making accusations

Escalate up the chain of command
- Reach out to the department chair, principal, district curriculum personnel, school board, state licensure board, or state legislature as needed to raise your concerns

Insist on transparency
- Curricula should be standards-aligned, balanced, and nonpartisan
- Consider a FOIA request

Community involvement
- Raise the issue at a school board meeting
- Form a coalition with like-minded parents
- Run for a seat on the school board

Consider removing your child
- Opt your child out of lessons that violate your family's values
- Request your child transfer to another class
- Remove your child from the school

Consider legal action
- Seek advice from a licensed attorney

Graphic by Josh Haverlock

V.

School Indoctrination Survey

This is meant to be an anonymous survey, in order to collect honest feedback, for sharing with school administrators and school boards. Feel free to adapt the questions to your school. Please do not include identifying information in your responses.

PARENTS

I have seen all of the course content from my child's classes.

Yes

No

Comments:

From what I have seen, I consider the course content used in my child's classes to be age appropriate and developmentally appropriate.

Yes

No

Comments:

The curriculum used in my child's school reflects my family's values.

Yes

No

Comments:

I am content with the amount of transparency from the school about the teaching materials and school activities that impact my child.

Yes

No

Comments:

I believe that the curriculum used in my child's school is good preparation for adult citizenship.

Yes

No

Comments:

I believe that the curriculum used in my child's school provides a solid academic grounding in the basics (reading, writing, arithmetic...)

Yes

No

Comments:

I believe that the curriculum used in my child's school is emotionally healthy.

Yes

No

Comments:

Have you noticed any physical or emotional effects of school curricula on your child?

Yes

No

Comments:

Has your child required any counseling or therapy related to school curriculum issues?

Yes

No

Comments:

I have concerns about some of the content being used in my child's classrooms.

Yes

No

Comments:

When I express my curricular concerns to my child's teacher or my school district, they take me seriously and are responsive.

Yes

No

N/A

Comments:

I think my child's school has become too politicized.

Yes

No

Comments:

Additional Comments:

STUDENTS

I enjoy the curriculum in my school.

Yes

No

Comments:

I am able to speak freely and openly in all of my classes.

Yes

No

Comments:

In class, I sometimes say what I think my teachers want to hear instead of what I really think.

Yes

No

Comments:

My teacher expects me to actively agree with his/her opinions.

Yes

No

Comments:

I believe that I have been graded down on assignments or tests for asserting opinions that differ from my teacher's preferred views.

Yes

No

Comments:

I fear retaliation if I stray from the teacher's preferred views in class.

Yes

No

Comments:

I have been retaliated against for straying from the teacher's preferred views in class.

Yes

No

Comments:

I find the curriculum used in my school to continually revisit the same themes.

Yes

No

Comments:

I have sat through lessons that are upsetting to me in school.

Yes

No

Comments:

I think that my teacher is trying to impose his/her personal views on me.

Yes

No

Comments:

My teachers present material in a fair, impartial, and academic manner in class.

Yes

No

Comments:

I disagree with some of the messaging I am being taught in my school.

Yes

No

Comments:

My teachers respect everyone equally in class.

Yes

No

Comments:

Some of the lessons I am being taught are in opposition to the values I bring to school/learn at home.

Yes

No

Comments:

I feel anxious and uncomfortable about going to school due to the political content there.

Yes

No

Comments:

I have been given school assignments that are offensive and/or up-setting to me.

Yes

No

Comments:

I feel targeted in the classroom due to my race, gender, politics, or other personal characteristics.

Yes

No

Comments:

I feel embarrassed in the classroom due to the topics the teacher chooses to discuss.

Yes

No

Comments:

I have received DEI training in my school.

Yes

No

If Yes, what did you think of it? Comments:

I think my school has become too politicized.

Yes

No

Comments:

Do you have any physical or emotional effects that you think are the result of school curricula?

Yes

No

Comments:

Additional Comments:

TEACHERS

I am being asked to teach things that make me feel uncomfortable.

Yes

No

Comments:

I am being asked to teach concepts that I disagree with.

Yes

No

Comments:

I am being asked to teach things that I think are not developmentally appropriate or emotionally healthy for my students.

Yes

No

Comments:

I am not allowed to cover topics in the way that I feel is best educationally.

Yes

No

Comments:

I am constantly looking over my shoulder and afraid of losing my job if I express doubts about new curricular commitments at my school.

Yes

No

Comments:

I have to be insincere and dishonest about my real views to keep my job and get through the day at my school.

Yes

No

Comments:

I think my school has become too politicized.

Yes

No

Comments:

I think my school tries to impose preferred political or ideological viewpoints on students.

Yes

No

Comments:

Additional Comments:

References

Abramson, L. Y., M. E. Seligman, and J. D. Teasdale. "Learned Helplessness in Humans: Critique and Reformulation." *Journal of Abnormal Psychology* 87, no. 1 (1978): 49–74.

Adams, Richard. "Teacher Suspended for President Obama Assassination Lesson." *Guardian*, May 19, 2010. https://www.theguardian.com/world/richard-adams-blog/2010/may/19/teacher-alabama-assasination-obama.

Ahmari, Sohrab. "Democracy Dies in Smugness." *Commentary Magazine*, January 17, 2018. https://www.commentarymagazine.com/articles/sohrab-ahmari/democracy-dies-smugness/.

American Council of Trustees and Alumni. *A Crisis in Civic Education.* Washington, DC: ACTA, January 2016. https://www.goacta.org/wp-content/uploads/ee/download/A_Crisis_in_Civic_Education.pdf.

American Council of Trustees and Alumni. *Free to Teach, Free to Learn: Understanding and Maintaining Academic Freedom in Higher Education.* Washington, DC: ACTA, 2013. https://www.goacta.org/wp-content/uploads/ee/download/free_to_teach_free_to_learn.pdf.

American Council of Trustees and Alumni. *Intellectual Diversity: Time for Action.* Washington, DC: ACTA, 2005. https://www.goacta.org/resource/intellectual_diversity/.

Anderson, Greta. "Survey Identifies 'Dangerous' Student Self-Censorship." *Inside Higher Ed*, April 29, 2020. https://www.insidehighered.com/quicktakes/2020/04/29/survey-identifies-%E2%80%98dangerous%E2%80%99-student-self-censorship.

Andrews, Lewis. "The Other Problem with Woke Schooling: It's Psychological Child Abuse." *Real Clear Policy*, April 6, 2021.

Arbeau, K. A., R. J. Coplan, and M. Weeks. "Shyness, Teacher-Child Relationships, and Socio-Emotional Adjustment in Grade 1." *International Journal of Behavioral Development*, 34 (2010): 259–269.

Asch, S. E. "Effects of Group Pressure upon the Modification and Distortion of Judgment." In H. Guetzkow, ed., *Groups, Leadership, and Men*. Pittsburgh, PA: Carnegie Press, 1951.

Asch, S. E. "Group Forces in the Modification and Distortion of Judgments." *Social Psychology* (1952): 450–501.

Asch, S. E. "Studies of Independence and Conformity: A Minority of One against a Unanimous Majority. *Psychological Monographs: General and Applied* 70, no. 9 (1956): 1–70.

Asher, Lyell. "How Ed Schools Became a Menace." *Chronicle of Higher Education*, April 8, 2018. https://www.chronicle.com/article/how-ed-schools-became-a-menace/.

Association of American Colleges and Universities. *Academic Freedom and Educational Responsibility: A Statement from the Board of Directors of Association of American Colleges and Universities*. Washington, DC: Association of American Colleges and Universities, 2006. https://www.aacu.org/about/statements/academic-freedom.

Association of American Colleges and Universities. "A Crucible Moment: College Learning & Democracy's Future: A Call to Action and Report from the National Task Force on Civic Learning and Democratic Engagement." USA: Association of American Colleges and Universities, 2012. https://www.aacu.org/crucible.

Association for Supervision and Curriculum Development. "Religious Liberty, Public Education, and the Future of American Democracy: A Statement of Principles." *In Connecting with the Community and the World of Work. Educational Leadership*, May 1995.

Associated Press. "John Kelly: Teacher 'Ought to Go to Hell' for Anti-Military Rant." *New York Post*, February 1, 2018. https://nypost.com/2018/02/01/john-kelly-teacher-ought-to-go-to-hell-for-anti-military-rant/.

Baker, J. A. Contributions of Teacher-Child Relationships to Positive School Adjustment during Elementary School. *Journal of School Psychology* 44 (2006): 211–229.

Barmann, Jay. "SF School Board Members Suggest Racism Is at Play in Blowup Over Lottery Admissions for Lowell High." SFist, October 14, 2020. https://sfist.com/2020/10/14/meeting-discussing-lotter y-lowell-high-school-gets-chaotic/.

Barnard, Anne. "1.1 Million Can Skip School for Climate Protest." *New York Times*, September 16, 2019. https://www.nytimes. com/2019/09/16/nyregion/youth-climate-strike-nyc.html.

Bawer, Bruce. *The Victims' Revolution: The Rise of Identity Studies and the Closing of the Liberal Mind.* New York, NY: Broadside Books, 2012.

Berne, Eric. *Games People Play: The Basic Handbook of Transactional Analysis.* New York, NY: Ballantine Books, 1996.

Berrien, Hank. "Philly Teacher: Parents with Access to Virtual Classrooms Would Do Damage to 'Honest Conversations about Gender/ Sexuality.'" Daily Wire, August 10, 2020. https://www.dailywire.com/ news/philly-teacher-parents-with-access-to-virtual-classrooms-wo uld-do-damage-to-honest-conversations-about-gender-sexuality.

Bildy, Lisa. "They Can't Cancel All of Us: How We Fought the Woke Thought Police and Won." New Discourses, June 11, 2020. https://newdiscourses.com/2020/06/how-we-fought-woke-though t-police-won/.

Black, A. E., and E. L. Deci. "The Effects of Instructors' Autonomy Support and Students' Autonomous Motivation on Learning Organic Chemistry: A Self-Determination Theory Perspective. *Science Education* 84 (2000): 740–756.

Bloom, Allan. *The Closing of the American Mind: How Higher Education Has Failed Democracy and Impoverished the Souls of Today's Students.* New York, NY: Simon and Schuster Paperbacks, 2012.

Bradley, Jennifer. "Resources for Teachers on the Days after the Attack on the U.S. Capitol." Beyond the Stoplight, January 6, 2021. https:// beyondthestoplight.com/2021/01/06/resources-for-teachers-on-th e-days-after-the-attack-on-the-u-s-capitol/.

Brion-Meisels, Gretchen, Margaret Kavanagh, Thomas Nikundiwe, and Carla Shalaby. *Planning to Change the World: A Plan Book for Social Justice Educators. Rethinking Schools*, 2020. https://rethinkingschools. org/books/planning-to-change-the-world-2020-2021/.

Buchanan, Gregory McClellan and Martin E. P. Seligman. *Explanatory Style*. Hillsdale, NJ: Lawrence Erlbaum, 1997.

Caldera, Altheria. "Eradicating Anti-Black Racism in U.S. Schools: A Call-to-Action for School Leaders." *Diversity, Social Justice, and the Educational Leader* 4, no. 1 (February 2020).

Caldera, Altheria. "Woke Pedagogy: A Framework for Teaching and Learning." Diversity, *Social Justice, and the Educational Leader* 2, no. 3 (November 2018).

Carr, J. G., F. D. Gilroy, and M. F. Sherman. "Silencing the Self and Depression among Women: The Moderating Effects of Race." *Psychology of Women Quarterly* 20 (1996): 375–392.

Christian, Matthew. "Florence One Teacher Removed Following 'Inexcusable' Facebook Post." SCNow, September 17, 2020. https://scnow.com/news/local/florence-one-teacher-removed-follo wing-inexcusable-facebook-post/article_f3011cf8-f91f-11ea-a31c-d712ec8f5d28.html#:~:text=FLORENCE%2C%20S.C.%20 %E2%80%94%20A%20teacher%20is,Schools%20following%20 a%20Facebook%20post.&text=O'Malley%20added%20that%20 the,any%20kind%20within%20the%20community.

Clarke, D. "Freedom of Thought in Schools: A Comparative Study." *International and Comparative Law Quarterly* 35, no. 2 (April 1986): 271–301.

Cochran-Smith, Marilyn. *Walking the Road: Race, Diversity, and Social Justice in Teacher Education*. New York, NY: Teachers College Press, 2004.

College Fix Staff. "Minnesota Police Group Rips State for Using Anti-Cop Book, Materials in Elementary School." College Fix, November 2, 2020. https://www.thecollegefix.com/minnesota-police-group-rip s-state-for-using-anti-cop-book-materials-in-elementary-school/.

Creeley, Will. "Dispositions in Teacher Education: Old Tricks, New Name." FIRE blog, March 14, 2007. https://www.thefire.org/dispositions-in-teacher-education-old-tricks-new-name/.

James Crowley, Student Confronts Teacher for Having Blue Lives Matter Flag in Classroom," Newsweek, January 12, 2021, https://www.newsweek.com/white-student-yells-teacher-blue-lives-matter-flag-classroom-1560865

Curry, Robert. "'Hey, Hey, Ho, Ho, Western Civ Has Got to Go.'" Intellectual Takeout, June 11, 2019. https://www.intellectualtakeout.org/article/hey-hey-ho-ho-western-civ-has-got-go/.

Delzo, Janissa. "School Bus Driver Who Led Prayer with Students Removed from Job." *Newsweek*, April 21, 2018. https://www.newsweek.com/school-bus-driver-george-nathaniel-fired-prayer-students-896215.

"Democratic vs. Republican Occupations: The Best American Infographics, 2016." Verdant Labs. Accessed November 15, 2020. http://verdantlabs.com/politics_of_professions/index.html.

A.P. Dillon, "Records Request Reveals 'Whiteness in Ed Spaces,' 'Affinity groups' at WCPSS EdCamp Equity," *Lady Liberty1885*, September 5, 2020.

Dobbin, Frank, and Alexandra Kalev. "Why Diversity Programs Fail." *Harvard Business Review*, July–August 2016. https://hbr.org/2016/07/why-diversity-programs-fail.

Duffy, Erin. "Area Students Stage Walkouts in Reaction to Florida Shooting; Papillion Principal's Approach: 'Let's Go Together.'" *Omaha World-Herald*, February 22, 2018. https://omaha.com/news/education/area-students-stage-walkouts-in-reaction-to-florida-shooting-papillion-principals-approach-lets-go-together/article_5f78274e-7b6c-5d9d-83b9-19015ec2bc1e.html.

Dunn, Joshua. "Free Speech Accountability and Public Trust: The Necessity of Neutrality." In Levinson, Meira and Jacob Fay. *Democratic Discord in Schools: Cases and Commentaries in Educational Ethics*. Cambridge, MA: Harvard University Press, 2019.

Dupuy, Beatrice. "Black Students in Suburban Schools Find Strength, Safe Spaces Together." *Star Tribune*, December 10, 2016.

Eden, Max. "Critical Race Theory in American Classrooms: The Radical Curriculum May Already Be at a Public School Near You." City *Journal*, September 18, 2020. https://www.city-journal.org/critical-race-theory-in-american-classrooms.

Eden, Max. "There Is No Apolitical Classroom: The Culture War Could Be Headed for Public Schools—Whether Parents Like It or Not." *City Journal*, June 19, 2020. https://www.city-journal.org/rise-of-woke-schools.

Eden, Max. "Public Education Has Gone 'Woke.'" Manhattan Institute, June 24, 2020. https://www.manhattan-institute.org/public-education-has-gone-woke.

Education Colleges for Justice & Equity: A Framework for Assessment and Transformation, version June 20, 2019. Education Deans for Justice and Equity, accessed November 25, 2020. https://education-deans.org/edje-framework/.

Eidelman, Vera and Sarah Hinger. "Some Schools Need a Lesson on Students' Free Speech Rights." ACLU blog, September 18, 2018. https://www.aclu.org/blog/free-speech/student-speech-and-privacy/some-schools-need-lesson-students-free-speech-rights.

Ellis, John. "A Crisis of Competence: The Corrupting Effect of Political Activism in the University of California." National Association of Scholars, March 30, 2012. https://www.nas.org/storage/app/media/Reports/A%20Crisis%20of%20Competence/A_Crisis_of_Competence.pd.

Ellis, John. *The Breakdown of Higher Education: How It Happened, the Damage It Does, and What Can Be Done.* Encounter Books, 2021.

Emmons, Libby. "Parents—It's Time to Speak Out against Critical Race Theory Indoctrination in Schools." *Post Millennial*, September 10, 2020. https://thepostmillennial.com/parents-it-is-time-to-speak-out-against-critical-race-theory-indoctrination.

Eromosele, Diana. "GA Teacher Allegedly Tells Students Their Parents Are Evil If They Voted for Obama; NAACP Wants Her Fired."

Root, April 29, 2015. https://www.theroot.com/ga-teacher-allegedl
y-tells-students-their-parents-are-1790859632.

Fain, Paul. "Deep Partisan Divide on Higher Education." *Inside
Higher Ed*, July 11, 2017. https://www.insidehighered.com/
news/2017/07/11/dramatic-shift-most-republicans-now-say-colleges-
have-negative-impact.

Fairley, Juliette. "Loudoun County Mother Homeschools Kids to Avoid
Critical-Race Education." West Nova News, October 26, 2020.
https://westnovanews.com/stories/559352192-loudoun-county-
mother-homeschools-kids-to-avoid-critical-race-education.

Ferrero, David. "How Private Prep Schools Get Diversity, Inclusion and
Social Justice Wrong." *Areo Magazine*, August 24, 2020. https://are-
omagazine.com/2020/08/24/how-private-prep-schools-get-diversit
y-inclusion-and-social-justice-wrong/.

Flett, G. L., A. Besser, P. L. Hewitt, and R. A. Davis. "Perfectionism,
Silencing the Self, and Depression." *Personality and Individual
Differences* 43 (2007): 1211–1222.

Forster, Greg. "Forming Teachers: The Education School Challenge."
Oklahoma Council of Public Affairs Perspective, August 2019. https://
www.ocpathink.org/uploads/assets/img/Forming-teachers-th
e-education-school-challenge.pdf.

Forster, Greg. "Who Teaches the Teachers?" *Oklahoma Council of Public
Affairs Perspective*, April 20, 2018. https://www.ocpathink.org/post/
who-teaches-the-teachers.

Foundation for Individual Rights in Education. "Columbia Embroiled
in Academic Freedom Controversy: FIRE Defends Student
Expression." FIRE blog, January 11, 2005. https://www.thefire.
org/columbia-embroiled-in-academic-freedom-controversy-fire-de-
fends-student-expression/.

Foundation for Individual Rights in Education. "Columbia University:
Ideological Litmus Tests at Teachers College." FIRE letter to
Columbia University. FIRE blog, accessed November 25, 2020,
https://www.thefire.org/cases/columbia-university-ideological-litmu
s-tests-at-teachers-college/.

Foundation for Individual Rights in Education. "Deficient High School Civic Education Contributing to Issues on Campus." FIRE Newsdesk, July 26, 2017. https://www.thefire.org/deficient-high-school-civic-education-contributing-to-issues-on-campus/.

Foundation for Individual Rights in Education. "FIRE Letter to Columbia University Teachers College Trustees, March 12, 2008." March 12, 2008. https://www.thefire.org/fire-letter-to-columbia-university-teachers-college-trustees-march-12-2008/.

Foundation for Individual Rights in Education. "FIRE Statement on NCATE's Encouragement of Political Litmus Tests in Higher Education." June 5, 2006. https://www.thefire.org/fire-statement-on-ncates-encouragement-of-political-litmus-tests-in-higher-education/.

Sierra Fox, "Prince William teacher on leave after Capitol riot comments during class," Fox5, January 22, 2021, https://www.fox5dc.com/news/video-prince-william-teacher-on-leave-after-capitol-riot-comments-during-class.

Freire, Paulo. *Pedagogy of the Oppressed*. New York, NY: Bloomsbury Academic, 2013.

French, David. "Religious Liberty: Not Just for Social Conservatives." *Dispatch*, February 5, 2020. https://thedispatch.com/p/religious-liberty-not-just-for-social.

Friedersdorf, Conor. "What Happens When a Slogan Becomes the Curriculum." *The Atlantic*, March 14, 2021.

Furrer, C. and E. Skinner. "Sense of Relatedness as a Factor in Children's Academic Engagement and Performance." *Journal of Educational Psychology* 95 (2003): 148–162.

Garcia, T. and P. R. Pintrich. "The Effects of Autonomy on Motivation and Performance in the College Classroom." *Contemporary Educational Psychology* 21 (1996): 477–486.

Garcia, Victor. "Journalist declares 'one-man war against critical race theory' after nuke lab holds 'white privilege' training." *FoxNews*, August 13, 2020.

Gnambs, T. and B. Hanfstingl. "The Decline of Academic Motivation During Adolescence: An Accelerated Longitudinal Cohort Analysis on the Effect of Psychological Need Satisfaction." *Journal of Educational Psychology* 36 (2016): 1691–1705.

Griffith, Keith. "Parents at Manhattan's $54K-a-year Dalton School Pull Their Kids after It Imposes Anti-Racism Manifesto That Focuses On 'Challenges to White Supremacy.'" Daily Mail Online, December 20, 2020. https://www.dailymail.co.uk/news/article-9072155/Parents-Dalton-School-balk-staffs-eight-page-list-anti-racist-demands.html.

Grolnick, W. S., R. M. Ryan, and E. L. Deci. "The Inner Resources for School Performance: Motivational Mediators of Children's Perceptions of Their Parents." *Journal of Educational Psychology* 83 (1991): 508–517.

Gross, Neil and Solon Simmons. "The Social and Political Views of American College and University Professors." In Gross, N. and S. Simmons, eds., *Professors and Their Politics*. Baltimore, MD: Johns Hopkins University Press, May 29, 2014.

Guelzo, Allen. "Pulitzer Overlooks Egregious Errors to Award Prize to New York Times' Fatally Flawed '1619 Project.'" Heritage Foundation, May 6, 2020. https://www.heritage.org/american-founders/commentary/pulitzer-overlooks-egregious-errors-award-prize-new-york-times-fatally.

Hadley Dunn, Alyssa. "Teaching on Days After: Post-Election Pedagogy for Equity and Justice." Michigan State University. https://docs.google.com/presentation/d/1hQ_aBr95gU6xf0OAHPBTOaSkThvzZexf6-dBrROODb4/edit?fbclid=IwAR2j0jjhAT7v2P2KrLMFSh85ye5r-rcg1T5BVFlnwzhV86I9zYOZb2KDzXwM#slide=id.g35f391192_00

Haidt, Jonathan. "The Age of Outrage." *City Journal*, December 17, 2017. https://www.city-journal.org/html/age-outrage-15608.html.

Haidt, Jonathan. "The Fine-Tuned Liberal Democracy." Wriston Lecture, delivered at the Manhattan Institute, November 15, 2017.

Haidt, Jonathan. "The Problem." Heterodox Academy, accessed July 21, 2016. https://heterodoxacademy.org/the-problem/.

Haidt, Jonathan. *The Righteous Mind: Why Good People Are Divided by Politics and Religion*. USA: Vintage, 2013.

Haidt, Jonathan. "Why Universities Must Choose One Telos: Truth or Social Justice." Heterodox Academy, October 21, 2016. https://heterodoxacademy.org/blog/one-telos-truth-or-social-justice-2/.

Ham, Mary Katharine and Guy Benson. *End of Discussion: How the Left's Outrage Industry Shuts Down Debate, Manipulates Voters, and Makes America Less Free (and Fun)*. New York, NY: Crown Forum, 2015.

Hancock, Peter. "Proposed New Teacher Standards Spark Controversy." *Capitol News Illinois*, November 10, 2020. https://capitolnewsillinois.com/NEWS/proposed-new-teacher-standards-spark-controversy.

Harris, Uri. "Wilfrid Laurier and the Creep of Critical Theory." *Quillette*, November 21, 2017. https://quillette.com/2017/11/21/wilfrid-laurier-creep-critical-theory/.

Harvard-Westlake Project. "Students, Parents, Faculty, Alumni of Harvard-Westlake: Speak the Truth." Accessed November 21, 2020. https://docs.google.com/forms/d/e/1FAIpQLScsP5ldZaKndBSLqhI24nxZD-Lhao5O0fxM-bCP_3VRc9BtWQ/viewform?gxids=7757.

Hayden, Jen. "Iowa Legislature Introduces Bill to Require University Faculty Applicants to State Party Affiliation." *Daily Kos* (blog), February 20, 2017. https://www.dailykos.com/stories/2017/2/20/1635991/-Iowa-legislature-introduces-bill-to-require-university-faculty-applicants-to-state-party-affiliation.

Haynes, Charles C. and Oliver Thomas. *Finding Common Ground: A First Amendment Guide to Religion and Public Schools*. First Amendment Center, 2007. https://www.religiousfreedomcenter.org/wp-content/uploads/2015/01/Religion-in-the-Public-School-Curriculum-Questions-and-Answers.pdf.

Hayot, Eric. "The Humanities as We Know Them Are Doomed. Now What?" *Chronicle of Higher Education*, July 1, 2018. https://www.chronicle.com/article/the-humanities-as-we-know-them-are-doomed-now-what/.

Hicks, Stephen. *Explaining Postmodernism: Skepticism and Socialism from Rousseau to Foucault*. USA: Ockham's Razor, 2013.

Hoadley-Brill, S. "The Cynical Theorists behind Cynical Theories." Liberal Currents, August 19, 2020. https://www.liberalcurrents.com/the-cynical-theorists-behind-cynical-theories/.

Hoffer, Eric. *The True Believer: Thoughts on the Nature of Mass Movements.* USA: Harper & Brothers, 1951.

Honeycutt, Nathan and Laura Freberg. "The Liberal and Conservative Experience across Academic Disciplines: An Extension of Inbar and Lammers." *Social Psychological and Personality Science*, March 2017.

hooks, bell. *Teaching to Transgress: Education as the Practice of Freedom.* New York, NY: Routledge, 2017.

Hudson, David. "Rights of Teachers." The First Amendment Encyclopedia, last modified September 2017. https://www.mtsu.edu/first-amendment/article/973/rights-of-teachers.

"Illiterate Revolutionaries," February 21, 2021, Man of Steele Productions: https://www.youtube.com/watch?v=vECN2oJ2gMU

Izumi, Lance T. *The Corrupt Classroom: Bias, Indoctrination, Violence and Social Engineering Show Why America Needs School Choice.* San Francisco, CA: Pacific Research Institute, 2017.

Izumi, Lance T. "Why Are Teachers Mostly Liberal?" Pacific Research Institute, April 3, 2019. https://www.pacificresearch.org/why-are-teachers-mostly-liberal/.

Jack, D. C. and A. Ali. "Introduction: Culture, Self-Silencing, and Depression: A Contextual-Relational Perspective." In Jack, D. C. and A. Ali, eds., *Silencing the Self across Cultures: Depression and Gender in the Social World.* New York, NY: Oxford University Press, 2010, 3–18.

Jack, D. C. and D. Dill. "The Silencing the Self Scale: Schemas of Intimacy Associated with Depression in Women." *Psychology of Women Quarterly* 16 (1992): 97–106.

Jack, Dana Crowley. *Silencing the Self: Women and Depression.* Cambridge, MA: Harvard University Press, 1991.

Jacobs, R. J. and B. Thomlison. "Self-Silencing and Age as Risk Factors for Sexually Acquired HIV in Midlife and Older Women." *Journal of Aging and Health* 21 (2009): 102–128.

Janis, Irving L. *Victims of Groupthink: A Psychological Study of Foreign-Policy Decisions and Fiascoes*. Boston, MA: Houghton Mifflin, 1972.

Kammerer, Annette. "The Scientific Underpinnings and Impacts of Shame." *Scientific American*, August 9, 2019.

Kayser, K., and Acquati, C. "Dyadic Coping across the Lifespan: A Comparison Between Younger and Middle-Aged Couples with Breast Cancer." *Frontiers in Psychology*, March 19, 2019.

Kirsanow, Peter. Letter to Edina High School from United States Commission on Civil Rights. August 24, 2017. http://www.newamericancivilrightsproject.org/wp-content/uploads/2014/03/Edina-High-School-letter-8.24.2017-final.pdf.

Klicka, Christopher J. "Decisions of the United States Supreme Court Upholding Parental Rights as 'Fundamental.'" *Connecting with the Community and the World of Work* 52, no. 8 (May 1995): 92–93.

Kors, Alan Charles. "The Enlightenment and Academic Freedom." Speech at Grand Valley State University, March 22, 2016. https://www.youtube.com/watch?v=fP1n5hElmSA&t=3708s.

Kohn, Alfie. *Punished by Rewards*. Boston, MA: Houghton Mifflin, 1993.

Kramer, Rita. *Ed School Follies: The Miseducation of America's Teachers*. New York, NY: Free Press, 2001.

Kuran, Timur. *Private Truths, Public Lies: The Social Consequences of Preference Falsification*. Cambridge, MA: Harvard University Press, 1997.

Labaree, David F. *The Trouble with Ed Schools*. New Haven, CT: Yale University Press, 2006.

Langbert, Mitchell, Anthony Quain, and Daniel Klein. "Faculty Voter Registration in Economics, History, Journalism, Law, and Psychology." *Econ Journal Watch*, 2016. https://econjwatch.org/articles/faculty-voter-registration-in-economics-history-journalism-communications-law-and-psychology.

Langbert, Mitchell. *Homogeneous: The Political Affiliations of Elite Liberal Arts College Faculty*. National Association of Scholars, April 19, 2018. https://link.springer.com/epdf/10.1007/s12129-018-9700-x?shared_access_token=gp2rvi_iDtlQtFfwLwOT9fe4Rwl

QNchNByi7wbcMAY6VS-9n0WALCjqT8pEbO7-xadb0R2
44aaF16x6E-Ch26FU5Z9ZKqKu88HBAJCKZSTb4_cMutGP
HtjmD0_OnmTYdgYS5-VdrB0XC1ka4Sl19hVSvhDo
pTS6_WZeCjiR0Sk%3D.

Leef, George. "A Racially 'Woke' Agenda Is Now Hardwired in Public Schools." Minding the Campus, November 4, 2019. https://www. mindingthecampus.org/2019/11/04/a-racially-woke-agenda-is-now -hardwired-in-public-schools/.

Levinson, Meira and Jacob Fay. *Democratic Discord in Schools: Cases and Commentaries in Educational Ethics.* Cambridge, MA: Harvard Education Press, 2019.

Lindholm, Jennifer, Katalin Szelenyi, Sylvia Hurtado, and William Korn. *The American College Teacher: National Norms for the 2004–2005 HERI Faculty Survey."* Higher Education Research Institute (HERI), September 2005. https://www.heri.ucla.edu/PDFs/pubs/FAC/ Norms/Monographs/TheAmericanCollegeTeacher2004To2005.pdf.

Liston, Delores and Regina Rahimi, eds., *Promoting Social Justice through the Scholarship of Teaching and Learning.* Bloomington, Indiana: Indiana University Press, 2017.

Lopez, F. G. "Student-Professor Relationship Styles, Childhood Attachment Bonds and Current Academic Orientations." *Journal of Social and Personal Relationships* 14 (1997): 271–282.

"Loudoun County Public Schools Spent $422K on Controversial Critical Race Theory Curriculum in Past Two Years." West Nova News. September 22, 2020. https://westnovanews.com/stories/555367615-l oudoun-county-public-schools-spent-422k-on-controversial-critical- race-theory-curriculum-in-past-two-years.

Lukianoff, Greg, and Jonathan Haidt. *The Coddling of the American Mind: How Good Intentions and Bad Ideas Are Setting Up a Generation for Failure.* New York, NY: Penguin Press, 2018.

Lukianoff, Greg. *Unlearning Liberty: Campus Censorship and the End of American Debate.* New York, NY: Encounter Books, 2014.

MacIverNews. "Questionable Curriculum: Schools Walk Out on Education." MacIver Institute, July 2, 2020. https://www.

maciverinstitute.com/2020/07/questionable-curriculum-schools-wal k-out-on-education/.

Mack, Tara and Bree Picower. *Planning to Change the World: A Plan Book for Social Justice Teachers 2010–2011.* New York, NY: New York Collective of Radical Educators and the Education for Liberation Network, 2010.

Magness, Phillip. "Here Is Proof That the Leftist Tilt on Campus Has Gotten Dramatically Worse." American Institute for Economic Research, May 1, 2019. https://www.aier.org/article/here-is-proof-tha t-the-leftist-tilt-on-campus-has-gotten-dramatically-worse/.

Martin, Jeanine. "Admission Test for TJHSST Eliminated." Bull Elephant, October 9, 2020. http://thebullelephant.com/admission-tes t-for-tjhsst-eliminated/.

"The Marxist 'Long March' into the Age of Identity Politics." *Parrhesia Diaries* (blog), February 1, 2020. theparrhesiadiaries.medium. com/the-marxist-long-march-through-the-institutions-and-into-t he-age-of-identity-politics-6a7042b235dc.

Maxwell, Bruce, Kevin McDonough, and David Waddington. "Broaching the Subject: Developing Law-Based Principles for Teacher Free Speech in the Classroom." *Teaching and Teacher Education* 70 (February 2018): 196–203.

McWhorter, John. "Don't Scrap the Test, Help Black Kids Ace It." *Atlantic,* May 9, 2019. https://www.theatlantic.com/ideas/archive/2019/05/ dont-abolish-nyc-high-school-admission-test/589045/.

McWhorter, John. "The Elect: The Threat to a Progressive America from Anti-Black Racists." *Substack,* Accessed February 23, 2021. https:// johnmcwhorter.substack.com/p/the-elect-the-threat-to-a-progressive.

Mill, John Stuart. *On Liberty.* London: John W. Parker and Son, West Strand, 1859.

Miłosz, Czesław. *The Captive Mind.* New York, NY: Vintage Books, 1953.

"Milwaukee Students Risk Arrest during Climate Protest against Banks Funding Fossil Fuel Industry." *Milwaukee Independent,* December 10, 2019. http://www.milwaukeeindependent.com/

articles/milwaukee-students-risk-arrest-climate-protest-banks-fundi ng-fossil-fuel-industry/.

Mitchell, Josh and Douglas Belkin. "Americans Losing Faith in College Degrees, Poll Finds." *Wall Street Journal*, September 7, 2017. https:// www.wsj.com/articles/americans-losing-faith-in-college-degrees-pol l-finds-1504776601.

Molina, Joshua. "Judge Strikes Down Portion of Fair Education Santa Barbara's Lawsuit over Implicit Bias Training." *Noozhawk*, July 15, 2020. https://www.noozhawk.com/article/judge_anderle_strikes_ down_portion_of_fair_education_implicit_bias_training.

Moshman, David. *Liberty and Learning: Academic Freedom for Teachers and Students*. USA: Heinemann, 2009.

Mounk, Yascha. *The People vs. Democracy: Why Our Freedom Is in Danger and How to Save It*. Cambridge, MA: Harvard University Press, 2018.

Mulraney, Frances. "Megyn Kelly Says She's Leaving New York City and Taking Her Kids Out of Their 'Woke' $56K-a-Year School after Letter Circulated Saying 'White Kids Are Being Indoctrinated in Black Death' and Will Grow Up to Be 'Killer Cops.'" Daily Mail Online, November 18, 2020. https://www.dailymail.co.uk/news/ article-8963261/Megyn-Kelly-says-shes-leaving-New-York-far-left-schools-gone-deep-end.html.

Murawski, John. "Disputed NY Times '1619 Project' Already Shaping Schoolkids' Minds on Race. RealClearInvestigations, January 31, 2020. https://www.realclearinvestigations.com/arti-cles/2020/01/31/disputed_ny_times_1619_project_is_already_shap-ing_kids_minds_on_race_bias_122192.html.

Murphy, Doyle. "Georgia Teacher Pulled from Classroom for Anti-Obama Rant." *New York Daily News*, April 28, 2015. https://www. nydailynews.com/news/national/georgia-teacher-pulled-classroo m-anti-obama-rant-article-1.2202604.

Murray, C. and M. T. Greenberg. "Children's Relationship with Teachers and Bonds with School: An Investigation of Patterns and Correlates in Middle Childhood." *Journal of School Psychology* 38, (2000): 423–445.

Nelson, Fraser. "Kemi Badenoch: The Problem with Critical Race Theory." *Spectator*, October 24, 2020. https://www.spectator.co.uk/article/kemi-badenoch-the-problem-with-critical-race-theory.

New Jersey Student Learning Standards. State of New Jersey Department of Education. Accessed November 23, 2020. https://www.nj.gov/education/cccs/.

Noelle-Neumann, E. "The Spiral of Silence: A Theory of Public Opinion." *Journal of Communication* 24, no. 2 (June 1974): 43–51.

Noelle-Neumann, E. "Turbulences in the Climate of Opinion: Methodological Applications of the Spiral of Silence Theory." *Public Opinion Quarterly* 41, no. 2 (1977): 143–158.

Packer, George. "When the Culture War Comes for the Kids: Caught between a Brutal Meritocracy and a Radical New Progressivism, a Parent Tries to Do Right by His Children While Navigating New York City's Schools." *Atlantic*, October 2019. https://www.theatlantic.com/magazine/archive/2019/10/when-the-culture-war-comes-for-the-kids/596668/.

"P.A.C.T. Inside Scoop!" Parents against Critical Theory. Accessed November 21, 2020. https://stoplcpscrt.com/crt-in-lcps-classrooms/.

Patrick, B., S. Stockbridge, H. V. Roosa, and J. Edelson. "Self-Silencing in School: Failures in Student Autonomy and Teacher-Student Relatedness." *Social Psychology of Education* 22 (2019): 943–967.

Pondiscio, Robert. "Teachers, Curb Your Activism." Thomas B. Fordham Institute, October 24, 2018. https://fordhaminstitute.org/national/commentary/teachers-curb-your-activism.

Professional Standards and Practices Commission. "Unit 3: The Teacher/Student Relationship." Pennsylvania Department of Education, Accessed March 25, 2021, https://www.pspc.education.pa.gov/Promoting-Ethical-Practices-Resources/Ethics-Toolkit/Unit3/Pages/The-Teacher---Student-Relationship.aspx

Quinn, D., et al. "Examining Effects of Anticipated Stigma, Centrality, Salience, Internalization, and Outness on Psychological Distress for People with Concealable Stigmatized Identities. *PLOS ONE* 9, no. 5 (2014).

Quinn, D. and S. Chaudoir. "Living with a Concealable Stigmatized Identity: The Impact of Anticipated Stigma, Centrality, Salience, and Cultural Stigma on Psychological Distress and Health." *Stigma and Health* 1 (2015): 35–39.

Randall, David. *Making Citizens: How American Universities Teach Civics.* National Association of Scholars, January 2017. https://www.nas.org/ storage/app/media/Reports/Making%20Citizens/NAS_makingCit-izens_fullReport.pdf.

Rantz, Jason. "Seattle Art Teacher Tells Kids 'Peace' Is 'Racist' and Trump Is Divisive." Mynorthwest.com, October 13, 2020. https:// mynorthwest.com/2220892/rantz-seattle-teacher-peace-racist-and -trump-is-divisive/.

Rantz, Jason. "Video Shows Teacher Telling 13-Year-Old That Trump's Comments 'Racist,' Immigration Policy Wrong." MyNorthwest, October 27, 2020. https://mynorthwest.com/2258047/rantz-vide o-teacher-trump-racist-immigration/?.

Rauch, Jonathan. *Kindly Inquisitors: The New Attacks on Free Thought.* Chicago, IL: University of Chicago Press, 2014.

Reid, Ellis, Meira Levinson, and Jacob Fay. "Talking Out of Turn: Teacher Speech for Hire." In Levinson, Meira and Jacob Fay, *Democratic Discord in Schools: Cases and Commentaries in Educational Ethics.* Cambridge, MA: Harvard University Press, 2019.

Reio, T. G., R. F. Marcus, and J. Sanders-Reio. "Contribution of Student and Instructor Relationships and Attachment Style to School Completion." *Journal of Genetic Psychology: Research and Theory on Human Development* 170 (2009): 53–71.

"Religious Liberty, Public Education, and the Future of American Democracy: A Statement of Principles." *Connecting with the Community and the World of Work* 52, no 8 (May 1995): 92–93.

Reynolds, Jeff. "Oregon School Districts Say White People Should Vote Democrat to Be Less Racist, May Have Broken the Law." PJ Media, July 7, 2020. https://pjmedia.com/election/jeff-reynolds/2020/07/07/ oregon-school-districts-say-white-people-should-vote-democrat-t o-be-less-racist-may-have-broken-the-law-n612452.

Riley, Naomi Schaefer. "My Kids and Their Elite Education in Racism." RealClearPolitics, September 16, 2020. https://www.realclearpolitics.com/2020/09/16/my_kids_and_their_elite_education_in_racism_523526.html.

Robbins, C. J. and A. M. Hayes. "The Role of Causal Attributions in the Prediction of Depression." In Buchanan, G. M. and M. E. P Seligman, *Explanatory Style*. NJ: Lawrence Erlbaum Associates, 1997, 71–98.

Rogers, Carl R. *On Becoming a Person: A Therapist's View of Psychotherapy*. Boston, MA: Houghton Mifflin, 1961.

Roorda, D. L., et al. "The Influence of Affective Teacher-Student Relationships on Students' School Engagement and Achievement: A Meta-Analytic Approach." *Review of Educational Research* 81 (2011): 493–529.

Romoser, James. "Middle East Studies: University Response to Controversy Focuses on Systemic Failures." *Columbia Daily Spectator*, March 27, 2013. https://www.columbiaspectator.com/2005/05/09/middle-east-studies-university-response-controversy-focuses-systemic-failures/.

Rotter, Julian B. "Generalized Expectancies for Internal versus External Control of Reinforcement." *Psychological Monographs: General & Applied* 80, no. 1 (1966): 1–28.

Rouse, Karen. "Teacher Caught in Bush 'Rant.'" Denver Post, last modified May 8, 2006. https://www.denverpost.com/2006/03/01/teacher-caught-in-bush-rant/.

Rowe, Ian. "The 1619 Project Perpetuates the Soft Bigotry of Low Expectations." 1776 Unites, February 10, 2020. https://1776unites.com/essays/the-1619-project-perpetuates-the-soft-bigotry-of-low-expectations-by-ian-v-rowe/.

Rufo, Christopher. "Woke Elementary." *City Journal*, January 13, 2021. https://christopherrufo.com/woke-elementary/.

Rufo, Christopher, "Subversive Education: North Carolina's Largest School District Launches a Campaign Against 'Whiteness in Educational Spaces." *City Journal*, March 17, 2021.

Ryan, R. M., J. D. Stiller, and J. H. Lynch. "Representations of Relationships to Teachers, Parents, and Friends as Predictors of Academic Motivation and Self-Esteem." *Journal of Early Adolescence* 14 (1994): 226–249.

Ryan, R. M. and J. P. Connell. "Perceived Locus of Causality and Internalization: Examining Reasons for Acting in Two Domains." *Journal of Personality and Social Psychology* 57 (1989): 749–761.

Samuels, Christina. "Selective Virginia Public High School to Drop Standardized Admissions Test." Education Week, October 12, 2020. https://www.edweek.org/leadership/selective-virginia-publi c-high-school-to-drop-standardized-admissions-test/2020/10#:~:- text=Thomas%20Jefferson%20High%20School%20for,the%20 school's%20enrollment%20more%20diverse.

Satterfield, Kolbie "Everyone Has a Right to Be Here: Protests Continue over Proposed Admission Changes to Prestigious FCPS High School." WUSA9, October 5, 2020. https://www.wusa9.com/article/news/ education/protests-over-proposed-admission-changes-to-thomas-j efferson-high-school-for-science-and-technology/65-a656b42 3-ef6d-4769-b3ff-d341b36d1564.

Schalin, Jay. "The Politicization of University Schools of Education: The Long March through the Education Schools." James G. Martin Center for Academic Renewal, February 19, 2019. https://www. jamesgmartin.center/2019/02/schools-of-education/.

Sedlovskaya, A. "Concealable Stigma and the Distinction between Public and Private Selves: Implications for Psychological Well-Being." *Dissertation Abstracts International* 72 (2016): 10-B.

Seligman, Martin E. P. *Learned Optimism: How to Change Your Mind and Your Life.* New York, NY: Vintage Books, 2006.

Sensoy, Ozlem and Robin DiAngelo. "Developing Social Justice Literacy: An Open Letter to Our Faculty Colleagues." *Phi Delta Kappan* (January 2009).

Shapiro, Eliza and Vivian Wang. "Amid Racial Divisions, Mayor's Plan to Scrap Elite School Exam Fails." *New York Times*, June 24,

2019. https://www.nytimes.com/2019/06/24/nyregion/specialized-schools-nyc-deblasio.html.

Shor, Ira. *When Students Have Power: Negotiating Authority in a Critical Pedagogy.* Chicago, IL: University of Chicago Press, 1996.

Shuler, Roger. "Anti-Obama Teacher Is Placed on Leave in Alabama." *Daily Kos* (blog), May 19, 2010. https://www.dailykos.com/stories/2010/5/19/867846/-.

Silverglate, Harvey A. and Jordan Lorence. *FIRE's Guide to First-Year Orientation and Thought Reform on Campus.* Philadelphia, PA: Foundation for Individual Rights in Education, 2005.

Simon, Roger L. *I Know Best: How Moral Narcissism Is Destroying Our Republic, If It Hasn't Already.* USA: Encounter Books, 2016.

Skinner, Victor. "White Middle Schoolers Forced to Stand in Front of Classmates, Apologize for 'Privilege.'" EAGNews.org, June 21, 2017. https://www.eagnews.org/2017/06/parents-teachers-slam-nc-school-districts-mandatory-white-privilege-training/.

Smart, L. and D. Wegner. "Covering Up What Can't Be Seen: Concealable Stigma and Mental Control." *Journal of Personality and Social Psychology* 77, no. 3 (1999): 474–486.

Smith, Emily. "Billionaire John Paulson Rips Elite Spence School for 'Anti-White Indoctrination.'" Page Six, July 7, 2020. https://pagesix.com/2020/07/07/billionaire-john-paulson-rips-elite-spence-school-for-anti-white-indoctrination/.

Soenens, B. and M. Vansteenkiste. "Antecedents and Outcomes of Self-Determination in 3 Life Domains: The Role of Parents' and Teachers' Autonomy Support." *Journal of Youth and Adolescence* 34 (2005): 589–604.

Sowell, Thomas. *The Vision of the Anointed: Self-Congratulation as a Basis for Social Policy.* New York, NY: Basic Books, 1995.

Spratt, C. L., M. F. Sherman, and F. D. Gilroy. "Silencing the Self and Sex as Predictors of Achievement Motivation." *Psychological Reports* 82 (1998): 259–263.

Steiner, David. "Skewed Perspective: What We Know about Teacher Preparation at Elite Education Schools." *Teachers and Teaching* 5, no. 1 (2009).

Stephens, Bret. "The 1619 Chronicles." *New York Times*, October 9, 2020. https://www.nytimes.com/2020/10/09/opinion/nyt-1619-project-criticisms.html.

Stepman, Jarrett. "Woke Math Aims to Teach Seattle Kids That 'Western' Math Is Racist." Daily Signal, October 24, 2019. https://www.dailysignal.com/2019/10/24/woke-math-aims-to-teach-seattle-kids-that-western-math-is-racist/.

Steward, Tom. "Edina Parents and Students Rebel against Politics in Classroom." Center of the American Experiment, July 11, 2017. https://www.americanexperiment.org/2017/07/edina-parents-and-students-rebel-against-politics-in-classroom/.

Sullivan, Andrew. "Why Is Wokeness Winning? The Astonishing and Continuing Success of Left Illiberalism." Weekly Dish, October 16, 2020. https://andrewsullivan.substack.com/p/why-is-wokeness-winning.

Swan, Rachel. "Mountain View Teacher Suspended for Comparing Trump to Hitler." SFGate, last modified November 13, 2016. https://www.sfgate.com/bayarea/article/Mountain-View-teacher-suspended-for-comparing-10610974.php.

Taylor, D. G. "Pluralistic Ignorance and the Spiral of Silence." *Public Opinion Quarterly* 46 (1982): 311–35.

Teachers College, Columbia University. "Academic Catalog 2022-2021," Department of Curriculum and Teaching. Accessed November 25, 2020. https://www.tc.columbia.edu/catalog/academics/departments/curriculum-and-teaching/.

"Teachers Unions." OpenSecrets.org. Accessed Nov. 22, 2020. https://www.opensecrets.org/industries/indus.php?ind=l1300.

Thompson, J. M. and B. I. Hart. "Attachment Dimensions Associated with Silencing the Self." Poster presented at the American Psychological Association Annual Convention, Toronto, Ontario, Canada, 1996.

Thompson, J. M. "Silencing the Self: Depressive Symptomatology and Close Relationships." *Psychology of Women Quarterly* 19 (1995): 337–353.

Tierney, John. "Social Scientist Sees Bias Within." *New York Times*, February 7, 2011. https://www.nytimes.com/2011/02/08/science/08tier.html.

Timpf, Katherine. "Seventh-Grade Assignment: Write Letters to Lawmakers Begging for Gun Control." *National Review*, March 29, 2018. https://www.nationalreview.com/2018/03/georgia-middle-school-gun-control-letter-assignment/.

Ton, Mai-Linh. "Expanding the Diversity Conversation." *Harvard Crimson*, May 24, 2018. https://www.thecrimson.com/article/2018/5/24/editorial-expanding-diversity-conversation/.

Torres, Christina. "All Students Need Anti-Racism Education." Teaching Tolerance, July 30, 2020. https://www.tolerance.org/magazine/all-students-need-antiracism-education.

Tosi, Justin and Brandon Warmke. "Moral Grandstanding." *Philosophy & Public Affairs* 44, no. 3 (June 2016.): 197–217.

Truesdell, Nicole. "Front Line in the Fight against White Supremacy: People Today Often Call for an End to Politics in the Classroom, Yet for Many Scholars, This *Is* Our Work, Argues Nicole Truesdell." *Inside Higher Ed*, December 22, 2017. https://www.insidehighered.com/advice/2017/12/22/faculty-trained-speak-about-systems-oppression-should-not-be-required-be-neutral.

Turner, Camilla. 'Victimhood Narrative' Taught in Schools Fuels Anxiety in Young Women." *Telegraph*, October 21, 2017. https://www.telegraph.co.uk/news/2017/10/21/victimhood-narrative-taught-schools-fuels-anxiety-young-women/.

Underwood, Julie. "School Districts Control Teachers' Classroom Speech." *Phi Delta Kappan*, December 4, 2017. https://kappanonline.org/underwood-school-districts-control-teachers-classroom-speech/.

Vallerand, R. J. and R. Bissonnette. "Intrinsic, Extrinsic, and Amotivational Styles as Predictors of Behavior: A Prospective Study." *Journal of Personality* 60 (1992): 599–620.

Vansteenkiste, M., et al. "Examining the Motivational Impact of Intrinsic versus Extrinsic Goal Framing and Autonomy-Supportive versus Internally Controlling Communication Style on Early Adolescents' Academic Achievement." *Child Development* 86 (2005): 483–501.

Vansteenkiste, M., et al. "Identifying Configurations of Perceived Teacher Autonomy Support and Structure: Associations with Self-Regulated Learning, Motivation and Problem Behavior." *Learning and Instruction* 22 (2012): 431–439.

Velotti, P., Garofalo, C. Bottazzi, F., and Caretti, Vincenzo. "Faces of Shame: Implications for Self-Esteem, Emotion Regulation, Aggression, and Well-Being. The Journal of Psychology 151: 2 (2017), 174-184.

Watkins, Chase. "Social Justice Program Says Teachers Should 'Reject and Resist' Parents Who Disagree with It." College Fix, November 29, 2019. https://www.thecollegefix.com/social-justice-program-says-teachers-should-reject-and-resist-parents-who-disagree-with-it/.

Weiner, Bernard, ed. *Achievement Motivation and Attribution Theory.* Morristown, NJ: General Learning Press, 1974.

Weiner, Bernard. *Human Motivation.* New York, NY: Holt, Rinehart, and Winston, 1980.

Weiss, Bari. "Stop Being Shocked: American Liberalism Is in Danger from a New Ideology—One with Dangerous Implications for Jews." *Tablet*, October 14, 2020. https://www.tabletmag.com/sections/news/articles/stop-being-shocked.

Williams, Scott. "Burlington High School Teacher Suspended; Allegedly Directed Students to Watch Video Questioning Election Results." *Journal Times*, January 7, 2021.

Wilson, Jamie. "Portland Teacher Forced to Remove Anti-Trump Message in Classroom." Fox 12 Oregon, May 16, 2017. https://www.kptv.com/news/portland-teacher-forced-to-remove-anti-trump-message-in-classroom/article_79f841d8-8b2b-5c97-b0d7-c5eeeec456be.html.

Wilson, Robin. "Social Change Tops Classic Books in Professors' Teaching Priorities." *Chronicle of Higher Education*, March 5, 2009.

https://www.chronicle.com/article/social-change-tops-classic-books-in-professors-teaching-priorities-1564/.

Woke at Harvard-Westlake (@wokeathw). Instagram, 2020. https://www.instagram.com/wokeathw/?hl=en.

Wolff, Robert, Barrington Moore, and Herbert Marcuse. *A Critique of Pure Tolerance*. Boston: Beacon Press, 1969, 95–137.

Wood, Vincent. "Teachers Presenting White Privilege as Fact Are Breaking the Law, Minister Warns." *Independent*, October 21, 2020. https://www.independent.co.uk/news/uk/politics/kemi-badenoch-black-history-month-white-privilege-black-lives-matter-b1189547.html.

Wright, Matthew. "Teacher Is Suspended after 'Segregating Her Students Based on Religious Beliefs and Whether They Supported Abortion.'" Daily Mail Online, November 4, 2019. https://www.dailymail.co.uk/news/article-7646177/A-North-Carolina-teacher-suspended-allegedly-segregated-students.html.

Yang, Wesley Twitter thread, Accessed May 24, 2019, https://twitter.com/wesyang/status/1132128661556142080?lang=en.

Zelevansky, Nora. "The Big Business of Unconscious Bias." *New York Times*, November 20, 2019. https://www.nytimes.com/2019/11/20/style/diversity-consultants.html.

Zilber, Ariel. "North Carolina High School Teacher Made Her Students Compare Speeches by Hitler and Trump, Say Outraged Parents." Daily Mail Online, last modified September 24, 2016. https://www.dailymail.co.uk/news/article-3804928/North-Carolina-high-school-teacher-students-compare-speeches-Hitler-Trump-say-outraged-parents.html.

Zimmer-Gembeck, M. J., et al. "Relationships at School and Stage-Environment Fit as Resources for Adolescent Engagement and Achievement." *Journal of Adolescence* 29 (2006): 911–933.

Zimmerman, Jonathan and Emily Robertson. *The Case for Contention: Teaching Controversial Issues in American Schools*. Chicago: University of Chicago Press, 2017.

Resources

Foundation for Individual Rights in Education
Civics Alliance
Civics Renewal Network
Foundation for Economic Education
Freedoms Foundation
Fairforall.org
Parents Defending Education
Free Expression Network
Free to Choose Network
No Left Turn in Education
Parents' Rights in Education
Schoohouserights.org
Institute for Free Speech
Bill of Rights Institute
Heterodox Academy
1776 Unites
Teachthebibleinschools.org
Undoctrinate.org
What Are They Learning.com
Yourlogicalfallacyis.com
ParentsUnited.org
LearnLiberty.org
Edlibertyall.org

Acknowledgments

I have many people to thank in the preparation of this manuscript. First, I'd like to thank the parents, students, and teachers who generously shared their stories with me. I also owe appreciation to FIRE for both the time and the go-ahead to pursue this project. More specifically, I'd like to thank the integral Greg Lukianoff, the indomitable Robert Shibley, the invaluable Adam Goldstein, the indisputable Ryne Weiss, the indispensable Sean Stevens, the inimitable Josh Haverlock, and the indefinable anonymous unicorn.

I also owe an inordinate debt of gratitude to the intrepid Beth Feeley and her infinite Rolodex.

Appreciation also goes to David Bernstein for believing instantly in the value of this project, to Kate Monahan for her detailed editing assistance, and always to Mark for supporting my lifelong writing habit.

To contact FIRE's High School Outreach Department, email highschooloutreach@thefire.org.